THE COMPLETE
POTTER'S
COMPANION

SPECIAL PHOTOGRAPHY
PETER KINNEAR

CONRAN OCTOPUS

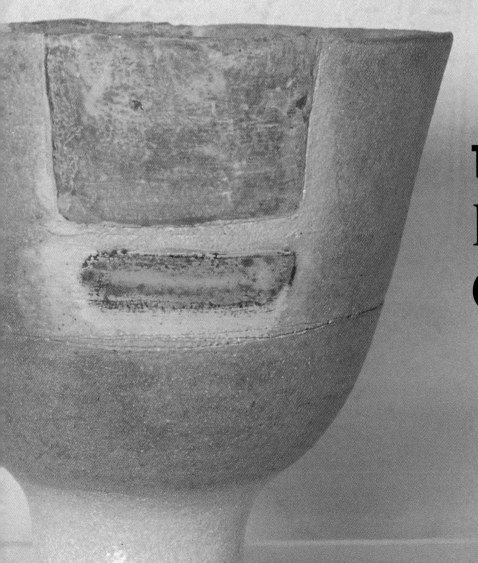

THE COMPLETE
POTTER'S
COMPANION
TONY BIRKS

Project Editor Mary Davies
Art Editor Alison Fenton
Design Assistant Alison Barclay
Special Photography Peter Kinnear
Illustrator Paul Bryant
Picture Researcher Abigail Ahern
Production Controller Julia Golding

Endpapers: A detail of a bowl by Lucie Rie, painted with
manganese dioxide to give gold.
Title spread: Small bowl by Robin Welch in front of a painting
by the potter. The bowl of T-material was washed with salt solution
before stoneware firing with medium reduction, and then painted with
lustre and refired to low temperature.
Title verso page: Composite earthenware jug by Betty Woodman.

First published in 1993 by
Conran Octopus Limited
37 Shelton Street, London WC2H 9HN

Copyright © Text 1993 Tony Birks
Copyright © Design and layout 1993 Conran Octopus Limited

Based on *The Potter's Companion*,
first published in 1974 and revised in 1982

British Library Cataloguing-in-Publication Data
A catalogue record for this book is available
from the British Library.

ISBN 1 85029 431 3

Typeset by Servis Filmsetting Limited, Manchester
Colour separations by Scantrans Pte Limited, Singapore
Printed and bound in Hong Kong

CONTENTS

INTRODUCTION

Half a century ago, craftsmen potters were on their knees. Factories produced plates and cups; no one wanted hand-made pots. Sculptors were using metal and stone. Ceramics departments were a rarity in art schools and colleges.

How things have changed. As the century comes to an end, clay is the most popular material for expressive art and craft. Every large town and many schools have thriving pottery classes. Studio potters are respected as artists, and their work is in great public and private collections. Clay, a still-abundant and cheap material, is enjoying an extraordinary renaissance as a creative medium. The pages of this book show how it has responded in the hands of modern artists to soaring flights of the imagination.

But not all would-be potters are concerned with pushing material to its limits, and instead settle for handsome hand-made utensils which adequately do a job. When I first wrote The Potter's Companion in 1972 it was intended to be a fully practical guide to help students who, in a two-hour evening class, had experienced the frustrations of too little time with their teacher, or too brief a session on the wheel, and wanted to extend what they had learned or reinforce it with reading at home. It was also intended to guide ambitious amateurs to self-sufficiency, and up to the point of organizing their own pottery. Over the years since the first edition many other pottery manuals have appeared, some specialized and some general, and my own approach to both teaching and pottery has changed. Revised editions of my original book reflected technical developments – particularly in kiln design – and the increasing overlapping of traditionally separate techniques. It is extraordinary how the once-clear demarcations between methods of making have become blurred, and how the most dynamic modern work is now almost always the fruit of combining techniques, like pinching and slab-building, moulding and throwing.

However, the intention of this entirely new edition is different. It is to encourage potters to experiment more widely and aim high, not to be satisfied with adequate results but to relate to the increasing throng of creative artists world-wide who make scintillating work, and for whom pottery is central to their lives. The illustrations show pots which, though recently made and extremely varied, should stand the test of time as outstanding works in their field.

There is, of course, a great deal more to pottery-making than can be conveyed in a single book. Becoming a potter does not happen easily or quickly, but the process of making pots is denied to no one, and it is to the new generation of pot makers that this book is dedicated.

T.B. NOVEMBER 1992

Marbled slivers made from white, red and black
clay, partially glazed and high fired, and separated
by clay discs to make a ceramic screen.
Construction by Cornelia Klein.
Overall height: 150cm (60in).

1

EARTH, FIRE AND WATER

The earth yields up pottery in a surprising way. Not only does every garden spade reveal an assortment of blue and white glazed fragments, but the earth itself is the very essence of pottery, and if undisturbed, pot fragments and clayey earth will lie together, unchanged, for centuries.

The pottery fragment may be worth looking at – for it can have a story to tell. Some years ago I picked up a dull fawn-coloured fragment which was the bottom of a hand-thrown pot, unglazed, with the marks underneath of the thread which had cut it from the wheel and on the side a fingermark made by the potter. I found it on a well-known Roman site, and the piece, like many more from the same area, came from the hands of a potter nearly 2,000 years ago. With pottery going back as far as civilization itself, there is nothing remarkable about such a find – the pot was not complete, after all – and since pottery does not decay like iron or wood, pottery sherds are often as common as weeds on an archaeological site. But the potter's fingerprints and the evidence of a continuing and timeless technique made the experience a moving one. It was the bottom of a vessel for liquid – probably a jug – and it was clearly made on the wheel, from local clay, just as it could have been made today.

Techniques have been refined, of course, and the ceramics industry is a highly precise one, but the basic principles have not changed. Nor has the attraction of pottery making lessened as it has become more mechanized, for clay, raw in its natural state or fired as a finished pot, has a strong tactile appeal, and making pottery can be an exhilarating experience.

This book is intended to be a practical guide and companion to the many people who, for whatever reason, want to understand the making of pottery. It is an immense field and many who take up pottery as a craft are rather hazy about both the essential materials and essential processes. Instructions begin in the following chapter and these are intended to be as full as possible for the beginner. The more experienced potter will find the later chapters deal with more advanced matters. Meanwhile, this chapter must help the beginner with a few definitions.

The raw material

Pottery is made from a common, naturally occurring material called clay which has been subjected to intense heat in a furnace. Clay does not become pottery until all the water it contains both in a free and a chemically combined form has been removed by heat, and when this is done, by firing in a kiln, the hard permanent result is in a stable state, and is more permanent than many kinds of rock. It can, of course, be broken up into pieces, but it is hard to get rid of the pieces. They will not dissolve or melt, or combine with other chemicals, and if they are covered with a surface of glass or glaze, they are even more impregnable.

The wonderful Waterweed bowl (*right*) from the Victoria and Albert Museum in London demonstrates to perfection the fluency of the painter in filling a curved space with an intricate non-symmetrical design. Around the banded rim swim 14 fish. It was made in Persia about 750 years ago. The Roman fragment (*below*) from Berkshire, England, is more than a thousand years older.

Clay is weathered, decomposed granite and consists mainly of alumina and silica. Where clay lies in deep beds near its origin it is likely to be fairly pure, as in the case of the china clay deposits which surround the granite outcrop of Cornwall's Bodmin Moor in south-western England. There the clay makes the streams run white, and the waste-heaps where it is mined are ghostly like the mountains on the moon. China clay or kaolin found in such areas is the 'mother' clay, composed only of silica, alumina and water. All its descendants contain impurities and, funnily enough, it is the impurities which give clays their character and value for the studio potter, affecting colour and texture.

The further the alumina-silica is carried by rainwater and the leaching effects of rain and gravity from its source rock, the more likely it is to pick up other elements. Clay which occurs widely as a deposited material (i.e. transported and sedimented under water), especially in geologically recent areas, contains grains of silica as sand. Revealed in road cuttings and often turned up in the garden, it is coloured yellow or blue-grey by the elements, notably iron, which have leached into it and become diffused. The coarse brick clays of the English Midlands, for example, show their iron content in the rusty pink colour they turn after they have been burnt or fired in the kiln, and many other elements – calcium, titanium, sodium and potassium – occur in small but significant proportions.

The potter does not need to be a chemist to discover that the more 'impure' clay, the better working quality it may have. This does not mean that a pot can be thrown on the wheel from clay containing roots, rotting leaves and shells, yet once the organic matter has been sieved out, the home clay-digger may have to put in additives such as fine sand or bentonite to make the clay 'plastic' or malleable again. It is very tempting to use clay which you have dug out of the ground with your own spade, but it is extremely tiring. At the end of the day it will still require a great deal of energy before it can be used. The clay needs 'conditioning' by years of exposure to the weather, and

Shrinkage is graphically shown when the same plate is photographed freshly made (*right*) and then after stoneware firing (*far right*).

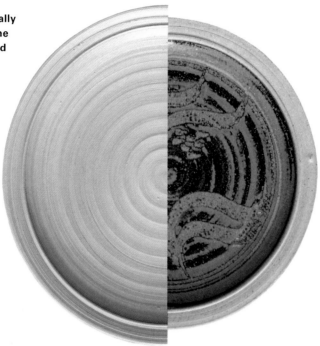

the sieving and homogenization of clay is a slow and laborious business. It has to be tested for its working qualities, its brittleness once fired and its shrinkage. When prepared and made plastic by additives, home-dug clay can still disappoint by losing its unusual colour in the kiln, and possibly by exploding or cracking under the strain of high temperatures.

The studio potter benefits by using clay which is carefully prepared for industrial use – often a blend of materials from several sources – and if he or she is interested in its chemistry, an analysis will be provided by the suppliers. The raw material is usually called the 'body' and this body is 'clothed' with glass, in the form of glaze, although in pots like porous flowerpots the body goes naked.

Making a pot
The process of pot making is as follows. The shape is formed by one of three methods. It is thrown on the wheel (see chapters 3–7), made by hand without mechanical aids (see chapters 8–10) or made with liquid or with plastic clay using moulds or other industrial tools (see chapters 11–13). After shaping the pot from clay in a wet or plastic form, the clay must dry out

completely in the atmosphere before it is heated in the kiln. It shrinks in size as it loses this 'free' water.

In the kiln it shrinks again when the chemically bound water leaves the clay at about 600° Centigrade – roughly the temperature of the element in an electric radiator or the tip of a smouldering cigarette. The temperature in the kiln is usually raised to about 1,000–1,100°C and after cooling the pot is taken out solid, insoluble, permanent and porous. At this stage it is known as 'biscuit' ware. The experience from which it has emerged is called the 'biscuit firing'. The pot is then covered with powdered glass or the ingredients of glass, and refired in the kiln so that the powder covering melts and resolidifies on the surface as a glaze. The resulting pot is no longer porous and is ready for use. This second firing is called the 'glaze' or 'glost firing'.

The two firings often take place one after the other in the same kiln, and the terms 'biscuit kiln' and 'glost kiln', confusing for the beginner, simply mean *the kiln packed for a biscuit firing* and *the kiln packed for a glost firing*.

Just to complicate matters, an important method of pottery making in studio potteries is the combining of the biscuit and glost firing in one process

known as 'raw glazing' or 'once firing', in which the pot passes only once through the ordeal of high temperatures. While it is economical on fuel, it can have a high failure rate.

Decoration of the ware can take place at any stage from the making of the pot from plastic clay to a patterning of the glazed surface. This latter practice involves a third (or second glost) firing, though it is normally undertaken only in industrial potteries.

Earthenware and stoneware
The terms 'earthenware' and 'stoneware' describe the two main kinds of pottery, and are the result of firing to different temperatures in the second (glost) firing. Earthenware is fired to between 1,000°C and 1,100°C, enough to melt the glaze but not high enough to change the character of the body inside. At around 1,150°C the clay itself begins to vitrify, or to become fused together as a solid non-porous mass, and when vitrification has taken place the pot becomes stoneware. Most stoneware firings are in the range between 1,250°C and 1,300°C, because it is at this temperature that the glaze takes on its best character.

At all temperatures between 650°C and 1,500°C it is possible to make pottery with satisfactory glazes, but most wares made industrially and in studios cluster in the two temperature zones 1,000°C–1,100°C and 1,250°C–1,300°C as these yield the most satisfactory results. In each case the clay body, the glaze and the kiln must be suited to the temperature. Glazes are formulated to 'mature' at precise temperatures, and give of their best only when within 10° of this temperature. On the other hand both clays and kilns work satisfactorily at all temperatures up to a known maximum. For example, above 1,000°C a certain clay may 'bloat' or blister or even explode, and a kiln may simply cease to increase in temperature or, if electric, its elements may burn out.

Stoneware pots are dense and relatively heavy, and the glaze colours are likely to be sombre, as in this jar by Richard Batterham. Height: 35.5cm (14in).

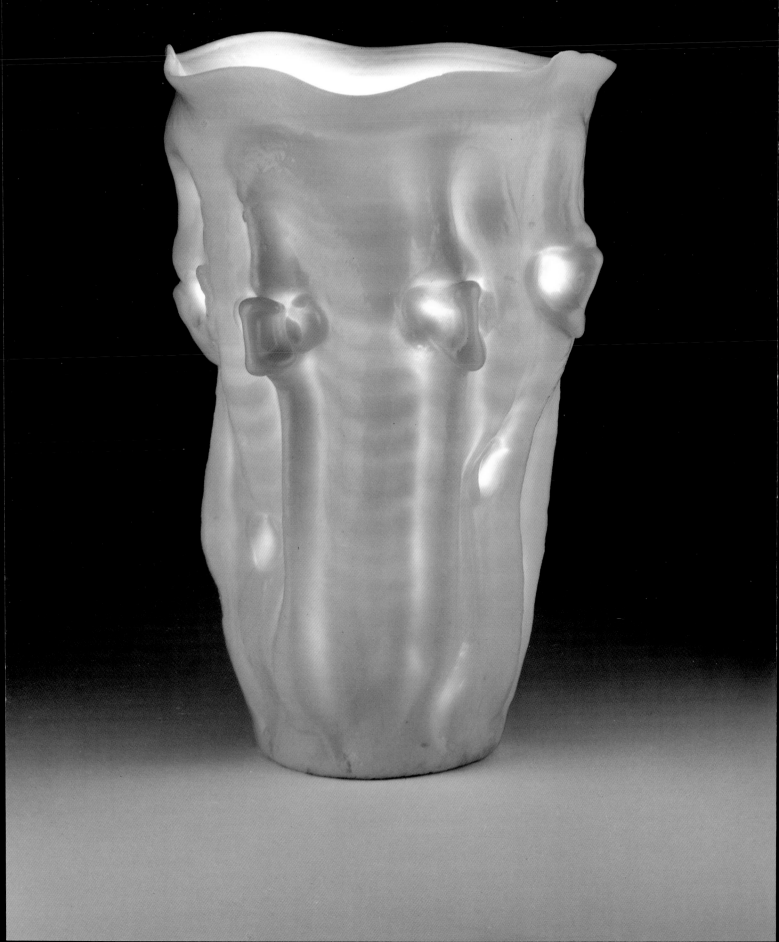

Clays and kilns are often known by these maximum temperatures and are called, for example, earthenware clays (1,100°C max.) or stoneware kilns (1,300°C max.). This does not mean that they cannot successfully be used for work at lower temperatures. An earthenware bowl can be made with stoneware clay in a stoneware kiln – provided it is fired to earthenware temperatures and has an earthenware glaze. It is really a question of common sense, and can be summed up as follows: do not try to fire a clay or a kiln to a temperature higher than its known maximum and make sure that the glaze is right for the temperature used. A 'hard' glaze which requires a high temperature will simply not melt if the temperature is too low, and it will run off into liquid pools (damaging the kiln) if the temperature is taken too high.

Earthenware is porous, not very dense or heavy and its glazes are usually shiny and bright. Stoneware is denser for the clay has fused together, and is therefore heavier than an earthenware pot of the same size; its glazes are usually duller and frequently mottled. A well-known branch of stoneware is porcelain, which is often translucent and light in weight because it is thin. It needs a special pure clay and glaze, but is fired at stoneware temperatures.

Provided the equipment is available, the beginner can work in any kind of pottery. It is very sad that earthenware is traditionally regarded as more suitable for beginners, with the promise of stoneware and porcelain as some kind of nebulous goal for the future. It is true that some potteries are only equipped with earthenware kilns and earthenware 'red' clays, though stoneware clays are no more expensive, but if it is practicable the beginner who works with coarse stoneware clays and simple stoneware glazes will gain most. Earthenware demands more precision of handling to achieve a result of the same quality. A great many individual potters and small studios specialize in stoneware. One reason why the vast majority of industrial pottery is earthenware is that it takes less energy in the kiln to produce the finished result. An expensive number of kilowatts is used up in producing the final 150°C of heat.

Perhaps it is the precision of industrial earthenware, coupled with its frequently lifeless design, which has caused liveliness of form to be linked with imprecision of execution. There is no need for a mass-produced pot to be lifeless and dull, and there is certainly no need for hand-made pots to be clumsy. A curious double standard causes some people to buy, with obvious satisfaction, mugs for drinking coffee and casseroles for baking in the oven of shocking clumsiness, whereas they would criticize a dining chair or an electric razor for the slightest fault. They have lost their ability to judge craftsmanship by the same high standards they apply to machine-made precision goods. The pottery studio is not the place for precision work, but this really need not be an excuse for a lack of grace or finish. Hastily or badly made pots are all the more unreasonable when you bear in mind the total length of time required to complete an individual pot.

To begin by insisting on the highest standards, however, is a mistake, for until you have completed a pot there is nothing by which to judge the next. Illusions are shattered at the very first lesson for the beginner hoping to go home loaded with coffee pots and useful dishes, and it is inevitably disappointing that the first term's work will probably consist of a few finished pots, produced near the term's end. Most beginners find progress tediously slow and classes frustrating. Learning pottery is not a steady and progressive climb, but a series of jumps, with the occasional backward slide. But when you make a jump and suddenly a whole host of pots appears from your own hands as if by magic, the frustrations and disappointments are all forgotten and there is a real sense of exhilaration.

Opposite: Porcelain can be translucent, and is often light in weight because its walls are thin. This vase by Rudolf Staffel was made on the wheel and its shape was 'altered' by hand while the clay was still soft.

Left: Some of the best-known types of earthenware – majolica and Delft – are characterized by cobalt oxide (blue) and white (tin) glaze. Lidded earthenware jar in red clay by Catherine Vanier. Height: 30.5cm (12in).

2

PREPARING THE CLAY

Like milk, clay is usually seen first not in its natural form, but ready packaged and treated for use. Chapter 1 outlined its origins, but most beginners first encounter pottery clay fresh from a polythene bag. Polythene, when intact and sealed, is airtight, and clay can be kept for many years in this way. As soon as the bag is punctured or the top left untied, however, it will begin to lose moisture and harden. Loss of moisture does not cause damage but the clay has to be softened up again before use and this takes time. It can of course be bought in powder form – the more normal practice in the United States – and this reduces transport costs but adds considerably to the labour of preparation. Nearly 30 per cent of clay in a plastic or malleable state is water, so a ton of powdered clay is more valuable to the professional potter than its plastic equivalent, but most beginners are not concerned with this sort of quantity, and will use new plastic clay straight from the bag, or second-hand clay from

the bin, where it is in the process of recycling. Quite a lot of clay never gets as far as the kiln, having suffered some accident in the making process, and this 'used' clay when recycled, usually by thorough mixing in a pug mill, is often more responsive the second time round. In any event, new or old, the clay will need preparing for use.

Wedging and kneading

Making the clay ready is sometimes hard work, and is too often skimped; inadequately prepared clay will usually fail during the making of a pot or at a later stage and in either case it is maddening. Plastic clay for pots is prepared in the same way whichever technique is to be used. The object of this preparation is to ensure that the clay has a perfectly even texture, and this is achieved by two processes: 'wedging', cutting the clay across with a nylon thread or a wire and forcefully pressing the cut lumps together again on the bench, and 'kneading', exerting pressure on the clay with the hands. This

latter technique is the very first one the beginner will learn, and it is a slight misnomer because dough and clay behave in different ways.

The potter takes a piece of plastic clay not smaller than the size of both fists and places it on a clean flat surface. Potteries usually have very solidly built wedging benches that can support a good deal of weight, and stand firm against the sideways pressure of the hands on the clay. The best surface for the bench top is slate, which is more absorbent than marble but less so than wood or plaster. The heel or pad of muscle at the base of the palms of both hands is pressed against the clay, away from the body. As the clay is pushed away by this action, the fingertips retrieve it and pull the edge of the clay over and back into position so that pressure can be applied again by the heel of the hand. Thus a continuous rhythmic and circular motion is set up.

The clay should not stick to the flat surface. If it does, it is either too wet (and should be replaced by a drier piece

KNEADING

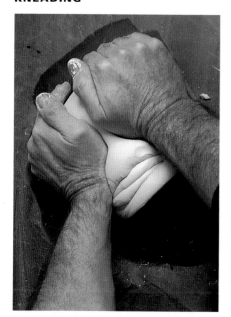

1 A lump of clay is pressed on to the bench to begin the kneading process. Pressure should come from the strong muscles at the base of the palm.

2 The fingertips pull the clay backwards and upwards, folding it over so the 'heels' of the hands can press down again.

3 When the pressure is even from both hands the clay takes up the characteristic shape which gives its name to 'bull's head' kneading.

or dried with additives – see opposite) or the potter is working too quickly on it and should attempt a more rhythmic movement. If the beginner's piece of clay becomes long and sausage-like, it should be stood on its end, pressed down into a more compact lump, and the process started again. Some beginners find the clay becoming 'greasy' and this is because they are stroking it and not using enough force; they should use the heel of the hand more and the fingertips less. Some manage to produce a combination of greasiness and cracking, and the reason here is usually that they have cosmetics on the hands. Clay does make some people's skin dry; it is best to let this happen while potting and use a moisturizing cream afterwards. A piece of clay which has become cracked on the surface is not fit for use and should be put back in the bin for reconditioning.

The classic technique of kneading is often learned in minutes. When this has been completely mastered, it can be varied if desired with the spiral kneading method. By putting more pressure with the heel of the right or left hand, a spiral shape will quickly emerge and if this can be controlled an even texture is very rapidly achieved. Clay which is kneaded spirally remains a constant shape throughout, which is more convenient. It is not necessary to learn the spiral technique, but it is this method which is usually adopted by experienced potters who want to prepare a lot of clay quickly.

A length of doubled, twisted bronze wire with a bobbin attached to each end, or a similar length of nylon thread as used by fishermen, is the tool used to cut through the kneaded clay, like wire through cheese, to investigate the state of the inside. If the wire is passed through the lump of clay at several levels, the slices can be peeled off and the cross-sections examined. Pottery-class clay commonly includes pieces of sponge, lumps of plaster of Paris, metal screws, hairs (very destructive to pots on the wheel) and other foreign bodies which must be rooted out. If the average-sized lump of clay is cut through at centimetre intervals, the slices separated and reassembled, and cut through again at right angles to the first cuts, it is likely that these hidden objects will come to light. So will cracks, air pockets and any hard lumps. A single slice, thrown down on the wedging table, will spread out on impact and any weakness in the clay will show up as a crack or cavity.

The cure for all such faults is simply to continue wedging and kneading the clay, and to slice up the lump at intervals until all the faults have disappeared. It is sensible, when reassembling slices to re-form the lump, to turn each slice over before joining it to its neighbour, so that the clay within the lump will be very thoroughly mixed. For the serious student, the exercise of mixing two different-coloured clays in slices, like a multi-decker sandwich, and then kneading them together clearly illustrates how the technique circulates the clay within the lump until it is perfectly mixed. If the kneading

SPIRAL KNEADING

By applying more downward pressure with the heel of one hand or the other, the clay will be kneaded into a compact spiral like an ammonite.

MAKING FLAWLESS CLAY

1 The purpose of kneading is to make sure the clay has a smooth consistency. When it is cut through, air pockets or hard lumps should reveal themselves.

2 A single cut through the clay will not find all the faults, so it should be cut several times with a wire into slices, like rashers of bacon.

process is done correctly, air pockets are not trapped in the clay by the continuous folding. Beginners often fail to see any improvement in the quality of the clay they are preparing, and the reason may be that they are trying to tackle too large a lump of clay. Halving the quantity is often the answer.

Additives

Certain additives can improve the working qualities of the clay or its texture or appearance. Most common of these is 'grog', which is quite simply ground-down pottery which has been fired in the kiln. This can be as fine as flour or as coarse as granulated sugar, and because it is absorbent it has the immediate effect of drying the clay. It is worked into the clay at the kneading stage, like fine currants into a pudding. Grog usually helps to give the clay a longer working life on the wheel. The pot will stay up longer without collapsing, and coarse grog (or silver sand) gives an attractive texture to the finished pot, although some beginners may find it distractingly scratchy to the hands. Colouring stains can be added to the clay at the kneading stage in the form of metal oxides or carbonates – small quantities are sufficient to affect the colour of the clay when fired – and the colours are described in chapter 14. Some potters choose *not* to knead the colourant too evenly into the clay, preferring the random appearance of coloured spots when the clay is fired.

You will soon find the optimum working hardness for clay. Clay which is too hard or too soft can only add to your difficulties. To test for hardness, try pressing with your thumb against the prepared ball. The clay should yield readily, but should not stick to your thumb when you take it away.

Storing prepared clay

The experienced potter who plans to work on the wheel will divide the lump of prepared clay into several balls, and the beginner should follow suit, having at least half a dozen pieces of clay ready, even if planning only a few minutes on the wheel. The life of a piece of clay when you are learning to throw may be only a few seconds, and it is frustrating and disruptive to have to leave the wheel to prepare more clay in mid-stream.

Clay loses moisture quickly and if put on to an absorbent wooden surface the underside of the ball will become dry and hard, so it is sensible to pile the balls together like cannon balls on a sheet of polythene, which can be wrapped around them if necessary. Once prepared, clay can be stored wrapped in polythene for a long time.

As wedging and kneading can be quite exhausting, many potters sensibly prefer to exhaust themselves first, and take a rest before throwing on the wheel. Others find a short period of preparation beneficial, for it puts them in the right mood, like a few minutes of yoga, or a warm-up before a race.

Hand-made pots such as coil pots are rarely completed in one session, and you should wrap and store enough clay for later use to complete the job.

EFFECTS OF KNEADING

WEIGHING OUT

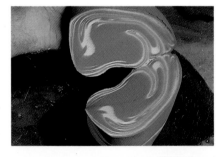

1–4 To understand how the particles of clay are moved around by the kneading process, try kneading two equal-sized balls of clay of different colours, and slicing across. As the kneading proceeds, the streaks of colour are progressively merged until the clay is uniform in colour and texture.

When the kneading is complete, divide the clay up into manageable balls. If you want to make pots of equal size, make sure all the balls weigh the same.

MAGIC OF
THE WHEEL

*The magic of turning a solid ball of clay into a perfect,
symmetrical pot in a matter of seconds draws most beginners
to the wheel. It is not necessarily the technique which makes the
'best' pots but it is the best way to learn how to handle clay.
Beginners, forced through lack of wheel facilities to start with
hand-made pots, can turn directly to the following section
for guidance, though my advice to them is to acquaint themselves
with the wheel and wheel techniques as early as possible.
The next five chapters take the beginner through the various
stages common to all thrown pottery, and illustrate with fine
examples what can be achieved when skills are learned.*

**Opposite: Fluency on the wheel takes
time and practice. The platter by Takeshi
Yasuda shows confident throwing.**

3

STARTING WORK ON THE WHEEL

Wheels

A great deal of strong emotion surrounds the question of choice of pottery wheels. Essentially, a wheel is a smoothly revolving platform capable of variable speeds of rotation, and generally turning a good deal slower than the beginner imagines. Power to turn the wheel can be supplied by the potter, using the feet on a pedal or fly wheel, or by some other source, such as electricity. For the beginner it is best to start on a good electric wheel. Pedalling, like riding a bicycle, usually shakes the body a bit and you need to be distracted as little as possible from the business of controlling what your hands are doing. Many potters prefer to work on a foot-controlled wheel, but usually only after they have learned to judge their 'power requirements' in advance and can use the fly wheel to advantage.

The greatest and most common defects of wheels are worn bearings, making the wheel-head shudder and wobble, and a jerky 'clutch', which starts and stops the wheel violently.

Both faults are trying to the best of potters and as a beginner, if you have any choice at all, you should avoid a wheel with these bad habits.

Centering

The first act in making a pot on a wheel is to centre the clay. There is no one way of centering, though one thing is quite certain: it is not possible to throw a perfect pot from a piece of clay which is not running true. It is essential to master a technique for centering at the outset. A beginner who can cope with some of the later stages of shaping and finishing the pot, but who cannot centre the clay without help is in a pathetic position; left alone, he or she can do nothing at all.

The difficulty of centering clay probably accounts for more despair and disillusion among beginners than anything else. This is because centering is a knack; once you have the knack it is not only easy but, when the clay is running true at all speeds and responding to the pressure of your hands, it is a positive pleasure. When you have reached this stage, you can congratulate yourself.

The centrifugal force of the revolving wheel will try to fling an uneven piece of clay off the wheel-head altogether, and the faster the wheel is turning, the harder it will try. Only when the weight of the clay is so perfectly balanced in the centre of the wheel that the centrifugal forces are equal on all sides will the clay revolve evenly, docile and gently obedient.

It is common sense to minimize the difficulties by making the lump of clay as round as possible before starting, and ensuring that the piece chosen is properly prepared, and not too hard. The amount of clay a beginner can control will depend on the size of his or her hands, but as a general guide a piece weighing about 0.45kg (1lb), or about the size of a large orange – rather larger than a tennis ball – would not be out of the way.

Do *not* throw the ball of clay on to a wheel that is spinning. You are almost certain to miss the centre of the wheel,

CENTERING THE CLAY 1

1 First place the ball of clay centrally on the dry wheel-head, and then wet its surface with water before starting the wheel.

2 With the wheel-head revolving quickly, place both hands together in a cup shape over the clay, and press firmly down.

3 The left hand has to work hard against the side of the ball of clay, while the right hand steadies it, but without pressure.

even at close range, and there is a good chance that you will miss the wheel-head altogether and the ball will land in the water bowl or on the floor. Start with the wheel stationary, and place the clay carefully in the centre of a dry wheel-head, pressing firmly against the surface without distorting the shape. Make sure that your hands as well as the wheel-head are dry before taking this first step. A layer of water underneath the clay will prevent it from sticking because water acts on clay as a lubricant, like oil on metal.

As soon as the wheel is set in motion, the unevenness of the clay will be apparent. Centering can now begin; no tools are needed, just hands lubricated with water. Though water will eventually soften and break down the structure of plastic clay, a film of water is needed on your hands to prevent them sticking to the clay when developing it on the wheel. If too little water is used, the clay will become stubborn and obtuse. Paradoxically, the more water, the less sticky the clay,

though a wheel swimming with water should be avoided as it makes working conditions difficult and soaks clothes.

If you hold your hands loosely over the clay they will wobble as the uneven ball goes round. If you were able to hold your hands absolutely rigid like a steel template, the clay would automatically centre itself underneath them, but it is quite difficult to hold your hands still as the wheel revolves, and the wobbles are apt to get worse and worse. Whether you are sitting or standing at the wheel, make sure that your elbows are firmly braced against the wheel surround – there is usually a rubber padding here for comfort. Encompass the whole of the clay using both hands; try, for example, positioning them either locked together at the fingertips with the thumbs covering the centre, or with the left hand at the side of the ball and the right hand over the top.

The wheel should be rotating quite fast; trying to centre a piece of clay with the wheel turning slowly adds to your problems, and an experienced

potter will centre the clay in a second or two with the wheel turning faster than at any later stage. A beginner using a kick wheel should get up a good deal of speed before touching the clay; you should not have to concentrate on speeding the wheel while your mind is on other things.

Pressure exerted on the clay inwards from the side will raise the clay up in a cone; pressure from above will lower it again, and this movement helps to remove the wobbles. The hands should not be separated but pressure should be applied alternately, first from the side and then from above, so that the clay can change shape underneath them. If you try a different technique and clasp both hands around the clay, drawing them with increasing pressure towards your body, the clay will rise rapidly upwards in a cone – it is taking the line of least resistance. Pressure evenly applied from the thumbs will reduce the cone to a low dome. By raising and lowering the clay several times using one of these methods, the clay

---

CENTERING THE CLAY 1

CENTERING THE CLAY 2

4–5 When the left hand has pressed the clay upwards to make a high mound, the pressure from this hand is relaxed, and the right hand is brought into play.

By pressing hard downwards with the muscles below the little finger, the mound will be flattened again.

Using both hands locked together and pulling the clay towards you is a popular alternative way of centering. Try both methods.

will be encouraged to centre itself. When the hands can be kept perfectly still while the clay revolves beneath them the job is done. In fact, there is no 'correct' way of holding the hands around the clay while centering – only the general rule that they must contain the clay, and be clasped in such a way that they can be held quite still while the wheel turns fast.

Those who find the experience of centering maddeningly difficult must persevere until they get the knack. A state of war with the revolving clay often ends in victory for the clay, but can be avoided if you forget your adversary and simply concentrate on holding your hands still.

Beginners sometimes find that some of the clay squeezes out between the two hands or thumbs as pressure is applied, making a mushroom shape. Or if the clay is flattened too severely with downward pressure, that a sticky, hollow 'navel' appears when pressure from the side raises the clay again. If either starts to happen, the position of the hands should be changed until the clay is comfortably contained. Air, or a pool of water, locked into the centred clay is bound to cause trouble when the pot is being formed, and to avoid this the clay must be kept in a compact shape.

Throwing from the lump

With all this emphasis on centering, how is it then, some beginners will ask, that when you see potters from Japan on television, or peasant potters in their workshops in Spain, they do not bother to centre the clay at all, or otherwise look as if they are throwing from the top of a wobbling mass.

The answer is that they are 'throwing from the lump'. To save time, they centre only the top bit of a large lump of clay, so that perhaps 12 small bowls can be made without having to recharge the wheel with clay each time. It looks as though they are failing to centre: in fact they are not using the part of the clay which is wobbling, and working only with the piece at the top.

Left-handedness

With two left-handed sons, I am aware of the problems presented to left-handers by the right-handed world in which we live. In engineering terms, it would be easy to make a powered wheel which revolves clockwise, but all are made to revolve anti-clockwise, to serve right-handers.

A kick wheel with a pedal or a fly wheel can be made to revolve either way, but a left-hander who makes it turn clockwise will be confounded when, on graduating to a powered wheel, he or she finds it turning to the left. In truth, both hands are more or less equally employed in throwing a pot, so the concept of a 'leading' hand is less significant than in, say, snooker, and it is not as unfeeling as it seems when a teacher adjures a beginner to 'pot right-handed'.

PREPARING TO OPEN UP

THROWING FROM THE LUMP

1 With the wheel turning, run a finger up to the edge of the centred lump to tidy up the clay near the base, and clean the wheel-head of slurry.

2 When the clay is running true, and your hands are not wobbling as the wheel rotates, you can bear down with both thumbs to make a central hollow.

This technique is useful when making very small items like lids. Only the top of the lump needs to be centred.

4

OPENING UP

With the clay spinning truly on the wheel-head the potter is ready for the next stage. Starting to open up the clay to form a pot provides another minor ordeal for the beginner. A hole is made down the centre of the ball with the thumb of the right hand, or with both thumbs together, and many find it hard to prevent the thumb wobbling on the way down. The hole must run as true as the clay, for if the hole is off-centre within the lump, the result is exactly the same as a perfect hole in an off-centred piece of clay – more material on one side than the other.

The first aid to learning this technique is to make a hollow in the top of the clay with the index finger of the right hand; lay it on the clay and move it towards the centre, pressing slightly downwards. Take it away gently and there will be a slight hollow. Now the thumb will have something to aim at when making the hole.

The next aid is to brace the forearms on the sides of the wheel, and to lock the hands together, with the left hand gripping the back of the right hand near the wrist. This should leave the right thumb free. Point it vertically downwards. Now lower it slowly into the ball of clay. Go too far and you will meet the hard surface of the wheel-head. Be too timid and the pot will have a base so thick that it will always feel elephantine, assuming that it does not crack in the kiln. Ideally, the hole inside should go to within 1.5cm (½in) of the wheel-head. Practice alone teaches you when you have gone far enough, though if you clear away the sticky clay from around the edge of the base of the lump at least you will see where the top of the wheel-head is.

Having made the hole, do not withdraw your thumb but push it sideways away from you to widen the base of the hole. Try to keep the tip of the thumb at a constant level, so that the base is flat, and make the movement *slowly*.

Everything done on the wheel is best done slowly. Rapid movements cause spirals which are ugly and destructive, and movements which are started slowly must also be finished slowly. A sudden end to the process of widening the base will be as destructive as a sudden beginning – and the pot will wobble.

Sometimes an airlock is caused at this stage. If you find that a vacuum is being produced as your thumb widens the base, withdraw it *slowly*, until the airlock is broken, and then replace it, along with a little water.

The fingers of the right hand, which have so far been left outside the clay, can now be used. Let them grasp the outside of the form firmly, on the far side away from your body. Then draw the hand slowly upwards and towards you. With fingers outside and thumb inside, about 2cm (¾in) apart, the clay will rise up between them and, if all is well, when the hand gently leaves the clay a hollow shape will have been made. Commonly called the 'inkwell' shape, it is probably easier to remember if likened to an upturned flowerpot. This process which takes so long to describe, and often takes hours to

---

MAKING A CYLINDER

1 Make a dimple with your forefinger in the middle of the centred clay. It is much easier to start opening up the clay in a hollow than on a hillock.

2 By linking hands, the thumb which is making the hollow in the pot will be steadied. An unsupported thumb wobbles and can make an eccentric hole.

3 When the thumb has been pressed down far enough it should, with the hands still linked, be pressed away from the potter to widen the base.

Right: A trim small cylindrical shape like this one by Ursula Scheid is not beyond a beginner's skills. Here the incised decoration and oxide spotting in the clay make the pot exceptional.

Opposite: A cylindrical pot by Herbert Wenzel. The carefully finished rim with its double-chamfered top gives the form its character. It is decorated by trailing glazes (see chapter 19) made from wood ash (see chapter 16).

MAKING A CYLINDER

4 Fingertips of the left hand are pressed against the clay inside; outside it is the side of the index finger alone which presses against the wall.

5 By bracing the hands together with the left thumb, both hands can rise in unison up the wall of the pot, a movement repeated several times.

6 Check that the top of the pot is level, using the index finger of the right hand. Do it gently, and support the wall with your other hand.

learn, should all be accomplished in a single movement lasting about five seconds. As you get more experienced you should aim at producing a firm corner to the inside of the base and an even thickness of wall.

Making a cylinder

The action so far has come only from the right hand while the left hand has been used for steadying. However, some potters prefer to begin opening up using both hands, making the same movements exactly together. At the next stage the two hands have different functions; make sure both are thoroughly moist by dipping them in the water bowl. The *left* hand is used *inside* the pot and the fingertips of as many fingers (not thumb) of this hand as you can get into the pot are pressed gently against the base of the wall. The *right* hand is used *outside* the pot, and the index finger is crooked so that the flat section between the first and second knuckles can be pressed down on the wheel-head. The side of the index finger will naturally fit against the wall or side of the pot. Both hands are then drawn upwards together. The clay, squeezed between the left and right hands, has nowhere to go but up, and in seconds a tall cylinder is made.

You are now in the very thick of it, and with so many things going on it is difficult to concentrate on three additional factors, but you will make great strides if you can maintain three constants: *constant speed of the wheel* (rather slower than for centering – perhaps half the speed), *a constant distance apart for the hands*, and *a constant speed of movement up the pot*. All three are factors in maintaining an even thickness in the wall of the pot. With practice, the hands will be able to withdraw slowly from the top of the clay to leave an even cylinder, running true, on the wheel. By repeating the same motion two or three times from the bottom of the pot to the top, the clay wall can be narrowed to a sensible thickness and the cylinder will reach its 'natural' height.

PROFILE OF A CYLINDER

The walls of a cylindrically-shaped pot should be of even thickness, but widening slightly near the base, and the base itself should be level. It is very **difficult and needs much practice, but from time to time it is worth cutting a freshly thrown pot down the middle to see how you are getting on.**

Putting shape into the cylinder can be described and understood very simply – though putting it into practice often takes a lifetime, for the potter's aesthetic sense as well as his or her practical ability is now tested. Stated briefly, greater pressure from the inside will make the pot swell and the walls belly outwards, whereas greater pressure from the outside will constrict the pot and make a neck or 'collar'. Left to its own devices the spinning cylinder, helped by centrifugal force, would eventually widen out and flatten itself like a torn pancake on the wheel. Therefore more pressure is needed to narrow the pot from outside than to widen the pot from within because you have to act against the centrifuge. For a really effective narrowing, both hands are used around the pot exactly as if you were throttling it, thumbs facing you, fingers round the far side. If the pot is closed up to a very narrow neck, it is important to check that all the water has been sponged out before it is too late to get the sponge inside.

These are the basic principles for making a pot on the wheel. Using the hands in concert, the potter lengthens and then widens or narrows the form. One aspect of the form is fixed by the technique; the wheel ensures that the plan of the pot is circular. The profile of the outside is the potter's affair, and practice will bring expertise in correcting faults as they appear, and anticipation so that they are avoided.

Learning from your mistakes

The commonest fault of all beginners is to make the wall of the pot too thin near the base so that the top ring of clay twists off and stays in the hands of the potter while the base turns merrily on. The temptation at this point is to alter your intention from making a vase to making an ashtray. Do resist it; there are infinitely better ways of making ashtrays, if you need them, and you learn nothing about throwing by fiddling with a sticky palette of clay close to the wheel-head. If this accident happens, as it surely will, the remainder of

the clay must be removed (easier to do with the wheel stopped, using a broad palette knife) and a new start made with a new ball of clay.

You soon realize why it is useful to have half a dozen or so balls of clay prepared for use, and you must not get depressed as one piece after another finds its way into the scraps bin. Neither clay nor time is wasted. When reconstituted, the clay can be used again, and dozens of mistakes are made before a pot is produced which is worth keeping.

A thin wall near the base simply will not bear the weight of the clay above, and if it does not tear apart it will probably sag like a spare tyre of flesh, or twist into a spiral pattern of ripples as strain is put on the upper part of the pot during shaping. Such a pot is useless – discard it (however much it hurts) and start again. The problem of spiral ripples often occurs when a pot is collared in too rapidly or with too much force. The clay, once widened out into a broad ring, especially near the top of the pot,

BELLYING OUT

COLLARING

More pressure from inside the pot will widen the shape, and this is how a pot is given a belly. The outside hand is doing a steadying job.

1 Both hands are needed to make a narrow neck. Imagine you are throttling the pot with both forefingers and thumbs and you will get the action right.

2 The distortion of the clay towards a triangular shape (*left*) is only temporary. It will regain a circular shape if the hands are released gently.

can only be narrowed down again with patience. If the ripples appear, discard the pot, start again from scratch, and next time collar the pot in more gently.

Under-prepared clay, very coarse clay, or indeed any clay at all may crack around the rim of the pot if it is forced outwards too quickly. The broken or uneven rim must be corrected immediately, or the cracks will run right down the pot. A simple technique for correcting an uneven top is to remove a complete ring of clay as the pot revolves on the wheel. This is done using a pin or needle with one end stuck for safety into a cork. If you hold the pin on the outside of the pot in the right hand and press it slowly through the wall of the pot until its point can be clearly felt by a fingertip of the other hand on the *inside* of the pot, a ring of clay will have been cut off. By raising the pin firmly, but not too jerkily, the ring can be lifted off and a new clean rim will be revealed below. This simple and rather appealing exercise floors some beginners completely because they attempt to lift off the ring

too soon, before the point has cut its way through a complete revolution. The technique can also be used to level up the top of a pot which has become lopsided through a fault in the centering or opening up. It will, however, be only a temporary expedient as the 'new' rim will be thicker on one side than the other and more work on the pot will bring up the unevenness again. Each time this happens the top will have to be cut off.

Almost anything can cause the beginner to make mistakes and spoil a pot at this stage. An air bubble trapped in the clay wall like a blister can throw the pot off-centre unless it is 'popped' with a pin, with the wheel stationary. Over-jerky movements, especially in releasing the hands from the clay, will set the pot wobbling towards destruction. Wobbles in the wall need not be fatal to the pot – by drawing the clay up again from the bottom with determined steady hands the wobbles can be eliminated, but they must not be neglected as they will only get worse. In time the

beginner's hands will learn sensitivity towards the clay as the nerves in the fingertips provide essential 'feedback'. Only practice will bring skill, though it helps if you can avoid bad habits. Two things to avoid are sitting with your hands on the pot doing nothing at all, and holding your breath. Beginners spend a great deal of time doing both, often at the same time, which is damaging to both pot and potter. The correct position for the body is forward, with the head above the pot and the elbows resting, if convenient, on the raised rim of the wheel surround.

LEVELLING THE RIM

3 Always release the hands from the clay gently. Beginners tend to jerk them away, which will make the pot wobble, or may cause the rim to tear.

1–2 If the rim has become uneven, press a pin mounted on a cork through the wall near the top, until you can feel its point with your finger on the inside.

Wait until the wheel has turned through a complete revolution and a ring of clay has been cut free before lifting it up and away.

5

SHAPES ON THE WHEEL

The natural shape which the clay most readily takes up is a flowerpot shape, wider at its top than at its base. The discipline of restricting the shape to a cylinder is a good one, though it bores many would-be potters off the wheel. If you can bring yourself to concentrate on this dull shape you will master the technique more quickly. If you cannot resist curved forms, however, it is quite probable that a rather dumpy rounded shape will take over and manage to assert itself in all your pots for a long time to come. Curves which come about by allowing the clay to go the way it wants to go will often 'sit down', or at least look as if they are going to, and wheel-thrown curves are all the better for being taut and vibrant. The hand techniques described in chapters 8 and 10 are more suitable for deep, bellying curves.

Choosing a profile

There is no grammar or rulebook of absolutes relating to the form of pots, but it is not difficult when comparing two thrown shapes to see the difference between a strong, clean shape and a hesitant faltering line, or to react to the grace of a curve or the impact of an angular shape. Some pots appear to have personality, even if their character is an unattractive one, and the elements which make up the personality are sometimes hard to define.

A shoulder or waist can improve the profile by adding a focus for the eye. Any curve which changes in pitch will be more exciting to the eye than a constant curve. Thus the catenary curve or parabola is literally more dynamic than a semi-circle, and a reversing or ogee curve is more lively if the two opposing parts are not matched. Students of harmony and proportion will make their own experiments in pottery and will be rewarded by the results. It is interesting how one shape seems to lead to another.

When the beginner departs from the cylinder, it is very important to have a clear idea of the shape which he or she wants to make. An outline or profile drawn with a clayey finger on the workshop wall is a useful guide, and a visible reminder of your intentions.

All the profiles shown here are 'possible' or 'natural' shapes which will withstand the pull of gravity.

MAKING A SMALL BOWL

1–2 An experienced potter will make a small bowl with a single outward sweep away from the body, using only the thumb inside. Beginners are advised to

follow a gentler sequence, pressing the clay away from the body and supporting the outside wall with the whole of the inside of the left hand.

3 As the bowl is widened, slow the speed of the wheel: the edge of even a small bowl is often rotating too fast for comfort.

Throwing a bowl

No basic pottery shape emphasizes the principles of harmony more clearly than the open bowl, a popular shape historically, functionally and aesthetically. Certainly beginners' bowls reveal more about their makers' skills and judgements than any other form.

A special technique is required to make open bowls on the wheel; it diverges from the 'normal' or upright pot method before the 'inkwell' stage. The potter allows the thumb to make an even curve inside the mound of clay and does not draw the clay towards him or her, but rather eases it outwards from the start so that the bowl form is obvious from an early stage. The drawing up of the wall is replaced by a stage in which the bowl is progressively increased in height and widened at the same time, with the hands at an angle to the wheel-head as shown. A shallow shape is difficult to make as there is a great deal of unsupported clay around the edges, and it is wise to give the bowl a fairly wide base, some of which can be removed during the turning process (see chapter 7).

As the diameter of the bowl increases so does the speed at which the circumference is revolving, and although the wheel itself should be turning slowly for bowl making the rate at which the clay is passing through the fingers at the rim is still considerable. To make the point clear, even if the wheel is revolving at only 60 revolutions per minute, the circumference of a 30cm (12in) bowl is passing through the fingers at the rate of more than 1m (3ft) a second – too fast for comfort. Pressure from the fingers, if jerky or not maintained, will have an uneven but rapid effect, or to put it another way, a mistake may well result in instant collapse.

With no way of supporting the structure radially, like a cantilevered grandstand, a thrown bowl depends for its stability on its body's capacity to withstand gravity. The clay should not be too soft, the rim should not be too fine, the cross-section should taper slightly towards the rim. The thickness of the base of a bowl can with advantage be greater than that of the 'upright' pot. A wide-open shape will appear lighter if it is raised slightly from the surface on which it stands. By removing some of the clay from the base when it is harder, the bowl can be given a slight foot (see chapter 7).

One useful rule to remember when making open or bowl shapes is to keep the form fairly high or 'upright' at the early stages of making; it is much easier to widen and lower a form from an upright shape than it is to close in a bowl that has been made too wide or too shallow. The final profile of the bowl should be left to the very last stage, and more attention should be given to the inside than to the outside, which can be made to match it later on (see chapter 7). The throwing of a very wide, very shallow bowl requires a great deal of skill – even most experienced potters need to be on the top of their form when making such a bowl – and it requires perfectly prepared clay.

4 Reverting to the more normal position of the left hand inside and right hand outside helps to refine the profile of the bowl in its later stages.

Opposite top: A wide shape rising from a small foot is more difficult to make than a deeply curving bowl. This flaring example is by Lucie Rie.

Above: The profile of a bowl is very important, and gentle curves, when thinly thrown, are best in porcelain, as in this example by the author.

The importance of the rim

Many beginners' pots, even the cylindrical variety, have a look of being 'short of clay' or too short overall for their form. Sometimes this is because the top has had to be cut off several times, and always it is because there is just not enough clay in the walls to allow the potter to finish off properly. It is really an aesthetic fault, overcome more quickly if you are aware of it, but it also has practical implications, because a thin rim is difficult to control, and easily damaged.

Massive stoneware pots by Edouard Chappallaz. The spherical pot with a celadon glaze (see chapter 16) depends for its character on the shape and finish of the rim. Here an annulus, raised in the throwing, emphasizes the small central hole. Height: 38cm (15in).

FINISHING THE RIM

GETTING THE SIZE RIGHT

1 Attention to the pot's top is important. Most beginners make too thin a rim, which gives a misleading impression about the wall's thickness.

2 One of the best 'tools' for finishing a rim is a strip of chamois leather. If it is held across the rim as shown, it will create a smooth rounded surface.

A measuring stick fixed with clay on the side of the wheel will indicate to you when your pot has reached the required height or width.

When the hands finally leave the pot at the top, an accent is given to the form as a whole, and character varies enormously according to the final line of the rim. If there is plenty of clay left over, the rim can have a full and luscious appearance, and certainly its thickness will give a clue to the thickness of the pot as a whole, and thus to its weight. The tactile appeal of pots is partly to do with their weight — a pot with really winning ways will insist on being picked up — and its weight in the hand should be exactly what you expect from its appearance. A beginner's thin-rimmed pot will give a nasty surprise as it has a thick base and feels like lead, and equally a thin pot should not have too thick a rim or it will feel lighter than it looks. However, a tight-lipped appearance is sometimes in character with the form as a whole, and so no rules can be set down about the tops of pots. But always bear in mind that the rim of a pot, like the muscles of a face, has the ability to give a pot its expression.

Do not be afraid of spending as long on the rim as you have on the shape as a whole, or of using tools to give a better finish or a contrast between the lip and the outside surface. A small strip of chamois leather held round the profile of the rim will give a smooth, well-finished appearance. A rubber or metal tool will give a rather starker one; a sponge is more gentle, and has the added advantage of soaking up the wet and sticky clay that often accumulates around the top.

Finishing the outside surface

The outside surface of the pot can also be treated or 'finished' with tools. Fingers characteristically leave throwing lines on both the inside and outside, and these are sometimes as personal as handwriting. Large bold throwing lines are often so beautiful and appropriate to a form that to touch them in any way would diminish the pot. A very large thrown pot seems to need its throwing lines to give it 'grain'. On smaller pots they are not always an

attractive feature, and a sponge run gently over the surface, as the wheel revolves, will remove them and replace them with its own finer striations.

Some potters like to use a rubber or metal tool called a 'kidney' (because of its shape). The rubber tool is sympathetic to the clay, leaving a fine smooth surface — it is especially useful for the inside of bowls. The metal one is more difficult to use, but a whole series of metal and wooden tools used on the profile of a thrown pot can achieve forms and surfaces impossible with the fingers. However, there are no nerves in the tips of a tool, as there are in the fingers, to provide a warning to the brain that the clay is uncomfortable and that something is about to go wrong. Sudden death by contortion can come to a pot against which a metal tool is being applied dry or too harshly.

A pointed metal tool will, if held with its tip against the side of a pot revolving on the wheel, cut a horizontal groove in the wall. This weakens the wall and should be done only when the walls have an adequate thickness. Such an incised line gives emphasis to the external form, but can also go some way towards concealing a lack of direction or intention in the profile of the pot, in which case it is a hindrance to the beginner rather than a help.

FINISHING THE SURFACE

1–2 The varying curve of the outline of a kidney-shaped tool allows the potter to use it to smooth almost any thrown shape. A metal tool (*above*) will ultimately scrape the surface very smooth. Many potters prefer a wooden 'kidney' or one made of flexible rubber (*above*).

Taking the pot off the wheel

The beginner who crosses all hurdles unscathed up to this stage may well meet with problems now. Removing the thrown shape from the wheel-head seems to induce nervous shivers in even the most placid, and unfortunately the essence of the operation is smoothness and confidence.

The inside of the pot is sponged dry of water with the wheel revolving. The fingers remove surplus sticky clay from around the base of the pot, also with the wheel revolving, leaving it as clean as possible. A metal tool can be used, if desired, to excavate a V-shaped nick around the very base of the pot before stopping the wheel, as a guide to the cutting thread.

A nylon thread or double twisted wire of the kind used in preparing the clay is then pulled underneath the pot as close to the wheel-head as possible, and out the other side. If the two ends of the wire are crossed over as it is being pulled through, the pot will be cut free at once, and can be lifted straight off the wheel, but this requires a certain amount of practice. The beginner may do better to pull the wire through without crossing it. A little water is then poured on the wheel-head and the operation repeated so that some of the water is pulled under the pot with the wire. This will free the pot from the wheel-head and the pot itself should start to move. The beginner will have looked anxiously inside the pot to see if the wire puts in an appearance on its way through. Pots without bases are not worth keeping and should be destroyed straight away. A slight movement in the clay of the base, however, as the wire passes underneath, is a healthy sign that the base is not too thick.

Any touching of the finished form with the fingers will mark it, and this should be kept to a minimum. A glazed tile or some other smooth surface placed on a level with the wheel-head will help, so that the pot can be slid sideways off the wheel. The tile *must* be clean, cold and wet. If it is dirty, or hot, or dry, or any combination of the three, the pot will stick to it as soon as it makes contact and will be distorted as it is pushed farther on. Similarly, if the pot, when pressed lightly in the direction of the tile with two fingers near to its base, refuses to move, it will also be distorted. The wire should be pulled under it again until it is free from the wheel. With one hand holding the tile and two fingers of the other hand pressing against the pot, the whole operation of transferring the pot sideways from wheel to tile should be completed smoothly in about three seconds. Make sure that the tile is being held level and be ready for it to take the weight of the pot.

Once the pot is on the tile, lift it away to a place where it will not get bumped casually by other potters, their overalls or their arms, but preferably, if there is space, to a position where it can be seen when you make the next pot. If the pot is allowed to dry on the tile, it will become immovably fastened to it, and it is best to guard against this by

SPONGING OUT

REMOVING THE POT

Lower the sponge carefully into the pot (with the wheel turning) so that you do not bump into the walls. When you have dried the base you can see if it is flat.

1 A smooth and confident action must be learnt when removing a pot from the wheel. Do not hesitate when pulling the wire under the pot.

2 Make sure that the surface you are going to put the pot on to is clean and wet, so that the pot does not 'snag' when it slides on.

running a cutting wire underneath the pot again, on its tile, so that it can dry and shrink without getting stuck.

Most pots look enormous when they are on the wheel, and appear to shrink to a realistic size when they are on the shelf. They also shrink in reality as they lose moisture, and again in the kiln, all of which has an effect on the self-esteem. Pots also look very different when seen from the side on the shelf compared to their shape when seen from above during the making, and it is a good thing occasionally to take a side-long look at an unfinished pot while it is still on the wheel.

Small pots are easier to take off the wheel-head than big ones; they can be lifted into the air with two fingers of each hand near the base, rather than slid on to tiles, and experienced potters will do this, to save time. Even experienced potters, though, will think twice about sliding or lifting a really large bowl from the wheel-head, as the distortion to the form is often very great.

The easiest way of tackling this problem is to stick (with wettish clay) a circular plywood disc or bat on to the wheel-head and make the bowl on this, so that it can be lifted off, plywood disc and all, simply by loosening the adhesive clay underneath. Clay makes a firm bond between wheel-head and disc by suction but this can be broken when the time comes by holding on to the disc and rotating the wheel. The pot, perfect and undistorted, can then be placed on the shelf with its disc, but it is a good idea to run the wire under the pot so that it can shrink away from the disc as it dries, otherwise it will probably never come off in one piece.

A thrown shape which is complete in itself may need attention as it dries, and the commonest process is that of 'turning' when the pot becomes as hard as firm cheese or leather. The whole process of finishing is described in chapter 7 and the beginner should look there for help in the finishing or leather-hard stage. However, many composite pots like teapots require elements which are made with plastic clay at the wet stage, and for the sake of completeness these are described first, in the next chapter.

THROWING ON A BAT

1–2 Lifting a shallow bowl or plate from the wheel is difficult. It is better to stick a circular wooden bat on to the wheel-head by placing it on top of a pad of clay, grooved for adhesion as shown. The thrown pot and bat can then be lifted off together (*top*).

GALLERY
THROWN POTS

Below
HEIN SEVERIJNS
A beautifully rounded pot,
well suited to the crystalline-
type glaze. Stoneware.

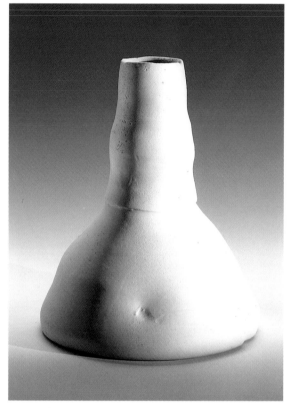

Above
ROBERT TURNER
'Beach', a thrown and
dimpled form, and part of a
series of soft-thrown forms
for which the artist is famous.
Height: 31.75cm (12½in).

Right
JANET MANSFIELD
A standing form, wheel-
thrown but showing the
marks of a metal tool used
while the pot was still wet.
Texture comes from a
granite-sand addition to the
body, and the patina and
natural ash glaze spotting
comes from slow firing in an
anagama-type kiln. Height:
30.5cm (12in).

Above
PETER VOULKOS
The most rugged of potters,
Peter Voulkos, made this
massive pierced plate,
wood-fired to stoneware
temperatures. Diameter:
59cm (22in).

Below
MICHAEL CASSON
This stylish bowl, with its
handsome rim, is a good
vehicle for the painted
decoration under a salt glaze.

Right
LUCIE RIE
The tall vase was squeezed
after throwing and raw
glazed. Manganese bleeds
through from the body clay.
Height: 35.5cm (14in).

6

LIDS, LIPS, HANDLES, SPOUTS AND COMPOSITE POTS

Many finished pots are the result not of a single wheel-made unit but of several items joined together when the clay has dried to the leather-hard stage. A teapot, for example, consists of a spout and a handle as well as a body and a lid. This chapter ends with the fascinating subject of composite pots – the making of complex sculptural shapes by joining together thrown or hand-made units, but it must inevitably begin with the more workaday business of describing lids, lips, spouts and handles for functional pots.

Compared with the general technique of throwing, learning to make all of these extras is very simple indeed. Integrating them into a fine single shape is much harder. The handle must not only fit the hand and be comfortable to hold, but it must also look as though it fits the pot. The lip of a jug must be in character with the shape of the pot it serves. The body of a teapot must only look complete when all its parts are assembled.

The extras contribute a good deal to the expression of the pot and each can be made in a variety of ways. By describing in detail first a jug, and then a teapot, much of the technique will be covered. The beginner is advised to try as many permutations as possible.

Lips

Making the pouring lip of a jug is done with the fingers while the pot is attached to the wheel and the wheel is stationary. It is disarmingly simple. The rim of the pot is stretched and bent outwards by one finger (usually the index finger of the right hand) while two fingers (usually the thumb and *second* finger of the left hand) restrain the rim from becoming too distorted. Provided the rim is not treated too roughly, and torn or cracked, an unsatisfactory lip can be erased and the circular rim restored by collaring and working the clay with the wheel in motion again, and the potter can then make another attempt.

Check that the handle and the lip are in a straight line when seen from above. If not, the jug will not pour properly.

MAKING A LIP FOR A JUG

1 The index finger of one hand pulls the lip outwards and down while the thumb and a finger of the other hand hold the clay back on both sides.

2 The restraining hand will raise the rim slightly, giving an undulating line and helping at the same time to funnel the liquid to the point of pouring.

3 If the finger and thumb are next slid firmly down the pot below the lip, they will make a 'throat' which emphasizes both function and form.

The index finger which does the stretching should leave as fine and sharp an edge as possible on the lip, even if the rim is a thick one. One of the perennial problems for potters and the ceramics industry in general is making a non-drip spout or lip. A drop of liquid will cling readily to a rounded surface when the liquid is being poured and will then run down to the foot when the pot is righted again. The elimination of this most irritating defect often presents the potter with an aesthetic problem, for the best pourers often look strained and ugly. The secret is to make a very fine edge at some point on the lip, even when the shape is a full one.

A thick ridge of clay below the rim will often help to give emphasis to the line of the pulled lip by underlining it, and this ridge also forms an aesthetically attractive attachment point for the handle (see page 40). The rate at which the liquid is funnelled towards the lip will also affect a jug's pouring qualities, and the funnelling effect is increased if, during the making of the lip, the two

restraining fingers are used firmly. By pulling back with these two fingers as the lip is drawn forwards, the surface of the rim will be made undulating, which often gives the pot more dignity. The beginner should practise with many shapes and compare the results to the 'cut' lip method, which is popular for coffee pots. This involves placing a folded triangle of soft clay against a cutaway shape in the rim of the pot and attaching it in the same way as a spout or handle.

Handles

On wheel-made pots handles are best made by the pulling method. This involves taking a piece of clay of throwing consistency shaped like a carrot, holding it firmly in one hand, and stroking it downwards with the other, rather like milking a cow. The need for constant lubrication with water makes it sensible to pull handles near the sink. However, on large pots they are best made on the work bench directly on the pot: the raw clay carrot is attached

Above: Pulled handles may be too floppy to be used immediately they are made. They can be hung up to dry a little.

Opposite: Casserole by Jane Hamlyn.

PULLING 'OFF THE POT'

1 Grasp the carrot of clay with one hand and pull the end downwards with the other hand, lubricated with water.

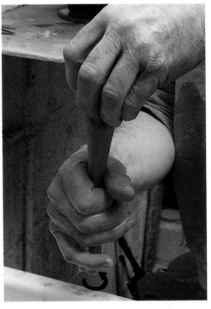

2 If you move the position of the hands through 180° (see arrow), the handle will have a symmetrical cross-section, which makes it more comfortable to use.

3 Try to avoid a handle which tapers to a point. The strip of clay should widen slightly towards the base.

directly to the pot at the desired point by scoring the leather-hard pot's surface with a pin, adding a little water, and pressing the thick end of the carrot on to it. The pot in question has to be stout and firm enough not to be distorted when the handle is pulled out to shape, and best results are achieved if the pot can be held at an angle and the handle pulled downwards.

Large handles 'pulled from the pot' appear to grow out of their source naturally, and when the handle is the correct length and thickness it can be bent over and attached at the base with the pressure of two thumbs. If the handle is too long, the extra length should be broken off before attachment, but the extra clay is usually removed when the thumb of each hand is used to 'splay' the lower attachment into the classic shape. The shape can be modified slightly after the handle is attached, but bending or squeezing usually spoils the 'arch' and if the pot is turned upside down to dry, sagging caused by gravity will be translated into uplift when the pot is righted again.

The bottom of the handle should never be made thinner than the top. Practice will teach the puller how to regulate the squeeze so that the handle is slightly slimmer at the centre than at the two ends. Pulling the handle on the pot is suitable also for small lugs on large jars, and for the kind of handle which sticks straight out like a lever. A straight handle can occasionally be used on a pot such as a coffee or milk jug, but it is only practical if the handle springs from a little lower than half way down the pot, so that the weight is counterbalanced about the handle as it is turned.

Beginners usually make handles separately from the pots which they are going to fit, but they should never be made in isolation. The potter who keeps an eye on the pot is more likely to make a handle of the right size and shape. The cross-section of the handle, made in the deep crook of the hand between the thumb and the forefinger, can be made symmetrical by turning the handle round through 180° so that both sides of the handle in turn meet the 'crook'.

MAKING A LEVER HANDLE

1–2 If you want to fix a straight handle to a small bowl it is a good idea to pull the handle from the pot (see top of text column), and then cut it to length afterwards. However, a knife cut will leave an edge uncomfortably sharp to the hand, and needs softening with sandpaper when dry.

Like throwing lines on the side of a pot, handle profiles are as personal as handwriting and most beginners take time to become fluent. Basic rules to remember are always to make sure you have enough clay in the carrot for the handle required, leaving a healthy lump at the top by which to grasp it while it is being made. Too many handles slip to the floor at this stage. When the shape is right, attach the handle firmly to a horizontal surface, letting it hang down like a dog's tail to dry a little before attachment. Finally, always make at least twice as many handles as you need to allow for accidents at the attachment stage. Many handles are forgotten in the pressure of events during class and go too hard to be used. To test for hardness, remember that the handle, hanging nearly straight downwards, should be capable of

Some of the decorative lugs on a fine pot by Wayne Ngan. They are made from worms of clay and fixed like small handles on the shoulders.

MAKING MATCHING HANDLES   ATTACHING A HANDLE

When you are making a set of pots with handles, be sure you have plenty of pulled strips matching in size and length.

1–2 Many beginners have difficulty in using soft clay without giving it a 'handled' look. Only experience will teach you how to stick a half-pulled

handle to a prepared patch near the rim of a jug. Pull it out with wet hands until it is elegant and pliable.

being bent to the appropriate arc without cracking across, but should not be so wet that it will inevitably respond stickily to handling.

When it has dried sufficiently, take a suitable candidate from its sticking place and remove the unshaped lump at the top end with the ball of the thumb. This makes a slightly concave shape well adapted to the curve of the pot. The concave face should be textured by scoring lines or making small holes with the point of a sharp pencil. It is now ready to be married to a correspondingly scored surface on the wall of the pot. A little water squeezed from a sponge on to both surfaces will help to make the bond a firm one, and water is a better adhesive than sticky clay or 'slip', though some potters keep bowls of sticky clay nearby especially for this purpose.

If the jug or pot is held 'face downwards', the lower attachment can be made by allowing the handle to arch over, pressing the end down with two thumbs, at the same time breaking off

An earthenware jug made by Theresia Hebenstreit. The bird is scratched on to the pot and the beak is part of the spout. Height: 71cm (28in).

any superfluous length. Beware too great a pressure, which can damage the shape of even a leather-hard pot, and take care too that the upper attachment does not spoil the circularity of the rim. It is important to ensure that the handle of a jug with a lip or spout is exactly opposite the lip or spout, or pouring becomes a messy business, and it is also important to check that the handle, when seen from above, sticks straight out. If it is bent, it will be uncomfortable in the hand.

Beginners find that pulled handles often break in the pulling and a common fault is to make a handle which tapers too much to a point. Early attempts are often lumpy and a disgrace to the pot, but the beginner can take comfort; the technique of making perfect handles becomes apparent with practice. They can also be made by the casting method (see chapter 13) and by the ingenious technique of pulling an oval loop of a very stiff wire, like a monocle on a stick but without the glass, through a block of prepared clay. This will release an even strip of clay, the profile of which can be adjusted by changing the shape of the wire loop. Try it. The handles are perfectly uniform and can be used more quickly after making than the hand-pulled ones, but they have little individuality and no soul. Circular handles with a similar lack of sensitivity can be made by slicing a thrown cylinder into rings and attaching a ring, like an ear, to the side of the pot.

A potter can spend a lifetime making jugs alone, fruitfully varying the size and relationships of handles and lips. The jug has a very strong appeal because it is totally self-justifying; as a storage vessel, adapted for the transfer of its contents, it answers a basic domestic need and puts in an appearance at all stages of civilization and in many cultures. Museum collections of medieval ware often include jugs and pitchers which are perfect forms, however coarse grained the materials; industrially produced jugs are often gawky or downright ugly by comparison, although in the 1930s and again in recent years they have often been the focus of much ingenuity and wit.

3 Bend the handle over to its lower junction point, which should have been roughened up, ready for a firm join.

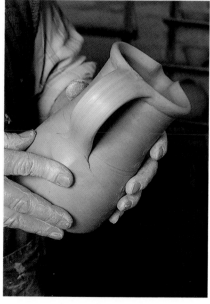

4 Break off the excess clay and splay the base with two thumbs, as shown. Then smooth over.

Lids

When the beginner can tackle a teapot he or she is really making progress, for this is the most complex of everyday pots. The basic form must be made to accommodate a lid, which should not fall out when the pot is tilted. Lid and spout should be made at the same time as the body of the pot; the handle made later. A suitable body for a teapot may well look rather dumpy without its additions; it will certainly have a specialized rim, usually with a recess or 'gallery' into which the lid can nestle. This recess is made simply, and in a few seconds, towards the end of the process of making the teapot body.

Rather more clay than usual is kept at the top of the shape, and the rim is flattened with the index finger of the right hand. The thumbnail on the left hand is then brought vertically down to split this rim in the middle, and a little downwards pressure makes a step in the rim. The edge of the recess should not be too fine and thin, though its profile should be fairly square and it should slope downwards slightly towards the centre. If the shape of the recess is an awkward one it may well be difficult to clean. The thumb and thumbnail are the most sensitive tools for this operation, though a wooden modelling tool can be substituted if the thumbnail is totally the wrong shape. Very long fingernails are a considerable encumbrance when making pottery, and very short ones are also unhelpful.

A chamois leather is useful for rounding off the inside edge of the recess, and the outside profile of the pot should be checked after the downward pressure of gallery making. It is difficult to do further work on the inside of the pot without damaging this recess, so make sure you are satisfied with the shape first.

When the pot is removed from the wheel, two measurements should be taken straight away with callipers. These measurements give the correct width for the lid and for its 'throat'. Only one pair of callipers is needed. The measurements can be 'stored' by pressing the calliper tips into a piece of plastic clay which should be kept nearby.

The teapot's lid should be thrown on the wheel straight after the body of the pot and made from the same kind of clay, to ensure the same colour and shrinkage. It will need a throat to stop it falling out of the pot as the tea is poured and, traditionally, it should also have a small hole to let out the steam. The top will need a graspable knob. The lid can be made on the wheel in two ways – either upside down or with its top uppermost. If the upside-down method is used, the throat is made first, by hollowing the middle and ensuring that its diameter matches the calliper measurement; the remaining, upper side will be completed on the leather-hard lid at the turning stage (see chapter 7). This is all much easier to do than it sounds – or looks. If the top-side method is adopted, a knob can easily be isolated by pressure with the thumbs slightly away from the centre, raising a lump in the centre. A lid made

---

MAKING A GALLERY

1 Jam pots, storage containers and teapots need snugly fitting lids, and these usually rest on a 'gallery' just inside the top rim of the pot.

2 Having widened and flattened the rim, it is easier than it looks to press part of this flattened rim down with the thumbnail, or a modelling tool.

3 Now measure with callipers the inner and outer edge of the gallery, so that you know how big to make the lid and its throat.

the 'right way up' on the wheel needs a very thick base, as the throat will have to be shaped out of it at the leather-hard stage (see chapter 7).

Lid making is rather a long-winded business, and for quantity production lids are usually designed so that they can be made quickly with little follow-up work. The design and technique, however, must relate to the form of the mother pot. The profile of the lid must continue or complement the pot as a whole and the potter should be able to see the main body of the pot while making the lid so the two are in sympathy. Lids made in isolation rarely look right when the pot is assembled.

A luscious porcelain espresso set by Carol Roorbach. Though traditional in design, it expresses modern hand-made pottery at its best, and sits on its own thrown tray. It has been salt fired to cone 10 (see page 137 and page 177).

LIDS: UPSIDE-DOWN METHOD

LIDS: TOP UPPERMOST

Making a lid upside down on the wheel is easy. You raise a 'throat' as shown here, making sure that its diameter accords with your calliper measurement.

1 If you are throwing a lid top uppermost, you must leave enough clay below the lid to provide for the 'throat', which is completed at the turning stage.

2 Check the measurement of your lid with callipers. Do not make it too small. You can reduce it when turning, but widening is impossible after throwing.

Left: Lid designs, made upside down (upper two) and topside uppermost. The yellow areas represent the clay removed by turning.

Above: Designs for storage jars, the upper one designed for safe stacking.

If the lid needs to be sharply arched, then it can be made upside down in the form of a bowl, perhaps flattening towards the rim, and its knob added later. Similarly, the lid can be made like a sort of beehive, the right way up. Getting the size right can be difficult – the lid should fit snugly with limited play in its recess. Neither is it easy to produce a knob which suits an elegant small teapot, but which is substantial enough to hold and robust enough not to break in the washing-up bowl.

There is no limit to the possible variations, though not all of them are practical. The higher the lid the more unstable when the pot is tilted, the smaller the knob, the less insulation it will provide for the fingers, and teapot lids can become very hot. The knob itself can be added by throwing when the rest of the lid has become leather hard. A small ball of clay will stick easily to the centre of the lid and, using a very little water, a knob can be shaped on the wheel, and any extra clay cut off (see page 63). The common-sense reason behind this rather curious approach to the knob is that it significantly reduces the amount of work at the later, turning stage.

Pots other than teapots have different requirements for lids. It is useful for storage jars to have lids which are flush with the top of the pot, or to have a recessed knob to help stacking. Rarely can ceramic lids be airtight unless they are aided with rubber or cork washers, and where hygiene is important, as in jam or mustard pots, it is a good idea to avoid profiles which are difficult to clean. Overlapping lids may be the most suitable here. Really wide lids for casseroles should be made on circular bats (see page 37) so that they can be removed from the wheel without distortion. It is the casserole lid which, manipulated as it needs to be in a hot and hostile oven, most usually falls short of the ideal. It needs to have a really large knob or strap handle which can be grasped, even through an oven glove, and which at the same time must be low or it is sure to tangle with the shelf above. Casserole bodies often have small lugs on the sides to help the cook, but the most helpful lid is a relatively deep-throated one which can be lifted from the side, without falling off the casserole base.

Spouts

Our teapot still needs a spout, and this can be made by casting (see chapter 13) or throwing. Any other hand method will probably be too crude for this delicate job. It is quite simple to throw a small hollow concave shape like a miniature cooling tower, using clay from the centred top of a lump. Open the clay with the thumb as usual but only use the smallest finger of the left hand inside for drawing up or the spout will become too big and clumsy. Finish the lip with a small outward curve, and cut through the clay near the base of the small tube, lifting it off and storing it on a tile. As with handles it is wise to make rather more spouts than you need so that there is always a spare in case of accidents.

Throwing on the wheel is the easiest part of the operation of making a spout. When it is leather hard, the wider lower part must be cut at an angle with a sharp knife to fit the belly of the pot body. The spout should then be placed roughly in position and a fine outline scratched on the pot around the edge of the spout. A metal drill-bit of approximately 5mm (¼in) diameter should be used to make the holes which will restrain the tea leaves, and this should be done by twisting the bit with the fingers very carefully, with a hand or finger on the inside of the wall to prevent it from giving way.

The pouring end of the spout can also be cut at an angle, although this is not

THROWING A SPOUT

1 Small fingers help when making a spout for a teapot. It is thrown like a miniature cylinder, and then squeezed to an appropriate shape by collaring.

Above: Tenmoku-glazed teapot by the author. A knob which is easy to grasp, and a throat so deep that the lid will not fall out, even when tilted, make for a friendly teapot.

Below right: An elegant cane-handled teapot by Geoffrey Whiting.

always necessary. A scored surface on both the pot and the base of the spout is needed to make a good bond and the two should be pressed firmly together with a little water on the contact surfaces. A comic and catastrophic fault is that of making the level of the top of the spout lower than that of the lid, so the pot can be filled to the point where tea gushes from the spout without tilting.

Spouts can be used on drinking flasks as well as tea and coffee pots, just as handles and lids are needed on a great variety of pots. These items can also be applied purely as decoration, but if they are to be practical they must function properly and feel right in the hand. The rhythmic ease with which a professional makes such additions takes much practice.

2 The final rim needs to be really fine to minimize drips, and confounds the usual principle of indicating the thickness of a pot by its edge.

ASSEMBLING A TEAPOT

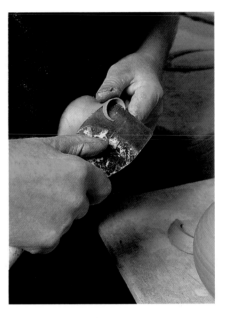

1 Hold the leather-hard spout against the body of the pot to judge the shape of the join. Remember the level of the spout must be above the gallery level.

2 Cut the base of the spout away at an angle. It needs to make a snug fit against the body of the pot.

3 Sometimes the pouring end is cut nearly horizontal before the spout is attached to the pot, the new sharp edge deterring drips.

4 A boring tool, which has a metal tube cut at an angle, is good for making the fan of straining holes at the base of the spout.

5 A scored edge to bond spout and body, and some water for adhesion, are essential before placing the spout and pressing it on.

6 The join is finished with a modelling tool or knife, and it may be necessary to add a worm of clay to make a smooth junction.

The teapot-maker's skill is shown in the cross-section (*left*) of a standard design by Julia and Bryan Newman. The unfired but finished pot (*above*) is also by the Newmans, the arch handle being made from a ring cut from the top of a wide thrown cylinder.

7 The pulled handle is attached in the normal way, but make sure that it is exactly opposite the spout.

8 Traditionally there is a small hole in a teapot lid. It can be made in the centre of the knob, or alongside.

9 Once the lid has been turned to fit, it can be placed in the teapot so that the two parts can dry – and shrink – in harmony.

Composite pots

A composite pot is the result of joining together units which were made separately. The elements may all be made on the wheel, or some may be hand produced or cast. An advantage of the composite pot is that it extends the potter's capabilities beyond the working limits of the wheel. Thrown cylinders can be joined to make towers more than a metre high. Or they can be cut up and set at right angles to the main axis or rearranged completely into sculptural structures.

The technique is extremely simple. Thrown pieces are cut when leather hard with a sharp knife, the contact surfaces are roughened or scored and joined together with a little water. Clay is heavy, of course, and gravity is an important factor in design. Occasionally composite pots may gain by appearing to defy gravity, but it is obviously not practical for ceramics which are going to be handled or used to have either a high centre of gravity or an unstable shape.

ASSEMBLING A COMPOSITE POT

1 A fruitière is a simple composite pot for beginners to try. Made from a thrown bowl added to a thrown stalk, you start with both parts leather hard.

2 The underside of the bowl and the top of the stalk are scratched where the surfaces will meet and wet to ensure a good join.

3 Central location of the stalk can be verified by turning the wheel (see page 58). It is not easy to make two thrown shapes combine into a harmonious unit.

It is possible, with a great deal of patience, to throw a very tall pot all in one piece, but soft clay will make such a shape unstable on the wheel, and the failure rate will be very high. It is much more practical to make two forms, joining them when the clay is hard enough to bear the weight.

Provided composite pots retain a single vertical axis, they can be completed on a revolving wheel with the use of a metal turning tool (see chapter 7) to smooth the join or by adding a ring of clay over the joined areas. The concept is straightforward in practice, though difficult to explain: if a sausage of matching clay is carefully arranged around the pot as a complete ring at the junction between the two thrown units, it can be worked with the hands using very little water and a perfect join can be made.

The many aesthetic problems which emerge from the composite technique are all-absorbing. How to combine two dissimilar and distinctive shapes into a satisfactory unit is a good exercise for the serious student and, indeed, it may occupy a lifetime. The technique may be simple, but it is difficult to combine shapes harmoniously. When you do succeed your composite pots will have a vibrant tension quite unlike that of a pot which is made in one piece. Thrown pots should be relaxed but composite pots can gain by this tension and the technique provides a unique opportunity for a potter's work to change its pitch and increase its scale.

The work of two contrasting potters is shown in these examples of composite pots. Bernard Leach's traditional oriental form (*opposite top*) is made by joining two flat press-moulded shapes (see chapter 12) and adding a thrown neck and a modified thrown foot. The totally original spade form (*right*) by Hans Coper is made from two thrown cylinders, one of which is flattened and inserted into the other.

GALLERY
TEAPOTS

Left
SHOJI HAMADA
A classic faceted body, echoed in the cut strap handle, makes for a stylish teapot with an oriental air.

Right
JANE HAMLYN
An impressed pattern and rouletting is used on the handle, lid and body of this pot, which was squeezed to a distinctive oval form after throwing, while still damp.

Left
WALTER KEELER
Even a teapot of fantastic form – and there are many historic examples – can function well. In this salt-glazed teapot an extruder (see page 99) has been used for the handle, spout and part of the lid.

Below
TAKESHI YASUDA
White slip and a shiny, transparent glaze cover the luscious curves of a pot decorated with navel-like sprigging and the green and brown staining of manganese and copper carbonate. The continuous-section handle was made with a wire loop, as described on page 45.

Left
ARNOLD ZIMMERMAN
'Teapot with Blue Swirl' – the handle, spout and knob do not always have to follow convention. Here the robust but quirky forms are an essential part of the design, complemented by the bold, wax-resist pattern.

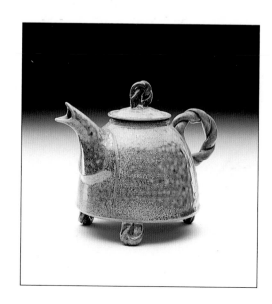

Right
MICHAEL CASSON
This appealing design echoes the form of a metal kettle, with its cut-back spout and added feet, but the lid and handle are made from twisted ropes of clay. A thin white ball-clay slip was used and the pot salt glazed.

7

TURNING, FINISHING AND FETTLING

When a pot has been removed from the wheel it can be allowed to dry completely and then fired in the kiln without further attention. More usually, however, there is work to be done on it as it dries. It can be altered in plan – either squared off or squeezed – while it is still wet but most of the work of cleaning up or 'fettling' the pot is done when the pot has dried to the 'leather-hard' stage.

The term 'leather' or 'cheese' hard is fairly self-explanatory: clay at this stage can be picked up and handled without damaging the shape; it can be pared easily with a knife. If the parings flake into small pieces instead of staying in long strips like apple peelings, then it is too hard. If the wall of the pot gives to gentle pressure, then it is too soft. The leather-hard stage is also the final stage at which major changes may be made to a pot's surface, and these include incised designs, fluting, perforations and the application of slips, described in chapter 18.

Drying the pot

Drying must be carefully controlled and should not be hurried. If directional heat is applied to a pot, the shape will be distorted as one side dries more quickly than the other, and this is irretrievable. The exposed parts of a pot will normally dry more quickly than the base, and to prevent strains and overdrying of the rim of a bowl it is a good idea to turn it upside down on to a smooth surface when the rim has become firm enough to support the pot's weight, as this will stop the rim drying and expose the base to the air.

Pots which have dried out totally cannot be turned, and damping down pots which have become too dry, by soaking them briefly under the tap, or immersing them for a second or two in a bowl of water, is a risky business. Ideally the pot should be caught at exactly the right leather-hard stage, and this poses a serious problem for the once-a-week student. Most home potters have 'damp cupboards' which should be airtight to keep the moisture in, but all too often are left with doors open. In damp autumn months a pot may take a week

or so to dry, depending on its size and thickness, but in summer a few hours is enough to dry a fresh pot to the leather-hard stage.

If a pot can only be attended to at weekly intervals, a fairly airtight biscuit tin is an essential part of the beginner's personal equipment as in this a damp state can be maintained for longer periods. The trouble with a biscuit tin, of course, is that its contents are invisible from outside and may be damaged if it is carelessly handled; pots are very vulnerable at all stages until they have been fired in the kiln, and any contact with the surface of a damp pot will leave its mark. A better, more expensive, protection is a rigid transparent and airtight plastic container, which is more likely to be handled with respect.

The purpose of turning

It is at the leather-hard stage that the extras such as spouts and handles are fixed to the mother pot, and thrown items can be joined to make composite

pots as described in chapter 6. But most people associate the leather-hard stage with 'turning'. In this process the leather-hard pot is again placed on the wheel and metal tools are used to remove surplus clay. The process can be a creative one, the entire form being refined, inside and out, with a turning tool, but more usually it is a corrective one, especially for the beginner, who has the opportunity to improve the shape of the base of the pot by cutting away clay.

Turning is a slower process than throwing, and often beginners will spend half an hour or more turning a pot which has taken only two or three minutes to throw. For a corrective process, this is quite ridiculous. Several new pots could have been thrown in the same time, and the potter would have made more progress. The beginner should try to avoid the pitfall of throwing crudely, and then trying to turn some aesthetic quality into the pot at the leather-hard stage. In classes,

RIBBING AND RESHAPING

The best tool for altering thrown forms while they are still wet will have a certain spring in it – a split bamboo 'rib' is better than a metal tool.

Inverting the pot and pressing the rim on to a plaster pyramid will square off the top of a wheel-thrown, or slip-cast, cylinder.

laborious turning can monopolize wheels for hours on end, with a bad effect on everyone's patience. Common practice is to use kick wheels for turning, reserving electric wheels for throwing. If an electric wheel is available, however, it is equally suitable, and will probably help to get the job done more quickly.

There is nothing sacred about turning; it is not an inevitable ritual. The pot should be judged for shape and weight as it stands. Only if it is found wanting should it be turned. Very simple forms, if well thrown, need no turning.

Centering the pot

As with throwing, turning involves fixing the object centrally on the wheel, working on it and removing it, and each stage has its minor hazards. Most open shapes will be fixed to the wheel upside down, and the rim of the pot, so carefully made, is now in contact with the metal wheel-head where it can be easily damaged. If the wheel-head is too wet, the rim may soften and buckle.

If the wheel-head is completely dry, the pot will have to be held in place by means of a long sausage of clay, like a rampart around the pot, or by a trio of balls of clay – perhaps a little harder than is used for throwing – pressed against the rim. The pot must be precisely on the centre of the wheel, and a good start towards achieving this is to make a series of concentric circles on a damp wheel-head with a fingernail. However, some metal or wooden wheel-heads are already inscribed with concentric grooves. If these rings are about 5mm (¼in) apart, one of the circles is bound to correspond closely to the rim of the pot, which can then be carefully positioned and the balls or sausages of clay added.

Many experienced potters will dispense with these buttresses and rely on the natural adhesion of a damp rim to a damp wheel-head, but the beginner is strongly advised to use them, taking care not to buckle or distort the rim with too much sideways pressure. It is maddening when turning a pot to

see it fly off the wheel-head and crumple up in the wheel tray. To avoid this it must be firmly fixed on the head, and supported. A disc of fairly hard clay completely covering the wheel-head, and completely level, can be used as a bed for very vulnerable or fine rims. Clay is kinder to rims than the hard metal of the wheel-head, but it must be firm enough not to stick permanently to a pot being turned, and sometimes a dusting of powdered clay between the turning 'bed' and the pot itself will usefully reduce adhesion.

Inversion of the pot allows its true base, inaccessible during the throwing, to be shaped, and this is particularly important for bowls. Vertical shapes such as vases, jugs and coffee pots, however, do not always need a concave or hollow foot, and if any tidying up is necessary around the base, it can be done with the pot the right way up on the wheel.

Leather-hard pots put on the wheel for turning must be centred, and running true. You can tell if a pot is off-

---

POSITIONING FOR TURNING 1   **TURNING A FOOT RING**

Your finger or a pointed tool will tell you if you have centred the rotating upturned pot correctly. The balls of clay keep the pot in place.

1 Only when the bowl is running true should you mark the base to indicate the inside and the outside edges of the foot.

2 Use a sharp tool held steadily in the hand. The thumb of the left hand is helpful as a brace, and the rest of this hand protects the pot.

centre when the wheel is revolving because it will wobble, but the wobble is hard to see when the wheel is brought to a stop to correct the fault. To check if a pot is centred bring the point of a needle or pointed turning tool towards its surface at its widest part as it revolves. Stop the wheel when the point has made contact with the clay. If the resulting scratch mark runs right around the pot, then the pot is truly centred, but if it is only a short cut, then the pot is clearly out of true and the pot should be pushed *away* from the centre of the curved scratch. How far to push it? Experience will tell, but it is usually less than you think. Adjust the clay wedges around the pot before you begin again. Hopefully the pot will now be running true, but check for centre again by the same method, and do not start until the pot is running true.

This burnished earthenware bowl by Duncan Ross was carefully turned to a smooth profile after throwing.

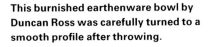

3 Turn away the clay from the outside as shown. The leather-hard clay should come away like apple peel. If it falls in small flakes, the clay is too dry.

4 Reverse the direction of the turning tool when you are making the inside of the foot. You are aiming to match the curve of the inside of your bowl.

5 Look carefully at the outside profile before you finish the turning process. It can change the character of a pot, not always for the better.

Useful turning tools. Round-headed tools will cut concave curves; straight ones are often used on convex surfaces. The hooped tool on the left is the self-sharpening tool made of banding wire designed by Hans Coper.

The tools for turning

Turning can be done with any tool capable of cutting through clay and a variety is made and sold for this purpose. Personal preferences vary enormously and it is quite likely that a broken or sharpened kitchen knife will outstrip all manufactured tools as a favourite. The veteran potter Lucie Rie always used a sharp needle and a razor blade for turning, until she was given, by Hans Coper, a self-sharpening, home-made tool which uses pallet banding-wire. Most turning tools are bars of metal bent at right angles at the end and shaped to make a blade, and all of them are better if they are sharp. Tools with a convex profile are the only ones which will carve out hollow curves, and straight-edged tools are better for convex shapes and straight sides. A minimum requirement, therefore, is one of each sort. Tools made of very heavy metal bring their weight to bear on the pot and, like heavy screwdrivers, they make light work. Wire-loop turning tools cannot be heavy but the wire at least must be very strong and not springy.

Most beginners learn to turn with the tools which are available at a pottery class. The inevitable wetness and untidiness of the working area make them rust quickly and get blunt, and they seem to get lost very easily. If you go to class with only one tool of your own, let it be a sharp turning tool, and make sure you put your name on it.

Checking for thickness

Before starting to cut away the clay you must have tested the thickness of your pot. How thick is it at the base? With a bowl it is relatively easy to tell, simply by feeling both sides at once and deducing how far apart your fingertips are. With an enclosed pot it is less easy, though a needle point pressed through the base will give some idea by its resistance how long it takes to go through the bottom, and a pinprick of these dimensions will soon fill in during the turning process.

POSITIONING FOR TURNING 2

MAKING REPEAT SHAPES

1–2 An alternative method of holding a leather-hard pot is to put a pad of stiff clay on the wheel-head first, and by marking it with concentric circles you can make the centering process easier. The clay on the wheel-head should not be too sticky, or it may spoil the rim of your pot.

Potters who repeat shapes in quantity will make a plaster chuck to hold their bowls for turning, and this is also a good way of checking the size.

Once the pot is inverted on the wheel there is no way of telling how thick the bottom is except by pressing it. Tapping the bottom provides information rather too late, because its note is dull while the pot is thick in the base, and changes its pitch only when it becomes membrane-thin, inappropriately thin for any pot. Most beginners turn their way right through the bases of several pots, and as soon as a hole appears you must discard the pot. Repairs can be made by adding clay of the same consistency, but it is better to learn to turn correctly than to learn to make repairs.

Turning technique

Always work on the right-hand side of the pot, as in throwing, and hold the tool in the right hand, steadying the blade if possible with one of the fingers of the left hand. The rest of the left hand can sometimes be cupped around the form, ready to catch it if it decides to jump off the wheel-head. The angle at which the blade meets the clay of the pot is important. The best angle will soon be obvious from experiment but it certainly will be an acute angle, much less than 90°, so that in effect the cutting edge is dragging clay from the pot rather than stabbing into it.

A tool held at the wrong angle may bounce rhythmically and uncontrollably against the clay, making ripples like those which water makes on a seashore, and these are called 'chatter markings'. Invariably ugly, they are sometimes tiresomely difficult to remove. As soon as they begin to appear the beginner must stop work, and find a remedy. Blunt tools and dry clay are also frequent causes of chatter marks. Sharpening the tool, dampening the clay with a wet sponge and changing the position and angle of the tool will help to remove the marks and restore a smooth surface.

The surface created by the turning tool is inevitably different from the one your fingers make in throwing, and a pot which changes texture at some point on its profile because of this often suffers aesthetically as a result. The whole profile can be turned lightly to remove this inconsistency, but such a form loses its life and looks more mechanical than when it showed the marks of throwing. It is best to keep the turning to a minimum on the side of a pot and to learn to make the merging of the two surface textures as sensitively as possible.

The base as thrown on the wheel, with the inevitable fingermarks left after it has been removed from the wheel, is often a more appropriate shape than a neatly turned base. A few minutes' work with a turning tool on the side of a pot can transform the proportions and, alas, this is very often for the worse. Because it is difficult to assess the effect you are having on the proportions of something which is upside down, a pot which is to be inverted for turning should be studied carefully before the process begins, and any change to its profile planned in advance of starting the work.

It is vital in the finished pot, however, that no really sharp edges come into contact with a table or other surface on which the form will finally stand. Glaze on a sharp edge can be as sharp as broken glass when it is fired and will cut hands and certainly scratch tables. All 'corners' should therefore be rounded off to avoid these sharp edges. The rounding is effective if only very slight, and crisp hard-edged forms do not need to look softened.

Making a foot ring

Although carving clay from the underneath of many upright shapes is quite unnecessary, with bowls the outside profile can be turned to follow the inside profile. The very base of the bowl thus remains convex, like an egg, and the bowl stands on a foot ring which is left when the clay within it has been turned away. It is sensible to mark with two fine incisions (which become rings as the wheel turns) the position of this foot on the upturned base, and to cut away the clay on the outside first and then in the centre, leaving the foot ring as a projecting ridge. This order is important, because it allows the outside profile to be determined precisely and satisfactorily without burning your boats.

Foot rings for bowls and other pots can have many different characters. They lift the main form up from the surface on which it stands, and this always lightens the appearance of the pot, but the potter should experiment with outward- and inward-facing, vertical, broad and narrow profiles in the foot ring, and study if possible oriental examples, which cannot be bettered for harmony with the form they have to carry. Small high foot rings are often elegant and graceful, but wide low ones are usually both more practical and stable.

A bowl thrown, turned and inlaid by Lucie Rie. It is thrown in one piece and the tall foot hollowed out by turning.

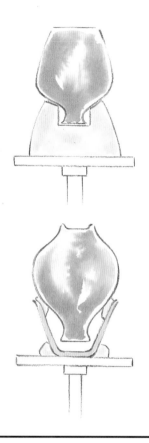

Using a chuck

If it is necessary, in order to make a foot ring or for some special purpose, to invert a tall slender shape, there is immediately a problem of stability on the wheel, and the usual method is to prepare a 'chuck' or recessed bed on the wheel-head.

Clay is used for this chuck, and it should be a little harder than throwing clay. It is not necessary to centre the clay for the chuck but the clay must be levelled at the top, without using water, with a metal tool like a steel ruler, and a centred hollow should then be made with a sharp metal tool and not with the fingers, in order to accommodate the top of the inverted pot. A perfect 'female' shape is rarely possible, but it is essential that the chuck should grip the pot firmly and hold it so that it is truly vertical. It is not necessary to use the same kind of clay for the chuck as was used in the pot itself. It is wise, however, to use a smooth ungrogged clay for this purpose, as coarse clay can be scratchy,

and a dark-coloured clay used for a chuck will occasionally stain a pot which is made of white clay (or vice versa) and so too great a contrast between the clays should be avoided.

Sometimes a tall pot which is to be turned can be inverted and lowered into the neck of a fired pot, itself fixed to the wheel with a ring of clay. This gives greater stability than a chuck when the load becomes top-heavy.

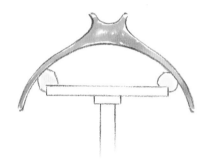

Above: Bowls and other shapes larger than the wheel-head can overhang, and need to be protected with a ring of clay from the wheel's unforgiving edge.

TURNING ON A CHUCK

1–2 Thrown shapes are not always easy to invert on the wheel. A clay chuck as shown in the drawing top left can help to steady a narrow-necked vase, or

a finished pot can be improvised as a chuck, illustrated in the drawing above left. The cylinder shown being turned (*above*) sits astride a clay cone.

TESTING FOR A LEVEL BASE

If the stem of a heavy turning tool wobbles when you hold it across the foot of your turned bowl, then the base is uneven. Press down to level it.

Occasionally the diameter of a bowl's rim will be greater than that of the wheel-head, and when inverted it will be very difficult to 'hang' it over the wheel without damage. In such a case, a centred lump of hardish clay, matching as closely as possible the inside profile of the bowl, should be used to grip the bowl firmly on the wheel, or a ring of clay used to cushion the wheel's unrelenting edge.

Handling a dry pot

When the pot has become completely dry it is fragile, brittle and no longer cold to the touch. In its unfired state the pot is known as 'green'. Handled carefully, a dry 'green' pot can be sandpapered. This is another corrective process, which in certain respects replaces turning, though it is much slower. The effect of sandpaper on the exposed surfaces is almost always unpleasant as the material is insensitive and attractive marks made in the throwing are quickly rubbed away. Fine sandpaper can be useful in smoothing the

Pots which are wheel made but then turned all the way up have a character of their own. This porcelain vase with inlay is by Nicholas Homoky.

joints of spouts and handles, but again only as a corrective measure.

The most sensible use of sandpaper is smoothing the uneven bottoms of pots which have not been turned. If the sandpaper is rubbed on the pot's base, the base will probably be rounded and the fault aggravated. If the sandpaper is fixed on a table and the pot rubbed on it, the surface of the base will be made smooth and the pot will stand firm. Loose grains of sand or grog on a hard smooth surface such as slate make an even better abrasive combination for the base of a pot, and if the green pot is ground carefully with a circular motion on to this the base of the pot will quickly be made level.

Experienced potters have learned by making mistakes how vulnerable green pots are to breakage. They will *never* pick up an unfired teapot or teacup by its handle, or a bowl by its edge. Beginners often do just this, and the pot breaks. At this stage in its life a pot cannot be repaired and all the effort of making it is wasted.

LIDS: UPSIDE-DOWN METHOD

LIDS: TOP UPPERMOST

1–2 It is very easy to add a knob to a wheel-made lid at the turning stage. Press a ball of clay on to the scored surface in the centre of the lid and, with a very little water, shape it with your fingers as the wheel turns, and the turning can then be completed.

If a lid is wheel thrown top-side up, it has to be inverted on to a clay chuck, and the underside and throat shaped by turning.

GALLERY
COMPOSITE POTS

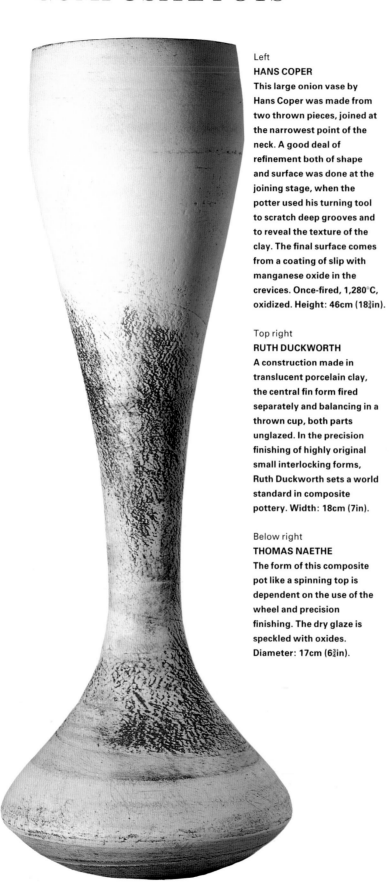

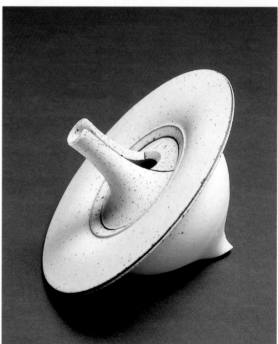

Left
HANS COPER
This large onion vase by Hans Coper was made from two thrown pieces, joined at the narrowest point of the neck. A good deal of refinement both of shape and surface was done at the joining stage, when the potter used his turning tool to scratch deep grooves and to reveal the texture of the clay. The final surface comes from a coating of slip with manganese oxide in the crevices. Once-fired, 1,280°C, oxidized. Height: 46cm (18¾in).

Top right
RUTH DUCKWORTH
A construction made in translucent porcelain clay, the central fin form fired separately and balancing in a thrown cup, both parts unglazed. In the precision finishing of highly original small interlocking forms, Ruth Duckworth sets a world standard in composite pottery. Width: 18cm (7in).

Below right
THOMAS NAETHE
The form of this composite pot like a spinning top is dependent on the use of the wheel and precision finishing. The dry glaze is speckled with oxides. Diameter: 17cm (6¾in).

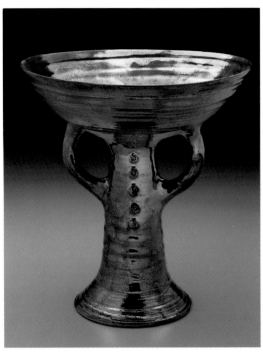

Below
PAULIEN PLOEGER
The use of thrown units to make figurative sculpture, particularly figurines, has a very long history. The combination of wheel-made units to build an abstract form is more recent, and is a test of the artist's sculptural ability. This handsome work owes much to its decoration, which uses a combination of paper resist, masking tape, exposed brush strokes and overlapping glazes. Stoneware, 1,250°C. Height: 30cm (11¾in).

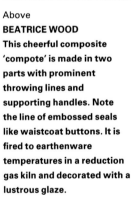

Above
BEATRICE WOOD
This cheerful composite 'compote' is made in two parts with prominent throwing lines and supporting handles. Note the line of embossed seals like waistcoat buttons. It is fired to earthenware temperatures in a reduction gas kiln and decorated with a lustrous glaze.

POTS
BY HAND

*The creative spirit is freed when hands and simple hand tools,
and nothing else, are employed in making pots. Without a wheel,
the discipline of radial symmetry disappears, and it is up to the
potter to create a form which is interesting and also well
enough balanced to stand without falling over.*

*Museums are full of hand-made pots, from palaeolithic beakers
through the continuing tradition of tea bowls in Japan to the
massive slab structures of contemporary artist potters. There are no
limits to size other than the size of the kiln. But wait – it is not
necessarily easy: the great Shoji Hamada wrote of hand-made pottery
enigmatically, 'Its simplicity makes it the hardest of all to make.'*

**Opposite: A hand-built form enriched
with metal oxides by Ewen Henderson.
Diameter: 43cm (17in).**

8

COILS AND COILING

It is a humbling experience to visit a gallery of African pottery such as that at Burlington House, in London, and be confronted by pots powerful and perfect, made for everyday use, and entirely by hand.

As a technical device the wheel may give speed and precision, while imposing discipline, but there is no question of its having elbowed hand-made ceramics into second place as far as worth and beauty are concerned. The would-be potter without a wheel must never for a moment feel he or she lacks the facilities to make pots. Some trepidation is justified, however, since, armed with a simple technique and the simplest of tools, the beginner is entering the arena from which have emerged many of the world's greatest pots, and much of the best modern work.

Alas, many pottery classes are so short of wheels that teachers often introduce beginners to pottery by starting them on hand-made shapes. The implication of this is not only that the technique but the *concept* is for the novice. Added to this is the inevitable association in a classroom between working clay by hand and the 'play-clay' of kindergarten. To be introduced as a beginner to the hand-shaping process when you have not become familiar with the characteristics of clay on the wheel is no fun. Clay will crack, sag, stiffen and stick to the table. It will appear obtuse and messy, and reluctant to yield up any reward. The sooner you can come to terms with it by mastering it on the wheel the better. At the same time, given the fact of limited wheel facilities, many beginners are obliged to start with hand-made pottery, and I hope that this section will be helpful to them, not least by classifying and describing some of the numerous different techniques.

There are several minor techniques of hand building, and two principal ones, both evilly named. 'Coiled' pottery allows the potter the freedom to build really large pots, as big as the kiln will allow. 'Slab' building (described in the next chapter) allows the potter to use hard-edged forms and plane surfaces of infinite variety. Some modern potters combine the two techniques.

Coiling, the traditional method of many African potters, usually produces pots which are circular in cross-section, or which approximate to a radial symmetry, like an apple or a gourd. Both are apt similes, for of all the pottery techniques this is the most organic. It does not lend itself to precision any more than the beauty of a woman or a whale can be invoked by following rules or numbers. The technique obeys the natural laws of gravity (unlike throwing which is often helped by centrifugal force to defy them) and has a more direct relationship between its structure and its form than other methods. The potter makes a number of long rolls of clay, circular and solid in cross-section. These are called 'coils' (though they are not twisted in any way) and, laid in rings one on top of another, they form the walls of the pot. Shape is controlled by the size of the ring.

Coiled pot by Jennifer Lee. Height: 25.5cm (10in). 'Because hand building necessarily involves constructing in layers, a line of distinctively coloured clay with its own individual minerals fired within it can form a stratum that may run completely around and across a pot from one wall to the other. And because Jennifer Lee does not use glaze, so her subtle colours and misty shades come not from a veil draped over the pot but from within its very substance, as in the face of a cliff.' Sir David Attenborough

Making the coils

Clay for making a coil pot is prepared in the same way as for throwing, although very plastic throwing clay is not necessary for this technique and most potters prefer a coarse grogged or sanded clay, which will have a better 'tooth' and texture. A favourite clay for coiled pots is called 'crank mixture', originally prepared for making the 'saggars' or protective drums in open-flame kilns. It is cheap and coarse to the point of being abrasive. Red clay is also popularly used for coiled pots, and is better if it includes grog (see chapter 2).

Because of the variations in the amount of shrinkage from one clay body to another, it is not easy to mix clays when coiling a pot, though potters can do so to good effect, as explained in chapter 17. It is usual, however, to use the same clay throughout, and important to provide yourself

Coiled raku pot by David Roberts. Diameter: 60cm (24in).

PREPARING THE COILS

The most widely used method of making coils is to roll them out under the fingers on a clean bench. Do not try to make them too long.

An alternative method is to roll a sausage of clay vertically, allowing gravity to help to lengthen it. It is speedy and quickly learned.

By pressing the clay between finger and thumb you extend it vertically without rolling it, making a 'strap' of clay which many potters prefer.

with enough clay to finish the job. Coiling is one of the slowest methods of making pots, and at a once-weekly class you may well spend three weeks or so on a pot. Put your store of clay away in an airtight bag with your work each week, or you may find the clay in the bins is of a different colour and type at the next session.

Both the diameter of the clay sausage and its length are important. It is not wise to make coils less than 1cm ($\frac{3}{8}$in) in diameter, and it is not practical to roll them under the hands when the length exceeds about 45cm (18in). The width of your hands placed fingers outstretched side by side so that the thumbs just touch indicates the maximum length of clay you can control. If the roll of clay is wider than this, the coil will become twisted and will probably break, as only the clay under your fingers rotates with rolling.

A lump of clay the size of a healthy carrot will make a roll of sensible length and the potter will make about seven or eight rolls before beginning the pot. To make more is a mistake, however, as rolls dry very quickly, especially if laid on a wooden table, and as soon as they are too stiff to bend freely they are useless and must be put in the scraps bin.

Some potters like to start their coils by squeezing a large carrot of clay held vertically into a rope, using gravity to assist in the lengthening process, or by rolling it between the fingers vertically. A simpler method of making coils is to extrude them through a template of appropriate size in an extruder or 'bulley' (see page 99). Hand-operated versions of these machines are now widely available, and opinions vary as to whether the uniform coils which they produce assist and speed the potter or deaden the work because they are inorganic and boring.

Building techniques

In some primitive societies potters walk backwards around the pot, feeding out the coil like a hosepipe on to the clay wall, but in confined spaces and certainly for smaller pots it is a help if the pot itself can be rotated as it is being made. The ideal help here is a 'banding' wheel made of heavy cast iron in two parts. Most potteries have them, and mostly they get broken as beginners lift them from bench to bench without realizing that the bottom will fall out and smash expensively on the floor. Without a banding wheel the wheel-head of a kick wheel will do. Failing that, a biscuit tin or any solid box placed on the bench to raise the pot up to a better working height will serve, and by moving the box every now and then the pot can be turned on the bench without itself being touched.

Most potters make the base of a coil pot by rolling out a disc of clay with an ordinary rolling pin. Silver sand or grog, canvas or simply a piece of newspaper should be put underneath the clay to prevent it sticking to the table while it is being rolled out. If the clay sticks to the rolling pin it is too soft, and firmer clay should be used, or the lump dried out. If the pot is to be truly circular, a circle can be made on the disc with compasses or

DIFFERENT TYPES OF COILS

STARTING A POT

In the foreground are extruded coils (see page 99), regular in cross-section. Compare them with the hand-made coils behind them.

1 The base can be rolled out or pressed with the side of the hand to a thickness which should match the diameter of your coils.

2 The first coil added to the base is firmly bonded with the thumb. The marks made by the potter's thumb need not be smoothed away.

by cutting the disc while it rotates on the wheel-head, the surplus clay being cut away. Do resist the temptation to draw round some handy plate, as this will fix the size of the base and will almost certainly not be the size you require. The thickness of the rolled-out disc should be the same as the diameter of the rolls of clay and certainly should not be less than 1cm (⅜in).

A roll of clay is pressed on to the base to form a complete ring and further rings are added to this. No 'glue' is required, just pressure from the fingers and the rolls will stick to one another. Any water or slip added to assist in gluing one coil on top of another will make both hands and clay sticky, and reduce the potter's control. Nor is it a good idea to use a continuous spiral of clay, as in this way the top of the pot will never be level, but continuously mounting. It is not at all necesary to have complete rings of clay each time, as small lengths can be added with ease to fill in the gaps. Obviously if a watertight vessel is to be made the walls must be even, without cracks or holes, and the best way of achieving this is to press down each ring of clay on to its neighbour until it becomes oval in cross-section. Then, after every four or five rings, you must join up the coils on both sides of the pot with downward pressure from the fingers or a tool. When an enclosed shape is made, it is difficult to smooth over the coils on the inside, but one side at least must be joined in this way.

The fingermarks or tool marks are like throwing lines, personal to the potter, and an enormous variety of surfaces is possible. Some beginners leave – indeed are encouraged to leave – the coils on the outside untouched, so that the pot looks like a clumsy sort of Michelin man, in the mistaken belief that this is a more traditional or generic form. I have never seen a pot made in this way look other than ridiculous, and it is naturally weaker in structure if the coils are not joined up.

Many beginners, unable to grasp the principle of widening the pot's shape by adding ever larger rings of clay, are paralysed into making a pot of constant diameter, like a wobbly umbrella stand or an elephant's leg. Others widen the pot over-ambitiously, and it responds quickly by sagging out of shape or collapsing because of its unsupported weight. Pots started on small bases often appear to get wider and wider but no higher as each coil in turn spreads outwards, sags down and adds to the diameter of the base. Thus are ugly hyacinth bowls made, annually, by the thousand.

When making wide coil pots, it is essential to anticipate collapse. If the wall begins to bulge slightly, or the top appears flaccid or lifeless, then the next step is to put the pot into shape around its rim, support the sagging profile with wedges of hard clay or sponge rubber if collapse is imminent, and then store it safely away on a shelf to dry. Depending on temperature and humidity, the pot will stiffen up in between half an hour and two hours, and work can then begin again. If the top coil

CONTROLLING THE FORM

1 Rings of clay of increasing diameter will widen the shape, but the wall of the pot needs support from one hand while the other does the joining.

2–3 Joining up the coils after every four or five circuits can be done by hand (or with a wooden tool). It needs to be done thoroughly on the inside of the form before the top is narrowed, when access is more difficult. The outside can be tackled later.

becomes as hard as cardboard, it should be softened with water from a sponge run around the rim. Avoid using slip, which always makes everything sticky, and use water very sparingly, as it will run down the walls and can do damage at the base of the pot.

The outward curve of a coil pot can be reversed simply by using progressively smaller rings of clay. The problem of collapse is aggravated slightly in the early stages of narrowing, for the pressure essential to join up the coils will be partly downwards, and as the top of the pot gets smaller it is harder and harder to get a hand inside to give the necessary support. Sometimes it is a good idea to fill the pot with crumpled newspaper, which has a supportive springiness and will, of course, burn away in the kiln. If the form is fairly spherical, a rubber balloon can be blown up and tied at the neck inside it. This provides much support for the shoulder of the coiled form, and can always be deflated or popped when the coiled form is dry. Other supports used at the making

A thinly coiled pot with droopy top by Betty Blandino. Height: 20.5cm (8in).

stage, such as props of clay, have a habit of getting jammed inside the pot, and if such a pot is fired it will rattle irritatingly for ever.

The use of props on the outside to support a generously bellying form while it dries causes no problem; these can be removed later. The potter should take care to use clay which is slightly harder than the working clay for these props so that they do not stick permanently to the pot.

A fat ring of clay, like an inflated inner tube or indeed a car-tyre inner tube itself, arranged around the pot will help to support it while it is being widened. If a really shallow enclosed form is planned, the walls can be permanently supported and strengthened inside with vertical ribs, like the balsawood 'fins' which separate the membranes of a model aeroplane's wings. A shallow hand-built shape can be successfully supported in a plaster mould, and many fine modern pots have been made in this way. The shape of the lower part of the pot is dictated, by the

CONTROLLING THE SURFACE

Coiled pots seem dull at the early stages, but remember that tall cylinders can be coiled to heights beyond the limits of wheel-made pots.

After the coils are joined the pot is receptive to decorative techniques – such as added ribs or impressing – at all stages until it is completely dry.

The texture which is put on to the coiled pot is almost as important as its form. Here the fingermarks maintain a regular angle.

mould, however, and it is best to make a mould specially for the pot (see chapter 12). A shallow curving base can also be achieved by making the first few coils over a football and inverting the shape when it has dried a little. Such a shape would need a coiled foot ring for stability.

It is quite difficult to get a pot stable about its centre when coiling. The problem does not arise in throwing, and may take the coil potter by surprise. Most pots which emulate natural 'vegetable' forms with radial symmetry, such as pumpkins or tomatoes, do not need a vertical axis, but if a finished pot is to hold water, stability is important. Unstable pots usually have a short life and it is not wise to make wide coiled pots with too small a base.

Finishing the top of a coiled pot demands the same care as the top of a thrown form. It should be emphasized, and a roll of clay, perhaps of smaller diameter, can be added to the top coil to give it extra width. Walls of constant thickness are desirable for the rest of the form, and they certainly must not be thin near the base. Coil pots can afford to be heavier in relation to their size than thrown pots, and a coil pot which feels uncomfortably light in the hand is a poor specimen. Making coil pots with walls which are pathetically thin is one of two major mistakes made by the beginner; the other is starting the pot without the faintest idea of what shape you want to make. It is essential to start the pot with a clear idea of its finished form, and it is a good thing to draw it on the bench top in pencil so that it is constantly before you. Although the finished result may not look like the drawing it will certainly be better than one made haphazardly without a preconceived form in mind, for in coiling, a good shape never comes about by accident. In the main the same principles of form apply to coil pots as to thrown pots (see page 31). Changes of angle, as in shoulders and flanges, attract the eye and often indicate strength. However, very rounded organic curves and forms which squat low to the surface on which they stand are often peculiarly appropriate to coiled pots, and not to

other techniques. A coiled pot need not be circular, but in my experience coil pots which deliberately diverge from the circular plan to be triangular or oval are often less successful. In that respect coiled pottery is rather like basket making.

Texture on coiled pots

Once the coils are joined together, the surface can be left alone or, as with thrown pots, it can be treated as it grows harder and drier. Of all the tools I have ever used, an old hacksaw blade is the best I know for working the surface of a coil pot. Because it is flexible it can cope with three-dimensional changes of curve, as can a plastic comb. A smooth piece of wood used to beat the surface may also be effective. The beginner must experiment. The texture left by fingers alone is not always very pretty but neither is a surface which is over-worked. Impressed designs made with seals or stamps are not as effective on coiled pots as designs in applied relief, such as fins or ribs, and sometimes projecting lugs or handles added to a coiled pot become an integral part of its form.

Coiled pots tend to take longer than thrown pots to dry out because of their extra thickness. Occasionally the base of a coil pot will crack if it has stuck to

Coiled pots can be as light as egg shells or as heavy as hand grenades. Good ones always cry out to be touched.

Opposite: A finely coiled pot by Alev Ebüzziya Siesbye, with a subtly out-turned rim. Diameter: 21.5cm (8½in).

Above: Massive pot by Ruth Duckworth – cobalt oxide in the dark brown slip burns through the glaze which runs over the outside surface.

the surface on which it stands, and it is therefore important to make sure that the pot stands free on its bat or base before putting it away.

I suppose that pottery classrooms are littered with more bad coil pots than any other kind, usually broken and unfired. These spectres and a general sense of apparent purposelessness about the slow act of making a coiled pot (pots made on the wheel, however bad, seem self-justifying) must turn most beginners off coiled pottery for ever, if not ceramics as a whole. A wheel is not needed in order to make good pots, but care and concentration are. A bonus for those who persevere is the knowledge that coiled pots can be made big – very big. But it is worth checking on the size of the kiln to be used for firing before you start.

GALLERY
COILED POTS

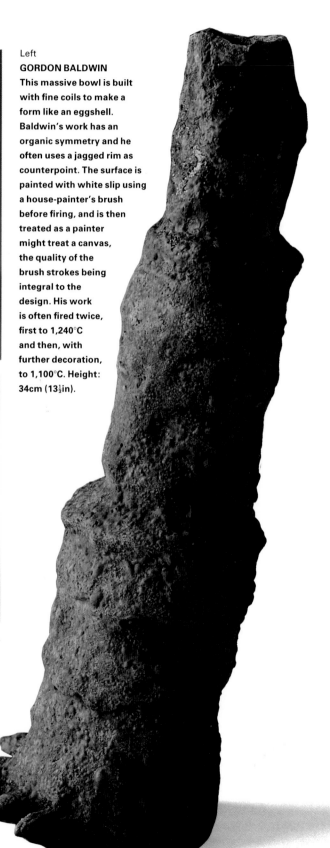

Left

GORDON BALDWIN
This massive bowl is built with fine coils to make a form like an eggshell. Baldwin's work has an organic symmetry and he often uses a jagged rim as counterpoint. The surface is painted with white slip using a house-painter's brush before firing, and is then treated as a painter might treat a canvas, the quality of the brush strokes being integral to the design. His work is often fired twice, first to 1,240°C and then, with further decoration, to 1,100°C. Height: 34cm (13½in).

Above
GABRIELE KOCH
Right
MARTIN LEWIS
Gabriele Koch's bowl is finely coiled and burnished to give a pewter-like patina. The complementary smoky decoration comes from a second sawdust firing in an outdoor drum-kiln. This immaculate pot contrasts with the craggy surface of the Martin Lewis pot. Made from several strips of oxide-rich clay in rings of diminishing diameter, it is carefully balanced, and poised with a series of 'claws' near the base.

Below
JENNIFER LEE
Hand-builder Jennifer Lee uses coils, and mixes oxides with the clay to achieve varied coloration in the once-fired end product. The clearly distinguished hoops of darker or lighter material in this bowl are the result of placing the coils at an angle to the axis of the pot. The level rim and very even profiles of the work are not the result of turning on a wheel – the pots are scraped down and burnished by hand, and fired to 1,270°C with reduction. They are sometimes refired in an oxidizing kiln, and always scrubbed with wet-or-dry sandpaper or abrasive cloth after firing.

9

SLAB POTTERY

The term 'slab' pottery is an unattractive one. Slab pots are neither flat nor undecorated, as the word seems to suggest. Put simply, slab pottery is the technique of making pots out of sheets of clay rolled out like pastry, often using a kitchen rolling pin. The technique taught to beginners is often illustrated with examples of dreary shallow boxes filled with cactus plants, or dishes shaped like hearts, to show that the sheets of clay can be curved. Any technique can be used to produce something boring or ugly, but pots made from sheets of clay can be exhilarating and lively, and it is this area of ceramics that has been one of the major growth points in recent years.

Slab pottery is not a 'natural' technique in the way in which coiling and throwing are natural developments to answer the need for practical vessels. Slabs of clay are not even as strong as pastry, but if they are handled when in exactly the right state of hardness, they can be most obedient materials. A rolled-out slab of clay is essentially a

Hexagonal slab pot by Shoji Hamada. The flat faces make good surfaces for brush decoration. Height: 20.5cm (8in).

flat surface and, therefore, like a plate, a splendid vehicle for decoration, whether incised, embossed or painted. At the same time sheets of clay are pliant and can be folded like leather into sculptural forms, though unlike leather they have no resilience to make them spring back again. Equally, while a pot made on the wheel is essentially abstract as it does not represent anything in nature, slab pottery can be, for example, both a ceramic form and representational at the same time.

The degree of precision achieved in throwing and turning is difficult to match with slab pottery, but the beginner is strongly advised to aim at a high standard of finish, and particularly at uniformity in thickness of slabs. Compared to the jointing of wood, slab building lacks all the sophistication of carpentry. It depends on butting clay together, and gluing simply with clay or water. The joins must be well made because unlike coiled pots, where construction is masked by textures, slab joins are often left bare.

ROLLING SLABS

SLICING SLABS

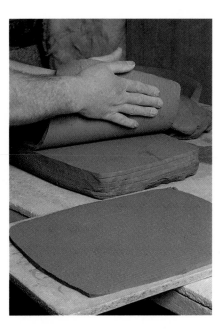

A block of prepared clay can be rolled into an even thickness if wooden guides of equal height are placed on either side of the clay.

1–2 Wire stretched between two notched sticks will slice the clay like cheese. By moving the wire down a notch and cutting again, a series of slices

of matching thickness can be cut. The top one should be discarded (for recycling) and the others separated out.

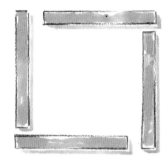

Above: Only if slab sides of equal size are arranged in a 'follow-my-leader' pattern (*top*) will they make a pot which is square in plan. The other arrangement makes a rectangular box – it can only be made square by cutting two sides shorter to allow for the thickness of the clay.

Below: Lasagne dish by Sandy Brown. The slabs are curved slightly to give the pot a soft appearance, and the flat rim and handles added to make a practical domestic piece. Dimensions: 40 × 25.5cm (16 × 10in).

Making a box form

The process of building a basic square or rectangular form illustrates most of the problems encountered in making a slab pot. Prepared clay should be rolled out on a surface to which it will not stick, and the best insurance against sticking is to spread a layer of grog underneath the clay, like flour under pastry. The grog can be as fine as flour or coarse like sand, but in each case it will cling to the surface. If a grogged surface does not appeal, then rolling the clay out on a sheet of newspaper is best. The clay will stick to this, but it can be pulled off when dry. The advantage of rolling out the clay on a piece of heavyweight canvas is that the clay sheets can easily be moved without damage by lifting the canvas. The clay, however, takes up the uniform texture of the canvas and this is not always attractive.

Two flat pieces of wood of equal thickness placed on each side of the clay will restrain the rolling pin as the prepared clay is rolled with the result that the slab of clay will be of even thickness all over. A good alternative method of making the sheets of clay is to pull a wire through a lump of prepared clay, raising the height of the wire by regular steps. The tools for doing this – a pair of notched sticks and doubled, twisted cutting wire – must be carefully used but can save the slab maker a great deal of time. The slices of

clay should be spread out so that they are equally exposed to the air for drying, and they must be turned over every now and then or, like slices of bread, they will curl at the edges as they dry.

The requirements for a pot with an open top are a base and four sides. Having allowed the slabs to dry a little, a clean, sharp, dry knife should be used to cut the pieces. A plastic set square will help to make the right angles at the corners and it is important to hold the knife vertically or the slab will have chamfered edges. The clay is pulled slightly by the knife and special care is needed, as when sawing through a plank of wood, towards the end of the cut. A slight distortion of the form at the corners can be corrected with the fingers, but it is best avoided in the first place. An alternative method, which avoids distortion at the corners, is to cut from either end of the slab, allowing the cuts to meet in the middle.

When assembling, the sides can either be stood on the base or around it. If the walls are raised from the surface on which the pot stands, either by chamfering or by fixing them away from the bottom of the base, then a shadow will be cast at the bottom of the pot, emphasizing it, like a line of make-up. By lapping the sides in a follow-my-leader pattern, sides of equal width can result in a square plan. The alternative system of butting the ends in pairs will produce a rectangular pot, even though the sides are cut to the same width.

The technique of joining sides is similar to that of adding handles. The surfaces to be joined together must be scored with a pin or knife (a cross-hatched pattern is effective) and then a little water or slip added to fill up these score marks before the two pieces are brought together. If a vertical wall is required, it is a good idea to have a heavy, smooth and reliably vertical object such as a brick handy so that the box can be rested against it to avoid collapse. Set up the walls one by one and use a wooden modelling tool to clean up the joints on the outside. A very fine roll of clay, about the thickness of a shoelace, can be added to the inside of each join and smoothed with a finger.

BUILDING A SLAB BOX

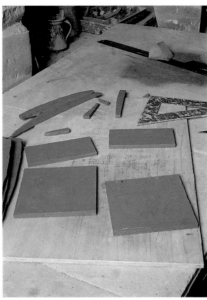

1 A plastic or metal set square is the best way of ensuring right angles when you cut the slab pot's sides from the sheet of clay.

2 Make the second slab of each pair of sides by placing the first on a sheet of clay and cutting round it. They will then be the same size.

3 A sharp tool is used to make hatch marks where the sides are going to abut. The grooves should be at least 3mm (⅛in) deep.

4 For speed, scratch the ends of two slabs at the same time. Doubling up the slabs makes it less likely that they will bend out of shape.

5 A tray of water wider than the slab is long will allow you to dunk the edge before fixing it. Hold the slab in the water for 2 seconds.

6 Water in the scratched grooves is essential if a permanent bond is to be made where the slabs meet.

BUILDING A SLAB BOX

7 The structure of the sides of the box is complete when the fourth side is attached. A bond is enhanced and the slabs are wriggled into place.

8 If the slab box is to be regular in shape, make sure the sides are at right angles before standing it on a prepared slab to make the base.

9 A hard-edged slab form needs clearly defined corners to look well finished. Fettling of the surfaces should help you to make the joints less visible.

10 Make sure there is some sand or grog on the baseboard so the pot can be moved easily as you work on it, and so that it does not stick when it dries.

11 Round the inside corners by adding to each a small 'worm' of clay from top to bottom. Fettle the top with a sponge or, when dried, with a surform tool.

12 So that the finished pot casts a shadow at its foot to emphasize the form, cut a small inward-facing chamfer at the bottom of each side.

This will give curved corners internally, which are much better for cleaning, without impairing the crisp right angles of the outside.

The pot can be given a fixed top as well, glued to the walls by the same method. It is important to note that any form of this kind will seal air inside it, and the whole lot will blow up in the kiln unless a small airhole is made in the pot somewhere, preferably in the base. This hole should not be less than 2mm ($\frac{1}{16}$in) in diameter. A top will have to take into account the thickness of the walls in order to be a perfect fit, and if it is to be a separate lid, it will need an additional wall on its underside to ensure that it grips firmly, like the throat of a thrown lid. A box with a precisely interlocking lid can be built by making first a sealed box, and then cutting through the walls, incorporating a 'key' section.

Above: A slab-built box with an integral lid. Built as a cube, the lid is separated from the container when a sharp knife, angled slightly downwards, is used to cut through the wall. Notches will ensure a good fit.

Surface details

It is often important to preserve hard edges, for aesthetic reasons, when the slab pot has dried. Sandpaper has a disastrous softening effect on the shape, and although you may want to use fine sandpaper on the sides of the pot, try not to blur its edges. The walls can be given a decorative texture if the clay is rolled out over a patterned base. Old dishcloths, coconut matting, a scrubbed table top, even a grid cover in the road provide good surfaces to experiment with. Surface detail need not, however, appear all over the pot and the plane surfaces of slab pots are well suited to applied and incised designs. Often a ridge of clay prepared in the same way as the slabs, fixed around the top of the pot or breaking up the elevation in a horizontal band, will improve the basic slab form.

Below: 'Two-Part Vessel', a sculpture made from soft slabs by Alison Britton. A bold painted design adorns the form.

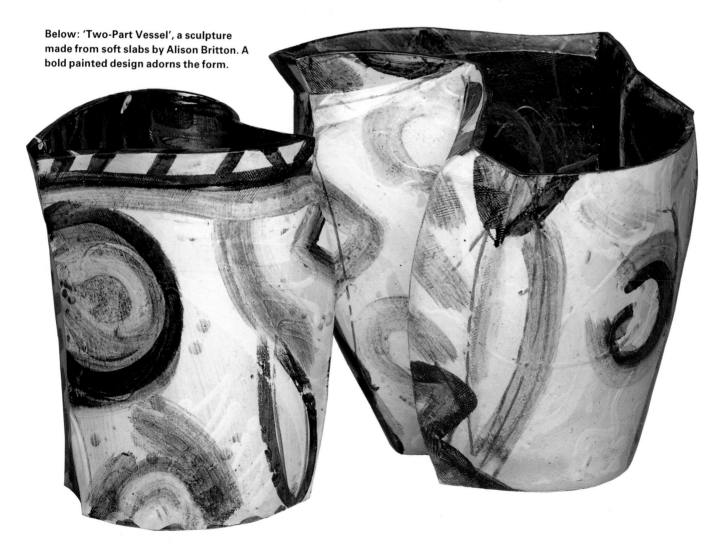

Making other shapes

Hexagonal, pentagonal and other plans can be made with slabs, as can irregular figures with many sides of different lengths. The joints will cease to be at right angles, but it is easier to cut the slabs with square edges first rather than angled ones, and to pare them to the correct angle at the time of assembly.

The slab technique is also appropriate for ceramic sculpture, and the range of possibilities widens if you consider using slabs as curved forms. Caught at the right time, clay can be persuaded to some extent into three-dimensional curves. Slabs which are curving, stretching, crumbling or breaking can be arrested in the act if the clay is supported while the slab dries.

Making slab pots, whether plain or complex, takes time and a lot of space. It also uses more clay than you expect. Cutting squares or rectangles from a slab rolled out with a rolling pin leaves much unused clay round the edges, though this can be reworked and reused immediately, before it dries, in narrow strips for decoration or lumped together and re-rolled to make additional slabs. All the slabs used in a piece must come from the same source, and preferably at the same time, as variations in clay may cause it to open up at the seams when it is being fired.

Above: Pots assembled from soft slabs have a different character to those made in leather-hard clay. Experiment by folding damp slabs.

Below: Hybrid pots by Cornelia Klein, made from wheel-thrown discs folded in half with a banana-shaped slab of clay inserted to complete the form.

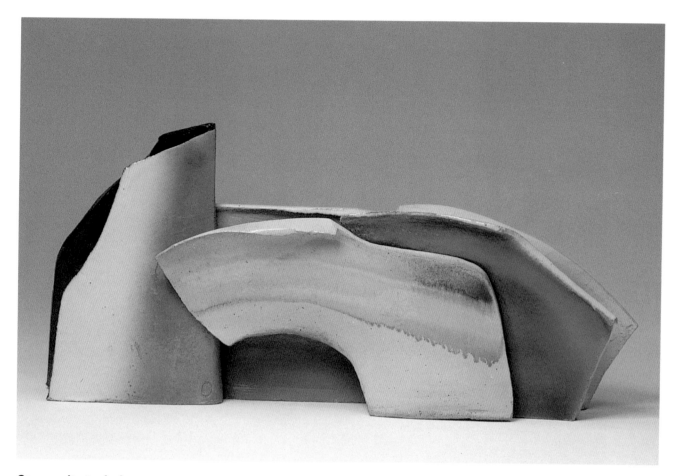

Composite techniques

The slab method is sometimes combined with other techniques, and a composite pot can be made partly from slabs, partly from thrown pieces. The results of such a mixture are not always attractive because it involves the pairing up of different characters, as hazardous an exercise as pairing up people.

Your own aesthetic sense is probably the best guide and it is a sense continually called upon by the potter undertaking slab forms. Thrown and even coiled pots make themselves to a certain extent. Never so slab pots, where the potter is master and the clay is completely passive. If you can muster up good judgement and inventiveness you will be amply rewarded.

The technique of rolling out and cutting shapes from clay extends from ginger-bread men and toys to the severe oriental ceramics representing houses, groups of buildings and farms, and finely articulated units which fit together to perform a function or just to delight the eye and hand. All cultures, past and present, show in their pottery decoration excesses of one kind or another, and the slab builder drawn into ever more elaborate use of clay should take stock of what he or she is doing. Is it to be pottery or clay modelling?

Above: Folded slabs of different thicknesses are used for this large sculptural form by Philippe Lambercy. Dexterous execution avoids an over-handled look.

Right: A cluster of porcelain needles seems to explode from a stoneware slabbed box by Evelyn Klein. This sculptural work shows how techniques can be combined, and also the special quality of slabs of clay when torn and twisted while still damp. The texture on the unglazed surface of the pot is enhanced by copper oxide.

SLAB POTS

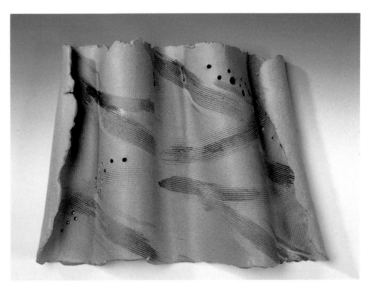

Opposite
CARMEN DIONYSE
The Belgian artist Carmen
Dionyse makes enigmatic
sculptural figures from clay
pieces, shaped by hand and
cracked because of the
texture and dryness of the
clay at the time of
application. The head is left
unglazed, with copper in the
crevices. Where the torso is
lightly finished with a semi-
matt pinkish glaze, the
copper burns through as
turquoise. Height: 69cm (27in).

Above
TORBJØRN KVASBØ
This standing slab form is
a marvellous example of the
dynamic use of texturing, the
recessed surface emphasized
by the ochre coloration of
the clay. The artist has
impressed his seal at
the top. Height:
75cm (29½in).

Above
ARD DE GRAAF
A soft-slab form with
perforations and combing.
Oxide painting under a
stoneware glaze.
32 × 45cm (12½ × 17¾in).

Left
PAUL SOLDNER
A raku standing form made
from soft slabs. The fine
texturing of the clay remains
unobscured by glaze.
75 × 68.5cm (29½ × 27in).

Left
ALISON BRITTON
On this slab-built sculptural
vase the bold decoration is
partly brush painted, partly
applied with a slip trailer. It
is glazed with a clear glaze.

10

PINCHING AND COMBINED HAND-BUILDING TECHNIQUES

'Take a ball of clay and, with your fingers and thumb, shape it into a pot. . . .' As easy as that. This humiliating exercise is often given to beginners in order to familiarize them with the material, and they soon find the ugly ball cracking and tearing, and rolling helplessly on its side. At best, a beginner may hope to produce something resembling a coconut shell, though if the walls are as thin as a coconut shell it will almost certainly break before firing, for unfired clay is very fragile.

The art of pinching a pot – making a pot entirely from a single piece of clay by hollowing it out – demands experience, or even a tradition, and is best shown by the ceremonial tea bowls of Japan, where the form, though thick in the wall, is studied to perfection. The rim, the profile, the base, the texture of the outside and the 'feel' of the finished pot in the hand can all contribute to the beauty of the whole. Concentration and sensitivity are essential if you are to make a pinched pot which

Wafer-thin porcelain bowl by Mary Rogers, a master of finely finished pinched pottery. Two of the four ribs which run down to the base to make a stable pot are visible.

is beautiful. A great deal of bogus nonsense surrounds the so-called qualities of lumpish shapes. Compare your work objectively with a Christmas pudding or a potato. Like other hand-made forms pinched pots can be magnificent, and some materials like porcelain body lend themselves well to delicate forms, but do not make pinched pots unless you can give them time and concentration.

It is rather easier to bash or beat a piece of clay into an interesting hollow shape, using a piece of wood or metal, though the achievement may not be much of a pot. If a lump of clay is fixed around the end of a piece of wooden battening (say 2.5×5cm or 1×2in) dusted with French chalk and this is then beaten carefully on a flat surface, a form with flat sides can be produced. The best way of describing the technique is to imagine that you are trying to turn a toffee apple into a lump of sugar, without touching it by hand.

Both techniques, which are capable of producing excellent pots, are at the

PINCHING A SMALL BOWL

1 If you are going to make a thinly pinched bowl from one piece of clay, the ball should be small enough to fit in the palm of your hand.

2 You start to open up the shape using the thumb of one hand, turning the bowl as you go, and making the shape thin near the base.

3 Use your thumb and a finger to pinch out the rim of a bowl. If it is made too wide too quickly it will easily flop down.

This very large vase made by squeezing clay is a characteristic pot by Richard De Vore. The folded clay, pressing against itself, shows the sensual potential of hand building. Height: 48cm (19in).

same time simple and complex. To do them full justice, you must first dispel the mistaken impression that pinching and bashing clay is some anguished act of a potter in despair. You should also banish the idea that this is a useful method of filling the last ten minutes of a class. The more thought and time given to such pots the better they are likely to be.

Pinching techniques

Some beginners appear to be 'natural' pinchers, their fingers so sensitive to the state of the clay that they know exactly when to stop before the rim starts to fray or to crack, or perhaps how to incorporate a splitting edge into an organic form. As with coiling, the potter who is pinching clay will be in a constant battle with gravity, and, as beginners soon learn, when the clay in a bowl shape is hard enough to resist gravity it is too hard to be pinched out between the fingers. One of the ways of cheating gravity is to work with your pot upside down, supported on a

A very thinly pinched flat sheet of clay can be placed inside a plaster mould or basin lined with cloth to prevent sticking. An undulating form results.

MAKING A FOOT RING

1 A tall foot ring on a thinly pinched shallow bowl is made separately, from a strip of clay, curved around and joined. It looks better if not perfectly circular.

2 When the bowl or undulating shape has hardened up sufficiently to be handled, you can join the foot by scoring and adding water or a little slip.

3 The junction can be blended with the fingers after adding a little clay. The pot's balance depends on the accurate positioning of the foot ring.

PINCHING A LARGER BOWL

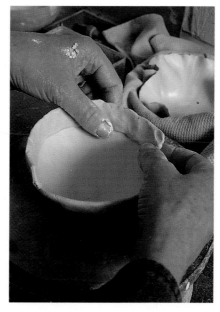

1 To increase the size of a pinched pot beyond that which the fingers can produce from a single ball of clay, first prepare straps of matching clay.

2 When the straps have been pinched out to the same thickness as the wall of the pot, and have dried a little, they can be added to the rim.

3 Take care! The walls of a pot which are soft enough to receive these additions will react to handling, and all too easily they will sag.

PINCHING ON A BALLOON

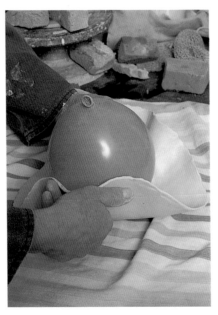

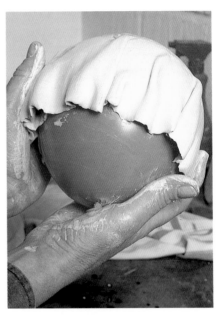

1 Pressing out a disc of porcelain on a dry towel with the thumb is a more appropriate method than using a rolling pin when making pinched work.

2 Do not pick up the clay like a sheet of pastry. It is better to place the balloon on the clay first and then invert it.

3 The reassuring bulge of the balloon will support the form while a little water is used to smooth the folds of clay.

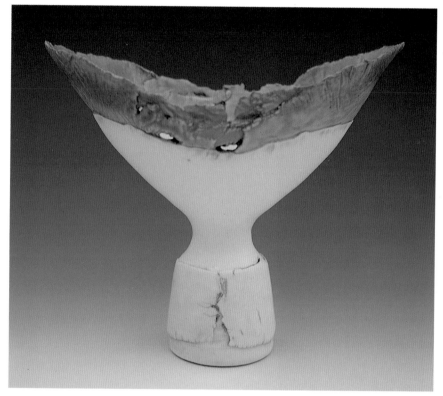

rubber ball or a balloon, or to work in stages, allowing the 'finished' bowl of the pot to dry harder while you keep the rim soft with strips of damp cloth.

The coarse grog (see page 17) which is frequently added to clay, and which assists coiled pottery in both texture and strength, is less suitable for pinched work, as it can cause the clay to dry too quickly. Fine smooth clay is usually preferred by pinch potters, and porcelain clay is best of all, rewarding the potter with translucency when it is very thin.

Many books suggest that inspiration be sought from nature – in seed forms, flowers and radially symmetrical organisms such as sea anemones. It is good to notice the intricacy of natural things, but too much biology can be bad for the creative spirit.

As with pots made from coils, stability is often a problem, and you learn from experience how to 'balance' the clay equally on all sides, so that when complete, the form *tends* to stay upright rather than *tending* to fall over. This does not mean that a pot has to be boringly symmetrical around the centre. Think of a spinning figure skater, the best example of balancing gravitational forces, and you will understand.

Mary White's porcelain form (*above left*) has a wafer of clay around its base and a clear strong profile, but most of its character comes from the hand-built rim. Bryan Newman pinched out the small bowl (*below*) and then attacked the walls with a ballpoint pen and other tools to give it a frenzied look. Diameter: 13cm (5in).

4 A dried seed head is used here against the still-soft clay to introduce a texture. This is only possible because the balloon gives under pressure.

5 Clay shrinks as it dries, and so must the balloon if the pot is to survive. A partial release of air from time to time is the answer. Pop it when the pot is dry.

GALLERY
PINCHED POTS

Balance is always a critical factor in hand-made pots, particularly those which are made by pinching. A pot, to survive, must be relied upon not to fall over. The pots illustrated here show three different solutions.

Above
ELSPETH OWEN
The beautiful rounded pot on a tiny base achieves stability by perfect balance around its centre. Height: 20cm (8in).

Above right
MARY WHITE
A frilly finned form like a whale's tail is given a heavy block on which to stand. Height: 27cm (10½in).

Right
MARY ROGERS
This small translucent porcelain bowl, with integral coloration in the clay body, stands on three small feet – a technique borrowed from the East. Diameter: 9cm (3½in).

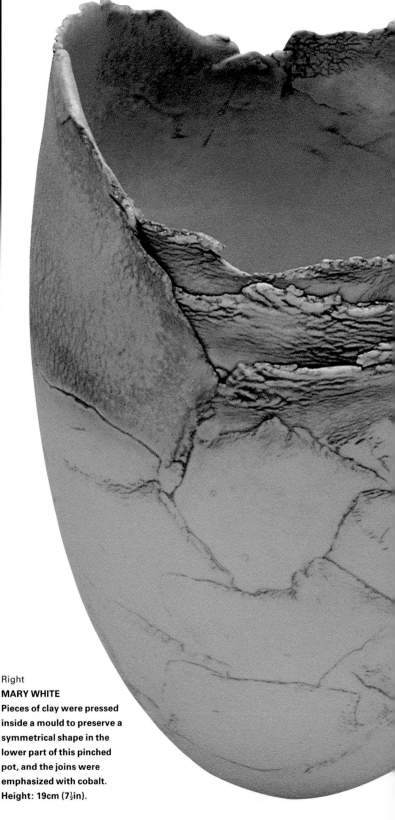

Above
DEIRDRE BOWLES
This wafer-thin porcelain bowl was pinched around a balloon to hold it together in the making stage, and stands squarely on a pinched foot. The simple dribble decoration of two contrasting glazes only partially covers the form. Height: 20cm (8in).

Below
JOHAN VAN LOON
This bowl form is made from thin straps of coloured clay, with the joins exposed, and glazed in blue only on the inside. Diameter: 32cm (12½in).

Right
MARY WHITE
Pieces of clay were pressed inside a mould to preserve a symmetrical shape in the lower part of this pinched pot, and the joins were emphasized with cobalt. Height: 19cm (7½in).

11

A LITTLE MECHANICAL ASSISTANCE

Up to this point, the pots and techniques described have involved the use of metal tools and only one mechanical aid – the wheel. If this assists the potter to tame centifugal force and to create hollow shapes with a circular cross-section, then other machines can assist the potter to other ends.

Tile cutting

Bricks and tiles are made mechanically, and while the studio potter is unlikely to want to make bricks, he or she may well want to produce tiles, either to decorate small panels or for more ambitious schemes.

Tiles are particularly susceptible to warping, a characteristic which is nearly always undesirable. To avoid warping, the thickness of the tile should be constant and its size must not be too large. Small-scale tiles, 5×5cm (2×2in) for example, can easily be cut from a slab rolled out with a rolling pin. If the clay is at least 1cm (⅜in) thick, then warping will be minimal.

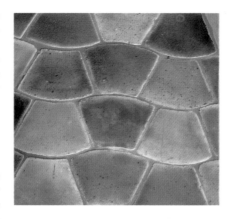

Tiles can be designed to interlock perfectly, even with curved edges.

Such tiles made by hand can be used for chess boards if glazed in alternate contrasting colours.

Circular and hexagonal tiles are inclined to warp less than square ones, but are difficult to cut precisely by hand, and this is where a tile cutter is really useful. It could hardly be simpler:

a metal frame which is pressed into the clay, much as a pastry cutter cuts out crimped circles for jam tarts. The tile cutter, however, is assisted by a spring-loaded back plate, which pushes the tile out, allowing the potter to produce tiles at high speed from rolled-out slabs of clay.

This is the only stage which is fast. The drying process must be extremely slow as a wet tile, left to its own devices, will curl up at the corners. The potter has to keep the tiles in an atmosphere which is not too dry, and turn them over regularly as they become drier. They can be stacked in a staggered pattern, so that the weight is carried by the corners, keeping them down while air gets to the centres.

A regular, even surface is essential for some purposes – for example, where a tile panel is used for a large painted design. Many potters buy tiles ready made for such use and paint designs on top of the manufacturer's clear glaze (see chapter 19). Floor tiles need to be fairly thick – at least 2cm (¾in) deep – in order to withstand wear.

Sometimes, however, the irregularities in a hand-made tile can be quite appropriate. Tiles used for wall cladding are often given textures, or even carved relief. Even when visual impact and appeal is more important to the tile panel than practicability the potter should remember the importance of ease of cleaning. Strong relief easily catches dust, and shiny glazed surfaces are simpler to wipe down than rough ones. When tile panels are used out of doors they have to face regular and sometimes extreme changes of temperature, although never as extreme as the temperatures experienced in the kiln. When rainwater turns to ice, spalling can result, which is why non-absorbent glazed surfaces are advised for external use. Small panels of tiles can be carved and decorated for house names, and make suitable projects for beginners. The original use of tile cladding was part practical, part decorative, and the decoration often consists of a design larger than any individual tile. The decoration of tiles is discussed in chapters 18 and 19.

USING A TILE CUTTER

1–2 Tile cutting looks easy, and it is, providing you have the right conditions. A perfectly prepared slab of clay must adhere to neither the bench nor the tile cutter when the tiles are being cut and pressed out. A little grog on the work top, and using clay that is not too soft, will help you.

Jigger and jolleying

A die stamper, which uses pressure to squeeze plastic material into a predetermined shape, can be used in pottery to impress a design on a clay surface. If two hinged dies are squeezed together by hand an entire piece can be shaped to a repeatable form, but it will be a solid rather than a hollow one. Using a device rather like a modern toasted-sandwich maker, shallow, hollow forms can be modified to crimp the clay only around the edges, and the technique has a history dating back to Roman times, when terracotta lamps were made in this way. It is a swift, but limited technique. Any studio potter designing a hinged press mould of this kind must choose the shape carefully. Undercut edges will not work successfully, and uninteresting shapes become very tedious when repeated *ad nauseam* from this kind of mechanical mould.

The pressing and squeezing of clay into shape has been combined with the wheel in one of the ceramic industry's

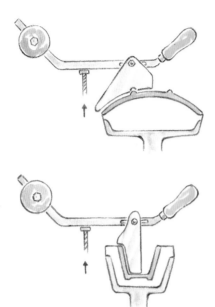

The jigger arm (*top*) can be adjusted to fit the jolley profile so the clay is squeezed to the right shape between the two; it is the stop (*arrowed*) which prevents the jigger from going too far.

most important techniques – jigger and jolleying. This process allows a series of identical pots to be made on the wheel entirely mechanically. Clay of a consistency harder than would be used for throwing is laid over a mould fixed to the wheel-head, and then pressed and scraped into shape by the lowering of a metal profile on an arm. This tool, the 'jigger', when held against the revolving clay makes pots much as the woodworker's lathe makes bowls or chair legs. It is a useful but rather an insensitive tool, not much used by studio potters. A shaping arm can also be used to form the *inside* profile of the pot, in which case the clay is cradled in an iron cup or 'jolley'.

Extruding

One machine which is gaining popularity is the wall-mounted extruder, which allows the studio potter by pulling a lever to press clay through a die, as toothpaste is squeezed from a tube, or cream from a pressurized can. By using a long handle, an enormous force can be exerted without a great deal of effort, and the results have applications in all forms of hand-made pottery.

By changing the die at the bottom of the cylinder the cross-section of the extrusion can be modified – from a circle to a square, or even a star. There is no limit to the length of the extrusions, other than that imposed by the siting of the extruder itself – its height above the floor – and the amount of clay it contains. Extruded ropes 60–90cm (2–3ft) long are usually as much as the potter will want to handle, however, and these are now much used by coil potters as ready-made coils.

The 'untouched by human hand' quality of the extrusion can be turned to the advantage of the studio potter, who will find that the extruded form can be bent and coaxed into shapes which are tense and springy and make other clay forms seem flaccid by comparison. This simple mechanical device can, for example, help a potter to make forms like those made in metal in a forge, though with a great deal less physical effort and also at high speed.

By inserting into the centre of the die a shape held on a strong tripod called a

---

USING A JOLLEY

1 Because the aim is to make identical forms, jolleying is not much used by artist potters. But standard wheels can be adapted with simple engineering.

2 Jolleying depends upon plaster moulds which must be clean before use. They absorb moisture from the clay, and must be replaced as they get worn.

USING AN EXTRUDER

'spider', the extruded form can be made hollow rather than solid. Thus tubes and quite intricate shapes can be produced. Manufacturers of hollow bricks use extruders and chop the sections up into manageable brick-sized pieces. Similarly a potter can experiment with clay extrusions, and by cutting them up into very short sections can use the pieces to make decorative panels which can be wall mounted or even used as room dividers, fired in sections and joined.

By using refractory fireclay in a hand extruder, the studio potter can produce his own kiln furniture (see chapter 20) and thereby cut costs, but it is in the area of sculptural and decorative ceramics that this machine is most useful. Extruders capable of holding 10kg (22lb) of clay can be quite expensive, but the mastic guns operated by hand and sold in hardware stores for extruding adhesives can be handy for working on a smaller scale. Alternative nozzles can be used to vary the section.

The dies for various shapes, with the resulting extrusions, are shown above; hollow extrusions can be made only by supporting an inner form on a metal spider (*below left*). Leverage produces long extrusions at high speed (*above*). Hollow extrusions are added to the rims of thrown plates by Emily Myers (*top*).

12

MOULDED POTTERY AND MOULD MAKING

By far the commonest form of pottery is that which is cast from moulds. Nearly all industrial pottery is made this way. For the studio potter and the beginner it is an interesting and useful technique, but it can be less directly creative and personal if you are using someone else's mould, and it is a good deal less convenient in the small workshop than it is in a large factory. The possibility of being able to make identical units is important to anyone who wants to market a product, and in industry the relationship between manpower and output is impressive. One man with a can of casting slip can fill up a thousand moulds in a short time, but a thousand moulds take up a great deal of space, and in a small workshop casting does not compare with throwing for productivity.

The cast-pot maker produces a form in clay from a mould — a mould which may well have been designed by someone else, perhaps even for another purpose. In industry the clay which is applied to this mould is liquid casting slip but studio potters may work with plastic clay, rolled out as for slab pots. Chapter 13 deals with the casting of pots using liquid casting slip. This chapter describes the casting of pots from an existing mould using plastic clay and the making of moulds.

Clay sheets laid inside or draped over another shallow form will take up the shape of this form, and provided it has a smooth surface the mould can be made of practically any solid material. Reasonably absorbent material has the advantage of helping to dry the clay, and plaster or unglazed pottery are the most commonly used.

A purist might say that casting a pot from the plastic pan of the kitchen scales or a large sea-worn pebble is an uncreative pursuit, but moulded dishes are very often vehicles for painted or other decoration, which is as creative as oil paint on canvas. If the source mould produces an adequate cast, it matters not what it is.

Press moulding

When a clay sheet is laid into a concave form to become a dish, the result is called a press-moulded dish. The term is confusing because it implies some kind of mechanical pressure; in reality it simply indicates that the clay is pressed into the dish.

The surface of the mould is in close contact with, and will therefore shape the outside surface of, the cast. The inside surface is exposed, and is worked up by the potter, whose aim is usually to create a smooth internal shape which follows the outside profile. If the sheet of clay has been rolled out to an even thickness, it should be a pretty good match, but the quality of the inside depends on the potter's skill in smoothing the surface with a tool such as a rubber kidney. Fingermarks inside usually spoil the surface, though textures can be added, and provided the cast is not intended for table use it can be finished with added relief. Think of a dish by Bernard Palissy.

USING A PRESS MOULD

1–2 Using a mould and a sheet of clay like thick pastry is often a beginner's first introduction to pottery. It teaches you how much handling clay will

tolerate, but it is not very creative; if you are using an ugly mould you are stuck with it, but a flat dish can be a good vehicle for decoration.

3 Butter muslin placed between mould and clay assists later removal. A sharp knife angled downwards levels the edges when cheese hard.

Skill and care are required in cutting the edge of the cast level with the top of the mould. The angle of the rim is important, and whether it is flat or angled, it must be maintained all round the shape, for any change in angle will be noticeable and ugly.

Soft leather-hard clay in a plaster mould will lose moisture to the mould, shrinking away from it as it dries and making it easier to remove. Often decoration of the inside surface is done while the clay is still in the mould, especially if it is to be slip (see chapter 18), but if some kind of foot or stabilizing bar of clay is to be added to the outside, the cast must be removed and the clay 'luted' or fixed on to the outside before it has dried out.

Hump moulding

When a clay sheet is draped over a convex shape, called a hump mould, it is the *inside* of the cast which is in close contact with the mould, and the outside surface which has to be worked on. Such a form can easily have a foot ring or base added, but since the cast shrinks against the mould, it has to be watched carefully and taken off early to avoid cracking.

Decoration for moulded pots

Pottery designs based on different textures and colours of clay are best achieved with casts from moulds. With even pressure used on the mould, the clays are less likely to separate after firing than with hand-built techniques and are more 'distinct' than in thrown ware. Both topics are described in chapter 17, but it should be mentioned that many other decorative designs are applied before the cast goes hard, or before the firing. Liquid slip, followed by slip trailing, is one method, and there is combing, either through the slip or on its own. A third technique is feathering, and inlaid or embossed designs can be used with both hump and press moulds, just as they can on hand-formed slabs of clay. All these traditional techniques are described in detail in chapter 18.

Making press moulds

There is no reason why a beginner should not make a mould in plaster of Paris, using either a ready-made master, such as a polystyrene food tray, or an original master made of solid clay. This is the first time that plaster has been employed (fine plaster of Paris, note, not builders' plaster) and it is necessary to say how inimical it is to clay. Bits of plaster mixed with clay will cause endless problems in throwing or in the kiln, and the work area where plaster is to be used must be kept well clear of the clay benches.

Moulds must be made on an absolutely flat and level surface. A smooth Formica table top is ideal, but a sheet of plain thin white paper should be laid on it to keep table and plaster apart. If the master is a ready-made form it, too, must have a smooth surface or rim to make good contact with the table. For instance, a leather bicycle saddle would not work, as it would not rest flat on the table, and poured plaster would run under the form. The master should also be a shallow shape; plastic clay slabs will form satisfactory casts only if none of the angles within the mould are too acute.

If you are making the master yourself, remember that plaster records every detail, and also that, because clay shrinks in drying and firing, your master must be 12–15 per cent larger than the finished pot you have in mind: 30cm (12in) is the maximum diameter, as casts which are too big will warp. The clay, preferably of a fine texture, should not end up more than 4.5cm (1¾in) deep.

A circular master can be made on the wheel out of solid clay, smoothed with a rubber kidney to a perfect surface, and it is best shaped on a large bat so that it is not distorted when it is removed from the wheel-head. If the master is to be some other symmetrical shape, say, an ellipse, you must draw the plan of the form on your ground paper with precision, with two centre lines indicating the quadrants, and build the form up carefully, using small balls of softish clay. You will need two cardboard (or thin metal) templates, one for the long and one for the

USING A HUMP MOULD

1–2 When using a hump mould you need to get at the edges to cut neatly around the form, and so the mould must be raised above the table top. This is why moulds are often made with plaster stalks, like mushrooms. It is important to maintain a constant angle when cutting the edge (*above*).

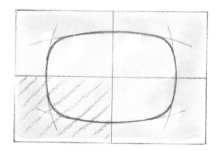

Plan the mould carefully. If it is to be symmetrical, draw the base out on card in quadrants (*above*). This will help you to make an accurate form. By designing and making your own mould you have the opportunity to make not only dishes but also, by joining two moulds together, and adding a foot, interesting standing forms such as the vessel (*right*) by James Tower. Width: 50cm (20in).

MAKING A MASTER

1 When you have decided on the shape and drawn the plan on the base board (*top*), build up the form with small balls of soft clay.

2–3 Cardboard templates pulled across the soft clay will shape the form more precisely than can be done by eye or hand. Regular rectangular shapes will

need at least two templates, one for the long side and one for the short. If the work is skimped at this stage you will regret it later.

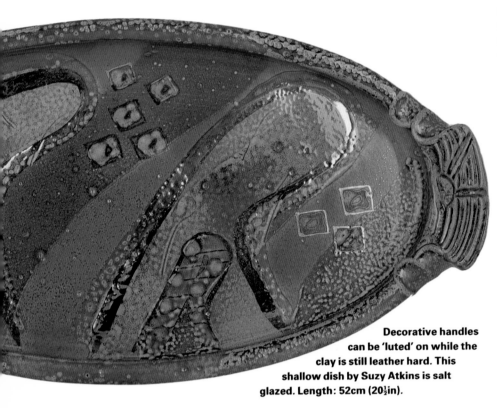

short axis, cut cleanly to indicate the exact section of the form, and these can be used as scrapers when the master shape nears completion.

It is boring to go on and on about the need for precision when making a mould, but if you give up your work too soon, before the shape is right, you will always regret it. The casts will come up time and again with the bumps or hollows that you failed to iron out.

When the master is ready, a high and thick wall of clay should be built around it about 5cm (2in) away from the edge of the form, and the height of the wall should be about 5cm (2in) higher than the highest part of it. If this wall of clay has any sharp corners to turn in going around the master, they should be buttressed, as should any long straight lengths of wall.

Plaster of Paris is weighty, and extremely messy if it breaks through the wall and cascades on to the floor. Clay walls are better barriers against this sort of accident than adjustable wooden boxes made specially for this

Decorative handles can be 'luted' on while the clay is still leather hard. This shallow dish by Suzy Atkins is salt glazed. Length: 52cm (20½in).

MAKING A MASTER

4–5 A master form can be burnished to a smooth surface when leather hard with a turning tool. A wall of clay or wood is then built around it.

6 You must mix enough plaster of Paris to make the mould from a single pouring. Follow the instructions in the text for a perfect mix.

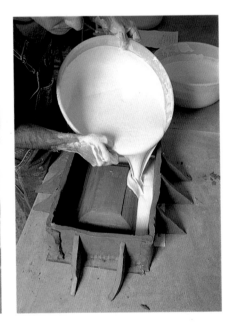

7 When the heavy liquid plaster is poured over the master you must be sure the walls are leak-proof and strong enough not to be overturned.

purpose, and I recommend them so long as they are thick enough. The clay in the wall should be at least 2.5cm (1in) thick and leather hard but not too special, as it is best thrown away after use, or at least not used for making pots, because it may contain plaster.

The plaster of Paris for the mould should be mixed in a single batch, adding plaster in a fine shower of powder from the hands in to a polythene bowl half full of cold water. When the plaster makes an appearance through the surface of the water, the mixture is almost thick enough, and when the island fills half the bowl, the two ingredients can be thoroughly mixed into a smooth white cream. It is possible and sensible to do this mixing with one hand only, and the left or minor hand at that, because when the plaster begins to become appreciably more viscous, it must be poured *immediately* over the master and within the clay walls. To have at least one hand clean and free from plaster makes this operation easier, and there

The plaster 'island' before mixing

is often at this stage no time to wash the hands.

A level white lake of plaster about 4–5cm (1½–2in) deep over the highest part of the master will quickly set, and within a few minutes the wall can be taken away and the bulky white object left to dry and also to cool, as heat is generated in the solidifying process. Turn the mould over so that the underside of the master is exposed. After an hour or two's drying the clay master will have shrunk enough to be lifted out of the mould. There is no further use for this form, and like the clay used for the surrounding wall, it should be discarded, or at least kept away from clay used for potting. The mould needs time to dry and if you attend a weekly class, it should be ready for the following week, provided it is kept in a dry place. The drier the mould the greater its absorbency and efficiency in use.

When you have finished, clean out the plaster mixing bowl, making sure you wash this well away from wherever clay is settling. And remember that plaster as it sets is a marvellous way of blocking up a sink.

Making hump moulds

A hump mould, if it is to be circular, can be made out of clay on the wheel, either as a shallow bowl, the outside of which becomes the mould surface when it is turned and biscuit fired, or as a solid form, hump side up, the inside of which is roughly hollowed out as it hardens, before firing, to prevent explosions in the kiln.

Many potters, however, prefer the familiar feel of plaster for the mould, and a hump mould can be made by pouring plaster into an existing hollow mould, having coated the interface with slip (or soft soap) to prevent the two plasters bonding inseparably together. If this method is used, it is worth putting a wide 'stalk' on to the hump mould like the stalk on a mushroom, by building a small wall of clay within the circumference of the plaster as it dries, and filling this up with freshly mixed plaster. The advantage of a hump mould on a stalk is that it is much easier to cut around the clay which is draped over the form, improving the rim of the resulting pot.

Regular shapes made in moulds can have designs inlaid into the clay wall. The dynamic diagonals in the bowl by Antje and Rainer Doss give this pot a tension it would lack if the lines were merely painted on. Chapter 17 shows more examples of such designs.

8 Plaster will find its own level, so that the mould, when inverted, will have a flat base.

13

SLIP CASTING

It has to be said that many potters, and not only beginners, find the whole performance of casting with slip or liquid clay too chemical, too industrial, too fiddly or too boring to interest them. Yet the results this technique can produce fascinate some potters, and can be achieved no other way.

The casts strongly reflect clay's ability to copy exactly other surfaces and forms – it is quite easy, for example, to cast an apple identical in its detailed form with the original. Many potters would say, 'So what? I do not want to make an apple. I want to make a pot.' Yet the nature of the slip-cast apple – its permanence, its readiness to accept a glaze and its sculptural potential – attracts many, either in the long term as a technique for making ceramic sculpture both large and small, or in the short term, simply as an experiment concerning the extreme limits of clay. Although it is a technique much used in industry, slip casting does not need much equipment and it can easily and simply be organized at home.

Slip casting does not mean cloning, nor must the results be soulless. Jeroen Bechtold combined clays, cut the rim and altered the shape of this porcelain vase. Dimensions: 30×23cm (11½×9in).

Preparing casting slip

Shrinkage is a major problem for the slip caster. The slip or liquid clay which takes on the form into which it is poured as a liquid must not shrink too much as it dries or it will distort or break apart. For this reason it has to be given very liquid characteristics while using the minimum amount of water. The ingredients, or 'deflocculants', which make this possible are sodium silicate, or water glass, and sodium carbonate or soda ash. The other ingredients of slip are ball clay, china clay, feldspar and flint in varying proportions.

Casting slip can be bought ready made, which saves a lot of trouble, or as a casting-slip kit, for home brewing, or it can be mixed up from a formula using dry ingredients. The casting-slip recipe on the next page makes a white, non-translucent porcelain which has to be fired to 1,250°C: porcelain is an increasingly popular material for studio pottery. For minimum shrinkage, the heavier the casting slip per litre of water the better. This slip should weigh

---

MOULDING READY-MADE FORMS

If the shape of the master does not come easily out of the mould, neither will a later cast – avoid undercut edges.

MIXING CASTING SLIP

1–3 Sodium silicate is a viscous liquid, but added in the correct quantity it has the effect of making the casting slip more runny. When the ingredients on

page 108 are mixed and sieved, the resulting mixture will develop a weird consistency which both runs off the fingers and clings to them (*above*).

1,800g per litre – water on its own, of course, weighs 1,000g per litre.

ball clay	300 grams
china clay	2,200 grams
feldspar (potash)	1,250 grams
flint	1,250 grams
sodium silicate	13 grams
sodium carbonate	13 grams
water	2.2 litres

First mix together the two deflocculants, sodium silicate and sodium carbonate, and dissolve the sticky mixture in half a cupful of warm water. Add most of this to the measured quantity of water in the recipe, and then add this liquid to the dry materials. With your hands, patiently squeeze out all the lumps in the resulting gluey mass, and sieve through a 100-strand mesh phosphor-bronze sieve or 'lawn'. Although the mixture appears to be far too gluey to be called a liquid, it is surprising how runny it becomes once it has been stirred. Like a modern emulsion paint, it is a thixotropic gel.

Add more of the dissolved deflocculants to the slip when thinned, until the material will run off your fingers in long syrupy strands. It may not be necessary to add all the remainder. Overloading the slip with these ingredients will cause it to change back from a liquid into an unmanageable jelly. The production of this rather unearthly material is an interesting experience for any potter. When it has been allowed to mature for perhaps a day or two the slip can then be used either in single- or in multiple-piece moulds.

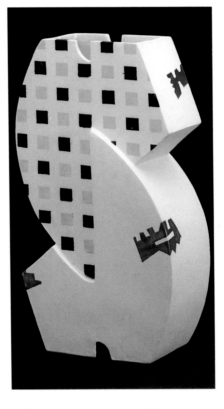

Using a one-piece mould

Clay which has dried inside a mould must be capable of being removed without breaking, and thus complicated shapes such as teapots or hands or even simple ones like top hats or china dogs are made from moulds which can be taken to pieces. Such moulds can be very complicated indeed, consisting of ten or more sections, sometimes lining the inside as well as the outside of the form.

Such moulds are beyond the scope of this book but several books deal with the subject specifically, and are available from ceramic suppliers (see page 190). The following instructions describe the use of casting slip in a single-piece mould as made in chapter 12. Casting-slip moulds are, however, typically both deeper and smaller than either press or hump moulds, and take a form which is quite unsuitable for the use of plastic clay sheets.

Left: Suitable shapes for one-piece moulds, the red areas showing the form of the masters.

The mould must be placed on a level surface because the casting slip, smooth, even and creamy when it is poured in, must fill it completely to the rim without running over one of the sides. The absorbent plaster soaks up moisture from the slip, and the surface level quickly drops. More slip should be poured in to keep the mould 'topped up' and this should be done gently, not from a height, into the centre of the mould. If done roughly, the cast, when it emerges later, may carry scars or pock marks on its inside surface, caused by pressure from the arrival of the 'topping up' slip.

The vital question is, of course, how long do you leave the slip to harden against the sides of the mould. This depends on the degree of absorbency of the plaster, the amount of water in the slip and how thick you want the wall of the cast to be. Only you can establish all these factors, but after a period of between 10 minutes and half an hour you will be able to pour the slip off into a bucket or jug by tilting the

TOPPING UP A MOULD

As moisture seeps from the slip into the walls of the mould, the level goes down, and after a few minutes you must top it up.

mould, and you will then see a residue clinging to the wall.

Running a sharp blade or palette knife around the rim of the mould will remove the surplus slip dribbles and make the rim straight and even. Experience will soon show how the blade should be angled acutely to the line of movement, so that the spare clay is lifted clear of the cast, and does not fall inside it to spoil the surface. As it dries, the cast will leave the wall of the mould of its own accord, and at any stage from leather hard to bone dry it can be tipped out. Needless to say, like any green pot, it is fragile at this stage and the thinner the wall or the more flat and open the shape, the more liable to breakage this new-born cast will be. But apart from being very brittle, slip casts from moulds benefit from minimal handling. There is a pristine quality about their surface which seems to disappear when they are held by the fingers. Casts are also, alas, very susceptible to warping at the drying stage, and directional heat will certainly cause distortion. The optimum thickness of the cast will depend on the shape and the use to which it will be put, but in general cast forms feel right in the hand if they are a little lighter and finer than thrown or hand-built forms.

Casting slip can be kept for several weeks or even months, but it should always be stored in a sealed container, with a narrow top, to minimize contact with the air. The carbon dioxide in the air helps form a skin on the surface, like that on emulsion paint, and this should be removed rather than stirred in when the slip is next used, and the slip sieved to ensure smooth consistency, which is the very essence of slip casting.

Decoration

Like press-moulded forms, slip-cast dishes are ideal subjects for decoration (see chapters 18 and 19). However, a decorative technique used by Jacqueline Poncelet and developed by Jane Waller is so much a part of the construction of the slip-cast pot that it is most convenient to explain it here.

By applying coloured casting slip from a slip trailer direct to the walls of the mould, patterns of a random or precise kind can be embedded in the walls of the cast when the slip is poured in the usual way. As the lines or dots of slip on the walls dry very quickly there should be no interval between completing the design and pouring in the body slip. The success of this method depends on the strength and colour of the slip forming the design, which will appear on the outside of the cast, sometimes burning through slightly to the inside if the cast is thin.

Opposite: S-shaped form by Dieter Balzer. Once the rules for making piece moulds are learned, almost any shape can be cast.

Right: Standing form by Johan van Loon. Casting slip is not only used in moulds. A thin solid object such as a raffia mat or a woven cloth can be soaked in slip and frozen into immortality when the original burns away in the kiln. The results are curiosities, but can be sculptural.

USING A PIECE MOULD

1 De-aerated slip injected under pressure will fill a row of two-piece moulds in no time, making casting the fastest process in large workshops.

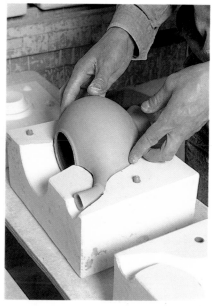

2 The gallery of the teapot is made by a third piece (see top left of picture). When leather hard, the cast is removed and the 'spare' cut from the spout.

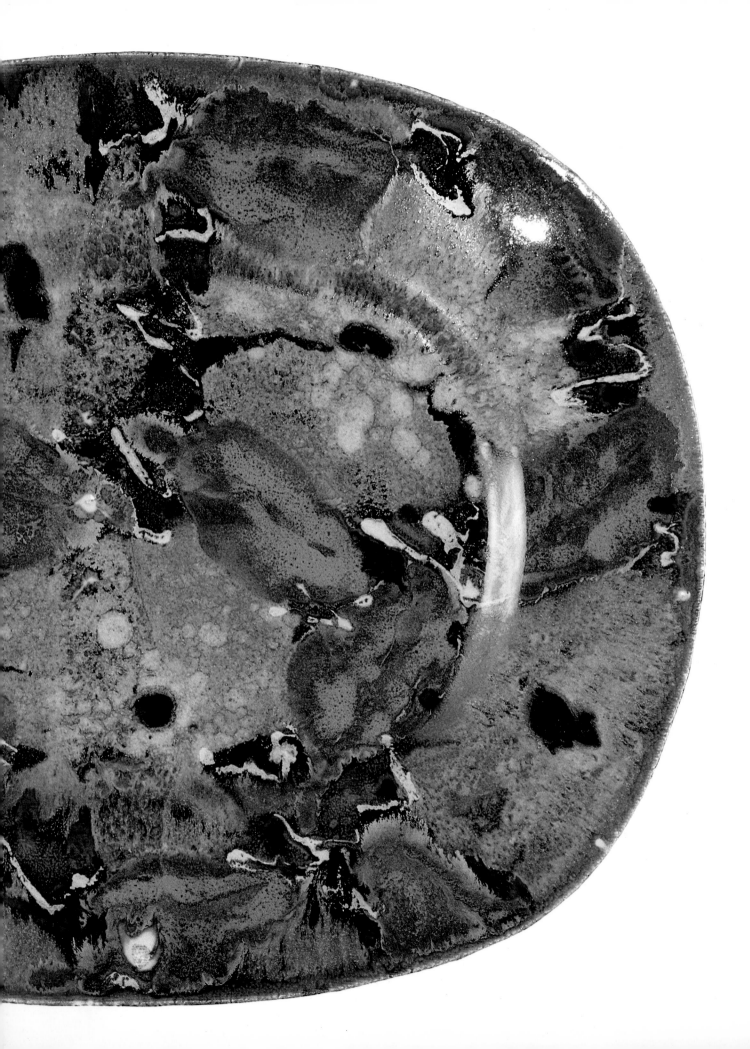

COATS OF MANY COLOURS

*The naked pot is rather like a naked body. What attracts the eye
is the form, and perhaps how it differs from expectations. The colour is
more or less the same all over, and predictable. A layer of glaze is
nicely described as 'coating the body', for glaze clothes the pot.
Glazes, like clothes, are both practical and an opportunity
for display, satisfying for those who are excited by texture and colour.
The next four chapters are for those who want to understand
the fundamentals – what glazes comprise, and how to make and
improve them – but those who simply want to get on
with the job need only read chapter 15.*

**Opposite: A combination of application
techniques and metal oxides enriches a
large moulded plate by Janice Tchalenko.**

14

WHAT'S IN A GLAZE

When a pot has been first, or biscuit, fired it is half made. The glaze, the style of glazing and decoration and the second firing complete the process, and there is a mating which is inseparable physically and aesthetically.

It is possible for a clumsy, lumpish biscuit pot to become beautiful if its glaze is a noble one, but more often a good biscuit pot becomes commonplace or downright ugly through poor glazing. The reasons can be many, including bad glazes, bad luck, an unpractised hand or just apathy. Potters of the world divide into two camps, the pot makers and the pot decorators, according to whether they are more interested in form or in surface, but those who primarily make pots for their shapes cannot afford to ignore the quality of the surface: glazes can play either a principal or a supportive role.

Glaze is glass, melted on to and then solidified on to the surface of a pot, and it provides a non-porous skin which lengthens the pot's life and makes it more hygienic and easier to clean. Like other forms of glass it is resistant to change and, however dirty or stained, can usually be cleaned without its own

nature being altered. Although pots buried in the ground may gain a permanent patina from slow chemical attack, glazed ware approaches gold in its immutability once made. The earliest known glazed pots were made over 3,000 years ago and are still sound.

Glaze consists mainly of silica, which is also a major constituent of clay. By itself it has a high melting point (about 1,700°C) but it can be persuaded to melt at much lower temperatures when a 'fluxing agent' such as lead, boron, sodium or potassium is present. The presence of alumina (aluminium oxide), also an ingredient of clay, with an even higher melting point, gives the mixture stability and adherence when it is in a molten state on the pot.

Variations in the proportions of alumina, silica and the flux, and the influence of a host of other elements –

titanium, calcium, copper, zinc, zirconium, nickel and iron – are responsible for the difference in 'quality' of a glaze, that is its colour, texture, opacity, gloss and feel. Another factor is the method of application to the pot, and yet another, the thickness of the glaze layer, both of which are explained in chapter 15, and, of course, there is the temperature to which it is fired.

The glaze ingredients, which the pottery student will encounter as pale,

Thrown stoneware bowls by Young Jae Lee, enhanced by a classic oriental glaze with the pink blush of copper in reduction. It is unusual for oxygen starvation in the kiln to be so great that the whole pot turns pink; areas of reduction are what many potters seek. Heights: 48cm (19¾in) and 35cm (13¾in).

finely ground powder in bags like flour, are mixed with water and applied to the pot as solids in suspension, the liquid conveniently disappearing into the porous surface of the biscuit pot, leaving the solid particles as a fine powder clinging to the outside. In this very vulnerable state the ware, with any painted or other decoration, is transferred to the kiln and refired so that the glaze melts and resolidifies on cooling.

For industrial purposes it is perfectly possible to grind up sheets of clear glass into a fine powder and spray this, mixed with water, on to ceramics, and cause it to re-form on the pots as glaze. Industrial mass production, with its insistence on uniformity, frequently requires chemists to make special glazes, using the known characteristics of elements to alter and improve results and calculating at a molecular level. Potters with a natural affinity for chemistry enjoy pitting their wits against the fire, employing their knowledge to make or alter glazes, but many beginners are alarmed by the thought of chemical formulae and molecular weights. This feeling of panic is unfortunate, as it is quite unnecessary to have any knowledge of chemistry in order to be a potter – it is much more to the point to be a good cook.

An analytical approach is more likely to be frustrating than fruitful at the studio pottery level, since the potter has little control over the precise chemical nature of the raw materials which he buys from suppliers. Bernard Leach in *A Potter's Book* says, 'To a craftsman it is more important to know what works well than to know in precise detail why it works well.' Thus a knowledge of the uses and effects of known materials is valuable in glaze making, and by experimenting you will come to know what to add, and in what quantities, without having to be able to reinterpret a chemical formula.

Right: Tin-glazed goblet by the master of majolica, Alan Caiger-Smith.

Opposite: Zinc and titanium show on the surface of a massive pebble pot by Edouard Chapallaz.

Glazes for earthenware

There are, as explained in chapter 1, two main types of ware, the result of specific firing temperatures. At the lower end of the temperature scale is earthenware, which matures between 1,000 and 1,100°C. Lead and borax are the commonest fluxes for earthenware glazes, and as raw lead is poisonous the studio potter knows it as lead 'frit', that is lead which has been combined with silica in a molten state and ground to a non-toxic powder.

Many classes now ban the use of lead in any form, and, although lead frits are still readily available from ceramic suppliers, at high prices, earthenware glazes in schools and colleges are based on borax and borax frits. The process of 'fritting' – combining the flux with silica – has a threefold advantage for the potter. Firstly a frit removes the health hazard of working with a toxic material; secondly it is insoluble, and so when as a powder it is mixed with water, it does not dissolve or lose any of its chemical ingredients; and thirdly it behaves in a very predictable way, melting at a precise temperature.

In the early years of this century, and until very recently in peasant countries, lead in the form of galena (lead sulphide) was used to make a simple glaze for earthenware, giving a 'soft' surface, especially over white slip. Unfortunately, it is easily attacked by vinegar, and even tea, releasing lead, and since its use has been banned for reasons of health, efforts have been made by potters and the manufacturers of ready-made glazes to find a good substitute which is safe to use.

If earthenware glazes are fired to temperatures higher than their recommended range, they become very liquid, run off the pot into pools on the shelf, and become volatile. If they are fired to temperatures below their recommended range, they will not melt at all, but stay on the surface, dry and hard, like old sandpaper.

It is the glaze ingredients which determine the melting point, but the character of the glaze reflects the temperature to which it has been fired. Earthenware glazes are mainly shiny, and the colours produced on them by metal oxides are clear and bright.

Glazes for stoneware

Stoneware glazes are much closer in character to clay, and in fact the glaze constituents are very similar indeed to the clay itself. The flux at stoneware temperatures (1,250–1,300°C) is either sodium or potassium, and the colour is rarely clear and even. At high temperatures very small quantities of metal oxides in the clay body burn through the glaze, making it spotty and blotchy, and colours are generally more muted and earthy. Fortunately, natural raw materials like feldspar (a constituent of granite) contain the necessary flux, and potassium is, of course, also found in wood ash.

As with earthenware glazes, colourants are mainly oxides applied either in a pure state, ground down as a powder, or in combined form as part of a natural material such as rutile, for example, which contains titanium. As a proportion of the basic glaze ingredients, colourants and opacifiers rarely account for more than 10 per cent. Their action and interaction is very complex, however. For instance, some metal oxides themselves have a slight fluxing effect, by slightly lowering the temperature at which the glaze will become runny.

Understanding glaze

The glazing room of an art school ceramics department or a large studio pottery is full of containers – small glass bottles containing apparently identical dark powders, and large bins or sacks holding yet more powders, mostly creamy-grey in colour. To the experienced potter, identification is easy – the glaze ingredients look and feel very different – but to the beginner it is something of a disappointment that there should be so much uniformity and drabness. It is sometimes hard to convince a beginner that a pale ginger-coloured liquid may produce a rich blue glaze. Only in the kiln are the true colours and capacity of oxides revealed.

Exactly what glaze materials can do in combination with high temperatures is not just a lifetime's study, but a total preoccupation that binds together such unlikely groups of people as craftsmen, museum curators, industrialists and antique dealers. No book for beginners

should dwell too long on what is in a glaze but, based on my own experience, the following descriptions of the materials found in every glaze room may help the beginner to find what he or she wants.

Opacifiers

Tin oxide is traditionally the glaze ingredient for making opaque white. The tin in the glaze does not dissolve, but simply reflects light and masks the colour of the clay. Tin glaze is the white background of the enamelled or painted earthenware pottery known as majolica. Tin is effective as an opacifier up to stoneware temperatures, but is less used in high-fired ware as many of the raw ingredients of stoneware glazes, such as dolomite, themselves act as opacifiers. White tin oxide is an expensive material.

Zirconium is much used in place of tin oxide for white earthenware glazes. It is cheaper and has a more 'fluid' look after firing. In combination with oxides

it helps to make earthenware glazes bright and reflective.

Zinc oxide, a slightly crystalline opacifier, is expensive and somewhat temperamental. It is often added to a glaze to reduce crazing, but may induce crawling (see page 138).

Dolomite, magnesian limestone, is a very useful opacifier in stoneware glazes as well as having other properties (see page 117).

Titanium dioxide, well known as an opacifier in paints, tends to create a mottled effect when in combination with other oxides, by separating dark areas with tiny white speckles. Used on its own as an opacifier it is creamy in colour. Rutile is a natural material containing both titanium and iron. The iron often shows as dark speckling.

Antimony oxide is a useful opacifier in earthenware glazes, though combined with lead-based glazes it turns yellow.

Cobalt carbonate (pale blue) and oxide (darker) on a dish by Catherine Vanier.

Colourants

Iron oxide in one of its forms is the commonest colourant in ceramics. Known as ferrous oxide, ferric oxide, magnetite, ochre, haematite and crocus martis, or just plain rust, this red, fawn, brown or black powder, according to its strength, colours glazes from pale straw to dark treacly brown or black. In quantities around 6 per cent of the total glaze volume, it is characteristically ginger. In stoneware reduction (see chapter 20) it helps to make the celadon pot green, grey or slaty-blue in colour.

Cobalt oxide is the bright blue colourant familiar on Willow Plate pottery and Meissen. It is an expensive pigment, but a very strong one and so only small quantities are needed. It is often used in combination with other oxides which reduce its fierceness. Cobalt carbonate is similar, though a little cheaper, and less strong.

Copper oxide, like most colourants, is black in its powdered form, but a powerful peacock green when fired. As it is strong, it is likely to go black if used in large quantities, and when used sparingly it is the pale green of oxidized copper roofs. In reduction stoneware (see page 178) it changes completely to become the auburn colour of a copper saucepan. Copper carbonate is less strong in colour.

Manganese dioxide is a dull purple when used thinly on its own. Used with other oxides it softens harsh colours and in combination with cobalt produces violet. At stoneware temperatures manganese dioxide has the useful property of acting as a flux, fusing on to a clay body without the help of a conventional glaze, thus making impervious vessels which are to be left unglazed. When painted on thickly, especially in combination with a small amount of copper carbonate, it fires to a rich browny-gold. It is also used as a clay colourant, turning red clay the colour of old plain chocolate.

Nickel oxide, green in colour in its powder form, has a greying effect, ugly on its own but useful to soften harsh colours in high-temperature glazes. In combination with chromium oxide it will make green.

Chromium oxide usually produces dull greens, though in combination with other oxides such as tin and iron it helps to produce pinks and yellows. I find it a nasty tiresome oxide which has often ruined glazes by bubbling, though some potters use it widely.

Vanadium and uranium oxide are useful in making yellow, especially in lead glazes. The latter is rather hard to come by nowadays.

The density of colour given to a glaze by different oxides depends on their inherent strength, and the amount of oxide used. One per cent of iron would scarcely be noticed, whereas 1 per cent of cobalt would certainly show up as blue. When colouring oxides, alone or in combination, exceed 10 per cent of the total the glaze becomes unpleasantly metallic, uneven in surface and is likely to have bubbles or 'craters' like the surface of the moon. Unevenness of surface is undesirable if the pot has to be used, and washed and dried, though varied or uneven coloration is sometimes sought after, and silicon carbide is sometimes added in small quantities to have a disruptive 'volcanic' effect on other oxides.

A mottled glaze may result from the inclusion of titanium dioxide or tin oxide with other colourants. A glaze will be spotty if the colouring oxides it contains are not finely ground. Most oxides are supplied already ground, but if they have coagulated into grains through moisture they can be ground again easily enough with pestle and mortar. When a randomly spotty effect is wanted, it is best achieved by adding the colourant to the clay body, simply by sprinkling it into the plastic clay as a powder. The oxides will burn through the glazes as spots of colour at stoneware temperatures.

Other essential materials

To complete the tally of stock materials in the glaze room, the following – and most important – will be found in bins or sacks.

Feldspar, probably in the largest sack, is the material used in many high-temperature glazes as the source not only of alumina and silica but of sodium or potassium, which act as the flux. Feldspar on its own will make a glaze at approximately 1,260°C, but not a very exciting one, characteristically milky. A natural material, feldspar's chemical formula is variable – for instance, potash feldspar and soda feldspar (with a slightly lower melting point) are both readily available from ceramic suppliers. But feldspar also varies from one source to another, and unfortunately from one batch to another. When I find a reliable and trusted glaze becoming dull and disappointing, I usually blame it on the shortcomings of the latest batch of feldspar – easy to say, and difficult to disprove.

China clay (kaolin) ought to be pure alumina and silica, and nothing else, but most commercially sold china clays have trace elements that have marginal effects on the material, which is mainly used in high-temperature glazes. Alone, it refuses to melt. It is, of course, a key ingredient in casting slips (see chapter 13). Light in weight and creamy in colour, it has a distinctive feel which an experienced potter can recognize blindfold.

Ball clay is greyer than china clay when raw, and contains a larger proportion of trace elements. Important in clay bodies – it is very plastic – and casting slips, its use in glazes is mainly for high-temperature ware.

Bentonite is a very plastic clay, used as a glaze suspender – it helps to prevent the heavier particles in a glaze sinking to the bottom if used in small quantities of 1–2 per cent. Too much and the glaze become jelly-like and unworkable. Bentonite is used to replace ball clay in porcelain to make it whiter.

Cornish stone (china stone) is an alternative source of both sodium and potassium as a flux for stoneware glazes. It is used therefore instead of feldspar and is traditionally stained a pale duck-egg blue in its raw state, for recognition purposes. It is crushed igneous rock, containing several trace elements, and cannot easily be given a precise chemical formula.

Dolomite contains calcium and magnesium, both of which promote mattness in stoneware glazes. Dolomite is also an opacifier which by itself has a slightly crystalline, distinctly oatmealy look, and often combines attractively with colouring oxides.

Whiting (limestone) is an important ingredient in stoneware glazes. It is a refractory material, with a very high melting point, but in combination with feldspar acts as a flux.

Flint and **quartz** are silica, ground from different sources. Either is added to glazes needing stiffener or hardener and because they do not melt when used alone are much employed as placing powders or batwash for kiln shelves (see chapter 20).

Nepheline syenite, being very rich in sodium and potassium, is a powerful flux for use in low-temperature or 'soft' stoneware glazes. It could be described as 'feldspar-but-more-so', and produces one of my favourite glazes.

Talc (French chalk) contains a high proportion of magnesium, like dolomite, and helps to make a matt surface in stoneware glazes. Trace elements such as iron and titanium usually give a glaze containing talc a creamy colour when fired.

It is quite likely that a final bin will simply be labelled 'Ash' and will hold the residual material from a bonfire. This 'potash', being a rich source of potassium, has such a complex and varied chemistry that it has led many would-be analysts on long wild-goose chases in search of a scientific basis for its special qualities. It is a flux which gives colour, texture and surface of enormous variety, and it also has a lot of personality, which endears it to some and infuriates others. Working with ash glaze is much more like cooking than chemistry, and so its collection and preparation are left to chapter 16 on recipes.

This deceptively simple piece depends upon an understanding of the effect of chemical ingredients. Claude Champy uses a pale glaze comprising (relative proportions) potassium feldspar (60), flint (60), whiting (40), titanium dioxide (15), zinc oxide (5) partly overlapping and reacting against a black glaze made of soda feldspar (120), whiting (30), china clay (15), cobalt oxide (3), chrome oxide (3) and red iron oxide (10). It is fired to 1,280°C.

15

DIPPING AND POURING

There are many ways of applying a glaze. For pots that will be used for food, it is important to get the glaze on in a smooth and even layer, and this cannot be done with a paint brush. Spraying with some form of atomizer like a compressed-air spray-gun is an efficient and economical method for industrial purposes, but is unsatisfactory for the studio potter. Carefully timed bursts of spray directed at a revolving pot can give an even surface, but in the small studio there is a great deal of waste, for the spray which misses the pot cannot be gathered and recycled, and as hand-held sprays cope badly with concave or intricate surfaces, the studio pottery is best advised to forget them. Immersion in the glaze is the best method of ensuring an even coat, and the hand glazer must learn the techniques of dipping and pouring.

Sieving a glaze

The beginner will probably first meet glaze as a liquid of creamy texture

Faceted pot by David Leach. The oriental tenmoku glaze breaks to a lighter colour to emphasize the form where the facets meet. Height: 23cm (9in).

made up either to a formula from ingredients mentioned in the previous chapter or from a dry pack on the 'just add water' principle. It should be kept in a bucket with a lid. The first thing to do is to sieve the glaze, as its various ingredients have different weights and will probably have separated out into layers in the bucket. The most important ones, such as lead frit in earthenware glazes, go persistently to the bottom of the bucket, and every bit of glaze must be brushed through a sieve into another bucket to give a perfect mix again. A phosphor-bronze sieve or lawn with a resilient, untarnishable 100-strand mesh in a wooden or plastic frame is needed for this, together with a scrubbing brush to help to push the stickier portions of the glaze right through the sieve.

The abrasive surface of phosphor-bronze mesh makes short work of rubber gloves and quickly wears through fingernails, so the scrubbing brush and lawn should be regarded as inseparable companions, like a pestle and mortar. Both must be kept scrupulously clean because specks of strong colourants like cobalt oxide left in the lawn or brush will show up in the next glaze which is sieved through it.

The act of glazing a pot appears simple and neat when done by an accomplished potter, but beginners find it a rather trying experience, and will learn faster if they have plenty of space on the bench in front of them, and plenty of glaze in the right type of container. A bucket is a handy shape in which to catch the glaze after sieving, since a 20.5cm (8in) lawn will usually fit comfortably into the top of it, and it is useful to have a jug handy and an enamel or plastic bowl approximately the size of a washing-up bowl.

Glazing a cylinder

If both the inside and outside of a cylinder have to be covered with glaze, the inside is normally glazed first. The jug should be filled from the bucket of glaze by pouring from the bucket into the jug. Most beginners want to fill the jug by dipping it into the glaze, but if they do they can contaminate the glaze if the outside of the jug is dirty. The

USING A SPRAY-GUN

Do not attempt spraying glaze unless you can use a specially constructed booth, as illustrated here, within which the pot can be revolved.

SIEVING GLAZE

Wooden sticks keep the 'lawn' out of the bowl while the glaze is being sieved, but make sure the bowl itself is big enough to hold all the glaze.

Not all pots need glazing all over. This cider flagon by John Leach is glazed inside, and over its lip, where the liquid it will contain may make contact. A traditional pot, it is fired to stoneware temperatures, and the unglazed exterior is not porous so it resists stains and can be kept clean.

glaze should be poured into the cylinder right up to the top and immediately poured out again into the bucket.

A quick rotating twist with the wrist as the liquid leaves the pot will shake off any droplets that would otherwise form on the rim. If any glaze runs on to the outside surface during this process it should be wiped away with a dry sponge, so that a double layer is avoided when the outside comes to be glazed. A biscuit pot will absorb the moisture from the glaze in a matter of seconds, and the glaze will be left dry on the surface.

The outside of a cylinder can most easily be glazed by inverting the pot, holding its base with the fingertips, and plunging it up to the fingertips in the glaze in the bucket, keeping it there for about a second before removing it. The airlock, as in a diving-bell, will prevent the glaze from coating the inside a second time. One of the most infuriating things that can happen at this stage is the discovery that there is not enough glaze in the bucket for you to

be able to immerse the pot completely. The pot must not touch the bottom of the bucket or its glazed rim will be damaged, so it is wise to compare the depth of glaze with the size of the pot before starting. Another twist of the wrist helps to shake off the surplus glaze again, and if the pot is turned upright in the hand the liquid on the rim will spread out evenly, rather than in a series of blobs.

This sort of care may seem obsessive, but you will quickly learn that glaze put on unevenly will show up clumsily after firing, and that flaws cannot easily be touched up. A certain amount of gentle 'fettling' of the glazed surface with the fingertips before the firing will improve matters by smoothing down rough edges and filling up cracks, but if this is done roughly lumps of glaze scale off altogether, and replacing them is difficult.

Marks on the outside of a cylinder where the fingers have held the pot are difficult to avoid if the glaze is to go right down to the base, and the earthenware pot, which needs a glazed base, may do better to be poured as described under Glazing open forms. A stoneware cylinder, which is not porous when fired, needs no glaze at the foot and the dipper's art is to grasp the pot firmly in the fingertips while keeping them within 5mm ($\frac{1}{4}$in) of the base. Fingermarks on a glazed pot are not the most ugly of flaws, but they do not suit all pots.

Once a glazed area is dry it can be handled sensitively without causing damage, and a cylinder can be glazed on the outside completely if it is glazed head-first up to half its height and then, when dry, base-first until the glaze lines meet. If the junction is a neat one it will not show, but if the glazes overlap there will be a change in glaze quality. Using two different glazes, of course, causes a decorative effect where they overlap, as described in chapter 19.

GLAZING A CYLINDER INTERIOR

1–2 If a jug is dipped into the glaze, make sure it is clean to avoid contamination. Fill the cylinder more than half full, and pour out the glaze immediately, twisting the pot as you go so that the glaze runs over all the inside.

Above: A tall porcelain vase by Young Jae Lee, glazed by dipping. Runny glazes must be cleaned off well above the base if they are not to glue the pot to the kiln shelf when they are fired.

GLAZING A CYLINDER EXTERIOR

WINDOW DIPPING

1–2 You can use two hands to immerse the cylinder in the glaze, but if you do, the finger which steadies the rim will leave a mark, and it is bound to need retouching, when the glaze coat is dry, with a droplet of glaze from the finger, as shown at top.

Dipping a pot at an angle several times into the glaze tub will never produce an even coat, but it may have a decorative value.

Glazing open forms

The glazing of an open form such as a large bowl demands more skill than glazing a cylinder. Since the circumference of the rim is relatively large when compared to the rest of the pot, the glaze poured inside has a long way to travel as it is poured out again if the whole surface is to be covered. The hand holding the bowl must be conveniently placed to allow the potter to twist the pot through almost a complete revolution as the glaze is poured out. Too much hesitation in pouring out the excess may mean too thick a coat of glaze, and pooling in the bottom of the bowl when the glaze melts.

Beginners are inclined to rush this stage, pouring out the glaze too quickly and leaving large areas of naked pot. If this happens, more glaze should be poured in straight away from the jug – the resulting overlapping will probably show, but the only other alternative is to wash all the glaze off with water, and begin again when the pot is dry, which takes a long time.

When the interior of the bowl is dry, it can be inverted on the fingertips and held like a mushroom, with the potter's arm as the stalk. Long fingernails will damage the interior glaze, but fingertips will not. The outside can be glazed in this position, the glaze being poured over the outside from a jug held in the other hand. Some potters prefer to glaze the outside of the bowl first, as this is more likely to produce a glaze coat of even thickness, both inside and out. Simply reverse the order of events, bearing in mind that the outside of the bowl will have to be handled carefully when the inside is worked on.

The pouring of glaze on the outside of a really large bowl is best achieved by resting the bowl, inverted, on two battens or thin strips of wood or metal (strong, long knitting needles will do), which lie across the rim of a plastic bowl. Glaze poured from a jug on to the outside will, if the jug is moved steadily round the pot, cover the naked surface without overlapping. The rim itself will probably benefit from a quick dip in the glaze when the outside is dry enough to be held by the foot, to cover up the marks left by the battens. It is a time for

waterproof clothing, for beginners can expect to spill glaze over the bench, the floor and their shoes in the excitement of the moment. A useful aid saving much time is a banding wheel, on which the plastic bowl, battens and inverted pot can all be rotated, giving the potter the chance to stand still while pouring glaze from the jug.

Small bowls and other open-shaped vessels can be glazed in one swift movement by immersing them completely but briefly in the glaze at an angle, holding them by the foot. A bowl so glazed should have a clean, even coat and an unblemished rim.

The many shapes which are intermediate between cylinder and bowl all demand individual treatment, and it is often wise to suit the shape and size of the glaze bucket to the pot, especially when the glaze is limited in quantity. When trying to roll a pot in an inadequate saucerful of glaze it is as well to remember that a good glaze poorly applied is usually worse than an ordinary glaze put on perfectly.

Above: A single dip in a deep bucket will glaze both sides of a saucer.

Opposite: Glaze can act like make-up, concealing or emphasizing the lines of the face. It runs darker into the grooves of a bowl by Tove Anderberg.

GLAZING A SMALL BOWL

1 Many beginners find glazing nerve wracking. Developing a sequence of smooth movements allows you to glaze the inside of a bowl swiftly.

2 By turning the bowl through a complete circle you cover the rim while pouring out the glaze. This avoids a messy second pouring.

GLAZING A LARGE BOWL

3 The pot's foot is held with the thumb and the rim with a fingertip to glaze the outside by immersion. An airlock prevents reglazing inside.

4 Using this method, the rim will need retouching. If you can hold the pot entirely by the foot ring, you can avoid this.

The exterior of a large bowl is glazed by inverting it over two sticks and pouring the glaze from a jug. The rim will be retouched later.

Jugs and teapots

Pots with handles, like jugs, are often a joy to glaze. With the handle immersed first, up to its junction with the pot, the rest of the pot can then be held by the handle when this glaze has dried, and immersed, inside and outside being covered in one operation with no fingermarks to spoil the surface.

Teapots, on the other hand, are more tiresome than most to glaze because of their spouts. The pot's pouring capacity will be tested when the glaze flows for the first time down the spout, and the potter *must* remember, when all the glaze has been poured out, to unblock the holes in the base of the spout, or glaze will fuse across them and no tea will ever be poured. If the lid of the pot, which may be dipped on both sides into the glaze, is to be fired sitting in the pot,

An unglazed handle allows you to immerse the pot in glaze without the need for retouching. A celadon-glazed fluted teapot by Geoffery Whiting.

GLAZING A TEAPOT

1 Traditionally the gallery and the seating of the lid are left unglazed, either by wiping the glaze off or by resisting with wax (*above*).

2 Glaze poured inside the teapot is rolled round up to the gallery edge, with the thumb over the spout.

3 The glaze is emptied out through the spout itself, but if the straining holes are sealed with glaze they should be reopened with a wire.

glaze must be wiped carefully off both the gallery and the throat with a sponge, or the lid will never come off and the teapot will be useless. Another method of keeping this area clear of glaze is to paint wax on to the seating before glazing (see chapter 19).

A sponge can be helpful for cleaning glaze off areas where it is not wanted, but it should never be used, either wet or dry, to smooth down unevenly glazed areas as it will pull the glaze away from the pot. A paint brush loaded with glaze can be used to re-touch areas from which the dry glaze has flaked away, such as the rim of a bowl, but it has to be used like an eye dropper rather than a brush, or it will remove more glaze than it replaces.

By now the beginner must feel bewildered by all the admonishments and advice, and unnerved to find that what should be a mere finishing stage appears to be the most difficult process of all. Hand-glazing is quite difficult to do well, but it should be encouraging to know that no tools are as good as your own hand for applying and 'fettling' the glaze.

Evenness of application

A smooth and even coat of glaze is essential for earthenware if it is not to remain porous, and such a pot, once glazed all over, should be seated on a 'stilt' or tripod (see page 176). The three points of this tripod leave only the finest marks on the base of the pot and do not affect its impermeability after glost firing. Once established on its tripod in a safe position, the pot should be handled as little as possible during any subsequent decoration, and put into the kiln for firing at the earliest opportunity.

Stoneware glazes vary more markedly in colour with the thickness of application than their earthenware equivalents, double layers showing up as lighter patches. At the same time the streakiness of uneven application is not always a fault and the stoneware potter is rarely aiming for a perfectly uniform coloration. The hand method is more appropriate to stoneware, and for beginners it is easier to learn dipping and pouring with stoneware glazes. Their ingredients have better adhesion to the surface of the pot when dry, and so they are less likely to get damaged on their way to the kiln.

Using a paint brush

On a stoneware pot which is unlikely to be used for food, for example a lamp base, the evenness of the glaze coat is less important, and glaze can be applied with a paint brush. A smallish, say 4cm (1½in), housepainter's brush is good, and the more thickly the glaze is applied the less the brushmarks will show: the result depends on the potter's intention.

Brush painting is very appropriate for the once-fired technique (see page 137) and adhesion of the glaze is improved if a small amount of gum arabic (about a dessertspoon to 2 litres/ 3½pt of glaze) is added to the mixture. You can expect a certain unevenness of the surface after the pot has been fired (which is why it does not suit earthenware) and this has to be borne in mind when choosing this method.

Potters who specialize in this technique, such as Lucie Rie, will ensure that the pot is turning (on a wheel-head or a banding wheel) as the glaze is painted on, and that the coating of glaze is quite thick. Remember, though, that the surface of the pot is absorbent like blotting paper, and if you try this method, experiment with different thicknesses of glaze up the walls of a test pot. That way you quickly learn how much to apply – it will vary from glaze to glaze.

Making a glaze

It may come as a jolt to the beginner whose mind is full of museum ceramics, or merely bent on completing a furnishing colour scheme, to be asked at a pottery class, 'What glaze do you want, shiny blue or shiny transparent?' It is unfortunately rather common for such classes to provide ready-made glazes of a very boring kind, and you will not always be popular if you want to provide your own. The reason is that damage to the kiln and other pots can

GLAZING A LID

1–2 A ring of wax brushed around the edge of an upturned lid raised on a banding wheel keeps the glaze neatly away from the edge when the lid is dipped. **Use wax when you have several pots to glaze or delay teapot glazing until you are heating wax for another decorative use.**

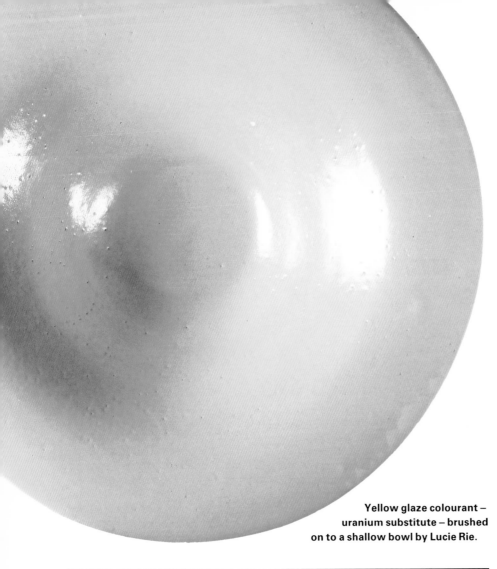

Yellow glaze colourant – uranium substitute – brushed on to a shallow bowl by Lucie Rie.

BRUSH PAINTING

1–2 All sorts of brushes – and brush strokes – can be used to paint glaze on to a pot. Biscuit and dry green pots soak up moisture, so add gum arabic to the mix to prevent the powder from flaking off. Brush painting only suits pots which benefit from an uneven glaze coat.

occur if a glaze is used which matures at a temperature lower than that to which the kiln is fired. Therefore the first step is to establish the firing temperature of the kiln, and to make sure that specially made glazes fit this temperature.

Many ready-prepared glazes can be bought from ceramic suppliers, and photographs in their catalogues indicate both their colour and their texture. They are reliable, with a known melting point, but there is not much joy in using them, and glazes can be made so easily from a small range of materials that it makes sense to try. The results, if not always perfect, will at least be as personal as the pots. Typical and useful recipes are given in the next chapter, and these are mixed by weighing out the ingredients and adding water. Glaze materials are supplied finely ground, though some of them are likely to go lumpy in their bags. It saves time and energy later if the lumps are crushed with a pestle in a mortar or between the fingers before weighing the materials.

I must confess that more than once I have started to make up a batch of glaze – 3kg (6lb) of dry materials is a sensible minimum quantity – only to find half way through that I have not got quite enough of a certain ingredient to complete the mixture. The result of being 'short' on one material can be interesting but it is more likely to make a disappointing glaze, so my advice is to assemble the materials in the sacks, bags or bins, and if supplies of one ingredient seem to be running low weigh that up first, and if necessary reduce the other ingredients proportionally, or wait until you have bought some more.

There is no significance in the order in which dry materials are mixed, but the weights must be right, so ensure that the balance is clean and your arithmetic correct. Metric measures are useful when dealing with recipes in percentages but, equally, 100oz of glaze can be made very quickly and simply by weighing out the appropriate percentages as ounces, and this weight of dry materials makes a sensible quantity.

Medium-hot water added to the ingredients will help to soften any remaining lumps and persuade the mixture to go through a lawn into another bowl or bucket. A 100-strand mesh lawn should be used and care taken that all the ingredients go through, for if any stay behind in the bristles of the scrubbing brush, for example, the glaze mixture will be inaccurate. Two or three sievings back and forth from bowl to bowl may take up to half an hour, depending on the ingredients. Adding more water speeds the process, but if it makes the glaze too thin and watery it must be poured off later when the constituents have settled; an over-thinned glaze cannot be used or even tested immediately it has been made.

The perfect consistency of glaze is impossible to define, since it depends on the porosity of the pot and the optimum glaze thickness on the surface. Stoneware glazes, particularly those containing ash, are usually applied thicker than earthenware glazes, and to describe the consistency as 'like thin cream' is meaningless since cream varies as much as glaze. However, if it is as thin as milk, it is too dilute for use, and some of the water must be removed.

Once the consistency is right, the ingredients must be kept thoroughly mixed by regular stirring, or by the use of a glaze suspender. Some potters add bentonite (up to 2 per cent by dry weight) in place of china or ball clay, as this has the fortunate property of holding all of the glaze ingredients in suspension.

Testing glazes

The first thing to do with a new glaze is to test it. Most studio potters have favourite shapes of clay on which they make their tests, varying from small egg-cups to flat and indented tiles. An arch of thrown clay cut from a cylinder is convenient since it will show the effect of concave and convex surfaces on the quality of the glaze, and also how the glaze changes its colour or 'breaks' on the edges.

It is wise to test a glaze on several clay bodies if more than one clay is to be used, since the glaze/body marriage is different in each case. Finally, it is vital to label the glaze test somewhere, by painting a number or a name on it in a metal oxide, which will stay legible after a firing. A glaze test is only any use if you know what it is. The same applies to the liquid glaze, of course, and glazes stored without names are a trial and a torment in almost every pottery studio or classroom. When you are in the middle of glazing, laying your hands on an indelible writing instrument is hard, and the best thing to do is to tie a felt pen on a string to something immovable, like a water tap. Numbering the glaze bucket or jar is enough for identification, but if you can bring yourself to write the whole recipe on a label it may help others to save time in making up new batches. Waterproof transparent tape stuck on the label on the side of the jar will help to keep a formula legible. Do not put the label on the lid of the jar, or bucket, for a reason too obvious to mention.

Storing glazes

I find that wide-necked sweet jars, which can still be bought cheaply for their replacement value from retailers, are admirable for storage, and two of these will comfortably hold 3kg (100oz) dry weight of glaze, mixed with water. The great advantage of these jars is that you can get your hand inside when necessary to prise out the sticky parts of the glaze which sink to the bottom when the jar has been standing for a while.

Glazes in jars or lidded buckets should last indefinitely, and so should plastic bowls and jugs. Phosphor-bronze lawns, however, which are expensive to replace, are soon ruined if they are left to soak in water, for their wooden frames swell and come unfastened at the sides. The fine mesh itself, though strong, can be punctured if tools are left inside, and it only needs a small hole for a lawn to become quite useless. This vital tool in the making of glazes should not be left in the sink, or flat on a shelf, but hung vertically on a short nail on the wall.

MIXING A GLAZE

1 Add warm water to the weighed ingredients in a polythene bowl, and mix and squeeze out the lumps with one hand.

2 If you use a plastic scrubbing brush with white bristles, you can easily tell if any bits of glaze are left in the brush after sieving.

DECORATING POTS 1

Left
VAUGHN SMITH
Hard-edge designs in contrasting colours are best achieved with a stencil or paper-resist technique, but the overlapping black cats here look like bold brush strokes. On the thrown lid are applied cats, cut from flat slabs, bent around, and painted in bright under-glaze colours. Earthenware. Height: 73.5cm (29in).

Opposite, top left
ROBIN WELCH
The dry coloured surface on Robin Welch's large thrown vase is the result of using pigments stable at high temperatures, while the gold in the reserved rectangle is applied later and the pot refired to 800°C.

Opposite, bottom left
JAC HANSEN
Wonderful and well-planned decoration using sgraffito, inlay and pigments under a galena-type glaze makes this animal figure exceptional.

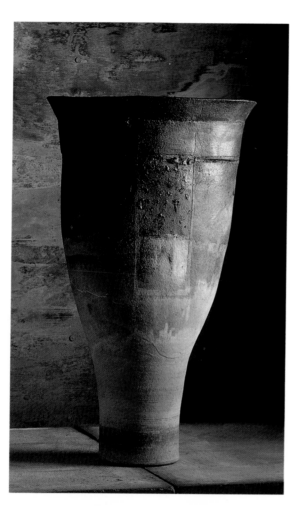

Right
GILLES LE CORRE
Large thrown platter,
decorated with coloured
glazes, brushed and trailed,
and fired to stoneware
temperatures in reduction.
Diameter: 48cm (19in).

16

RECIPES, RESULTS AND REMEDIES

The collection of wood or vegetable-matter ash to make a glaze has the faintest flavour of alchemy, mainly because the books which treat it in detail scorn to tell the beginner what to do with the ash when he or she has collected it, and just how to turn it into one of the bland grey powders which are mixed together for a glaze.

Potassium-rich wood ash is a flux or glaze-melter, and is usually combined with clay – alumina or silica – to make a stoneware glaze. For the beginner or amateur potter the fascination of ash glazes is that there are very few ingredients, and the wide variety of colours, textures and qualities come from the trace elements in the wood ash, so the potter, in collecting and preparing the ash, is truly participating in the creation of something unique. Because different kinds of ash and different batches vary enormously in what they contain, the ceramics industry, which needs to be able to repeat or sustain a colour indefinitely, is not interested in ash glazes. The studio potter, therefore, experiments alone, but fortunately no technical help is needed to develop and 'invent' a range of glazes.

Experimenting with ash glazes

The possible permutations of alumina-silica ingredients are numerous, and experiments to see how ash from one source compares with another must stick to a standard recipe such as that given on page 136 so that there is a 'control' and comparisons are valid. The variable is the ash, because different species of tree contain different trace elements in their wood, as do grasses and other vegetable matter. The local soil conditions, which provide the chemicals for the tree in the first place, also vary widely, so it is not possible to predict results accurately. We only know that ash glazes extend from creamy-white through greens and greys to bright orange, in both oxidized and reduced stoneware firings. (In an oxidized firing there is an adequate supply of air for combustion; in a reduced firing air flow is restricted.)

All wood ash provides a flux, with the trace elements making the colour, but

Sprinkling fine dry wood ash by hand on a dampened biscuit pot (*opposite*) will produce the handsome stoneware glaze above. The inside is separately glazed.

unfortunately the ash of other materials (such as coal) spoils the result, and it is essential to be sure that the ash is composed of vegetable matter and nothing else. Wood fires often contain a mixture of several woods, which does not in any way spoil the end glaze; it simply makes it impossible to get the same result again.

Anyone with a log-burning stove or fireplace is well placed to collect pure and controlled ash – simply by catching it on a foil sheet placed under the fire-bars – but the plight of the flat-dweller is not hopeless. Outdoor bonfires, the fires of wood scraps after tree-felling and even autumn fires of garden leaves yield perfect ash, provided that it is collected before rain has leached valuable chemicals out of it, and that no earth is scooped up with it.

Since it takes an enormous amount of wood to produce sufficient ash to make even a small amount of glaze (0.45kg or 1lb of ash is a minimum working quantity) enthusiastic beginners are inclined to scoop up roots, sand and grit from the base of the fire in an attempt to get all of the ash, and thereby they waste the lot by including

impurities. It is best to leave suspect ash behind, and to collect only the fine white or ochre-coloured powder in a metal tin, preferably while it is still warm. There is nothing magical about this super-freshness; it simply ensures that nothing has leached out or blown away before collection.

Plunging all the ash in water in a polythene bucket immediately separates out the light, unwanted charcoal from the dense ash, and this charcoal, together with the grey scum that surrounds it, should be scooped off. At this stage the ash has to be treated with respect for, mixed with water, a fairly powerful alkaline solution has been formed (caustic potash, or potassium hydroxide). If your hands or scrubbing brush are left in the liquid, they will begin to dissolve, and most potters know the characteristic soapy feeling of the fingers when they have been fishing pieces of charcoal out of the ash for a minute or so.

A potter I know in Portugal makes unglazed earthenware, in the traditional amphora shape, for holding drinking water, kept cool by evaporation. His kiln is fired by solid fuel, mainly wood, but in the appropriate season he burns almond shells. Once every two or three minutes throughout the duration of this firing, shovelfuls of almond shells go into the firemouth, very black oily smoke comes from the chimney and the small mountain of almond shells, delivered by the lorry load, becomes imperceptibly smaller. The white ash which accumulates below the fire is of no use to him as a glaze flux, since he makes no glazed stoneware, but he once gave me some to make a glaze test.

If the potassium in ash is very concentrated, the alkali can have quite spectacular effects. The almond-shell ash my Portuguese friend gave to me quickly removed all the green paint from the metal bowl in which I soaked it, and did not stop there. Wanting to reduce its weight and size for transport by air back to England, I dried the stuff to the shape and texture of a damp brick, and wrapped it carefully in polythene bags, newspaper and a rush basket. In a few hours spent on the wooden shelves of a left-luggage hall it ate its way through all this packing and made a nasty mess on the shelf.

The taming of this ash had by now become a challenge, especially with the possibility of some truly unique colour or texture as the reward. Alas, when the ash was finally mixed according to the standard formula on page 136 the result was one of the nastiest, oiliest, muddiest glazes I have ever seen, unpleasant to touch and heavily crazed. One of the lessons to be learned from this is that the greater the potassium content of the ash, the more powerful the flux in the glaze and the more 'glassy' the result is likely to be.

Potters reduce the potassium content in the ash once it has been sieved in a very unscientific way – by pouring it off as potassium hydroxide when the solid matter has settled. This process is known as 'washing', and could be said to require the intuition of a good cook. The more often water is added to the bucket of ash, and then poured off when the ash has settled, the more potassium is lost, though there is no easy way of measuring this. The resulting glaze will become 'harder' (that is, it will need a higher temperature to mature) and will probably become more matt with each potassium loss. This may lead to a more exciting glaze, or the reverse, and is certainly the reason why one potter's ash glaze will never be the same as another's.

To pour away potassium so prodigally may seem a waste, but feldspar, a major ingredient in most glazes, also acts as a flux, and the potter may only be interested in the colourants which are locked in the chemistry of the tree. No one can state precisely how much potassium hydroxide should be poured off an ash to get the best results, but if half a bucketful of dry ash is filled to the top with water, half the resulting liquid can be poured away when the ash has settled, the bucket filled up again, and the process repeated three or four times with advantage. Remember that the liquid you are pouring away can be a highly caustic alkali, which dissolves clothes and burns skin. So make sure that it is disposed of carefully, with plenty of water to dilute it.

The ash has to be turned back into a dry powder before it can be weighed against other dry ingredients such as feldspar, ball clay or china clay, so the clear liquid should be poured away carefully after the final 'wash', leaving the sediment behind. This needs time to dry out, and the process of preparing an ash is spread over several weeks, especially if it is done at a weekly class. Ash appears in only six of the glaze recipes which follow, but the small saga of collecting and preparing it is recommended to the beginner. The results can be truly superb, and they are always personal.

One most memorable experience was the making of a batch of glaze from the ash of peat blocks dug on Sedgemoor in Somerset in the south west of England, and burnt in one weekend in my own living-room fireplace. The glaze test produced a rich orange, with depth and a fine surface, and the subsequent pots were a joy. The source of those peat blocks has gone, and the glaze cannot be made again. I only regret that there is not a drop left to include with the tests shown here.

After such a long description of a single glaze ingredient, the reader may fear a similar treatment for all the others. There would be little point, however, as the studio potter or beginner is dependent on a supplier for these other materials, and they vary widely, though the supplier is quite likely to provide an analysis if requested.

Introducing the recipes

For those beginners who are encouraged by chapter 14 to make their own glazes, I have included 20 glaze recipes which I have used and found satisfactory. Because of variations in kilns and ingredients, it is unlikely that your results will be the same as mine, but they should certainly be interesting. The figures below represent relative proportions; they do not necessarily add up to 100. They can be grams, ounces or pounds, according to the quantities required. Where additions

'WASHING' WOOD ASH

1–2 Making ash glaze is like entering a lottery – something marvellous might turn up from the remains of a wood fire. But always wear rubber gloves to protect your hands from the caustic potash when 'washing' the ash, and use an old kitchen sieve to lift out charcoal, nails and staples.

(of oxides, for example) are referred to in the instructions, the proportions indicated represent percentages of the given recipe.

Most handbooks for serious potters contain sections on glazes, and there are many books devoted to the subject. It can be confusing to be confronted with so many options, but such books are valuable sources of information, as, of course, are the recipes given by other potters.

However seriously or sporadically you intend to pot, do keep a glaze notebook which records your experiments. It should include ingredients and their sources, recommended temperatures, dates and comments. Add recipes given by others too. Even if you have no time to test them when you write them in, one day you may.

Above: 'Three Little Girls from School' by Betty Woodman, with the bright colours and characteristic shininess of earthenware. Height: 25.5cm (10in).

Earthenware glazes

Honey Glaze   1,000°C

80 lead bisilicate   20 body clay

A clear to honey-coloured glaze, the colour depending on the body clay, which should be the same as that used for the ware. Because of its low temperature, this glaze can be useful for home-made kilns with uncertain maximum temperature (see chapter 20).

Leadless Glaze   1,140°C

56 feldspar	10 barium
33 flint	carbonate
25 colemanite	1.5 calcium
(contains borax)	nitrate
12 calcined zinc	
oxide	

Many communal potteries now prefer to use leadless glazes. This one matures at a temperature well above normal earthenware.

Transparent White Glaze   1,060°C

56 lead bisilicate   7 china clay
30 feldspar   5 whiting

This is a useful transparent glaze, good on slips. With the addition of 10 per cent tin oxide it is an opaque white majolica glaze.

Good-tempered Clear Glaze   1,050°C

75 lead   18 china clay
   sesquisilicate   6 flint

This glaze was developed by Mary Wondrausch for use on slipware. She describes it as good tempered, or well behaved, because it does not craze or run. By adding 1 per cent iron oxide it becomes golden; 2–3 per cent and it is amber. It should be given a one-hour soak at 1,050°C.

Stoneware glazes

1 BNO
oxidized 1,250°C

50 Cornish stone	10 quartz
35 china clay	5 whiting
20 dolomite	

Matt glazes sometimes look under-fired. This one does not. Dolomite gives it its oatmealy quality and also softens and modifies the normally strong oxide colourants. It is better, and whiter, when used thickly. An addition of 8 per cent iron oxide produces a useful brown (see 1a in the key below), not too shiny and good for tableware. Adding only 5 per cent iron oxide, plus 2.5 per cent tin oxide, gives a waxy Indian red.

2 Red Reserve
1,280°C

26 ball clay	16 whiting
26 quartz	12 red iron oxide
21 feldspar	

A lustrous purple-red glaze, it has a golden sparkle if titanium dioxide is painted on thinly.

The key below relates to the numbered glaze recipes on this and the facing page. Do not expect identical results.

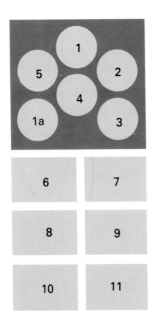

3 Ruth's Green

1,250–1,280°C

40 feldspar	20 whiting
38 china clay	4 copper oxide

An excellent glaze for tableware, the green becomes stronger if the copper oxide content is increased until it becomes a metallic black.

4 Abrey Crackle

oxidized 1,250°C

40 feldspar	5 titanium dioxide
30 whiting	0.25 cobalt oxide
25 stoneware body clay	0.25 nickel oxide
25 ball clay	

Gerald Abrey, a metallurgist, gives his name to this glaze, which has for many years been a favourite of mine for tableware. It is pale speckly grey-blue. 'Crackle' in this instance refers to the granular appearance which comes from the titanium dioxide. If the cobalt is increased to 5 per cent, and the nickel omitted, it is a brighter blue. If both are omitted, the texture remains and the colour pales.

5 'Clear' Felspathic

1,250°C

58 feldspar	6 ball clay
17 whiting	5 zinc oxide
14 flint	

This glaze is translucent rather than transparent, with the characteristic 'milk and water' look of a felspathic glaze. When it is thick it has fine bubbles trapped in the glaze which give sparkle, and it combines well with copper oxide (1 per cent) to make grey-green – a celadon without reduction.

6 'Hamada' Tenmoku

1,250°C

40 quartz	11 whiting
21 feldspar	8 ash
15 iron oxide	5 china clay

The massive loading of this glaze with iron oxide produces a dark brown shiny glaze which is handsome on tableware or jugs. It is best used in reduction firing.

7 Lucie Rie's White

oxidized 1,250°C

58 soda feldspar	10 tin oxide
14 china clay	8 whiting
10 zinc oxide	8 flint

This glaze is the famous glossy white glaze used on Lucie Rie's tableware, often stained brown with manganese and copper carbonate on the rims. It can be tried with less tin – 5 or even 2 per cent – but is expensive to make, and inclined to crawl when used on biscuit ware, perhaps because of the high zinc content. Lucie Rie's pots, of course, are once fired (see page 137), which avoids this problem.

8 Gill's White

oxidized 1,250°C

50 feldspar	10 whiting
20 zinc oxide	10 tin oxide

This is a simple formula for a beautiful shiny white glaze. A little quartz (2 per cent) may be needed to counteract crazing because the formula does not suit all bodies. It is excellent and less shiny as a glaze for once-fired ware. Like all glazes including tin oxide, it is expensive to make.

9 Bryan's Gold

1,250°C

54 china clay	13 feldspar
27 whiting	6 yellow ochre

Modified from a glaze used by Bryan Newman, this gives a very dry surface because of the high china clay content, but the yellow ochre (a weak form of iron oxide) creates an interesting mottled effect. If it is thin, it is brown; if it is thick, it is cream.

10 Dark Green

oxidized 1,280°C

48 feldspar	10 flint
22 china clay	3 copper oxide
20 whiting	

This handsome dark green glaze with a very smooth surface has small black mottlings where the copper oxide shows its strength. The addition of 1 per cent cobalt oxide and 1 per cent tin oxide instead of copper makes an equally rich dark blue.

11 Bryanston

reduced 1,280°C

50 feldspar	9 ball clay
18 quartz	8 whiting
10 china clay	5 talc

I was given this glaze by Steve Sheridan, the Australian potter who teaches pottery at Bryanston School in Dorset, England. He uses it in reduction, and it produces a magnificent smoky green with the addition of 2 per cent iron oxide. In oxidation, without the iron, it is a good white, very stable for pigments. Steve Sheridan emphasizes the crazing lines by rubbing his pots with sepia ink.

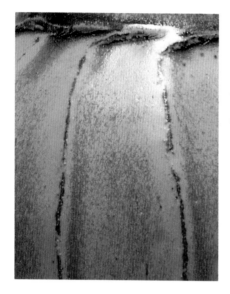

Ash glazes

Standard formula 1,250°C
40 ash   20 ball clay
40 feldspar

Shiny ash glaze 1,250°C
(with crazing)
50 ash   50 feldspar

Dry ash glaze 1,250°C
50 ash   50 china clay

Ash on its own will make a glaze, usually runny, best used inside and on the top of the outside of a pot, so that it does not stick the pot to the kiln shelf. If you have a wood ash strong in potassium, the shine will be reduced according to how much china clay you add.

The problem with ash glazes is that you cannot ever repeat them exactly when the source of the ash runs out. It is worth sticking to the standard formula, but you can experiment with china clay, whiting and talc instead of ball clay, and of course oxide additions will make their presence felt. For instance, 1 per cent tin oxide will produce fine white lines in the glaze. Ash glazes will usually look better in reduction firings. As explained in chapter 20, it is the changed colour of the body clay under the glaze which makes the pot look richer – deeper and more 'smoky'.

The dry ash glaze (formula left) is unsuitable for tableware, but can be used for sculptural pieces, though it is impossible to get an even colour. The thicker it is, the paler it will be. Wonderful colours can be produced by adding small percentages of iron (brown), cobalt, or cobalt and nickel (grey-blue).

Porcelain glazes

Please do not be confused by this name. Porcelain is a clay, and it does not require a special glaze, only one which matures at the appropriate temperature of 1,250–1,300°C. Therefore all the stoneware glazes, including the ash glazes in the previous section, can be used on porcelain, although many of them are less successful than on coarser stoneware clay. The following glazes are especially successful on porcelain – I love them both.

Gilbert's White   1,250–1,280°C

40 feldspar   15–20 well-washed
38 china clay   wood ash
20 whiting   0.1 copper oxide
                        (optional)

A beautiful waxy or dry glaze, this one shows very white on sharp porcelain edges. The copper oxide makes pale turquoise, if the ash does not produce its own strong coloration. Well-washed ash will be low in potassium, and this will contribute to the matteness of the glaze. The recipe came from Gilbert Harding-Green and is a modified version of Ruth's Green glaze.

Takeshi Clear   1,250°C

20 feldspar   15 china clay
20 whiting   15 quartz
15 nepheline   10 talc
   syenite   2 bone ash

This transparent glaze from Takeshi Yasuda is my favourite glaze for porcelain. It is a bright-eyed glaze which crazes beautifully. A little iron oxide will turn it greenish (in reduction) or brown.

Top left: An ash glaze, made using the standard formula and poplar ash.

Left: Ash and porcelain glazes (*top, left to right*): shiny ash glaze with crazing and dry ash glaze; (*bottom*) Gilbert's 'White' and Takeshi Clear.

Opposite: A salt-glazed plate by Jane Hamlyn. The pale mottling on the rim is typical of salt glazing.

Salt glazes

Salt-glazed pottery is found at both extremes of the world of ceramics, used by sculptural potters, who admire its surface quality and range, and also by the manufacturers of clay drain-pipes, who find it a cheap and easy way of waterproofing land drains. By shovelling common salt (sodium chloride) into the firemouth of the kiln, a skin of glaze forms from the sodium on the ware and the kiln walls alike, while the chlorine burns off as a poisonous gas. Needless to say, such glazes require the exclusive use of an outdoor, fuel-burning kiln with a flue. The resulting glaze, which forms at stoneware temperatures, is mottled, varying between grey and brown with a lustrous sheen, and used to be seen on stone ginger-beer jars, as well as the famous Bellarmine ware. A similar but more pinky glaze is made by using soda ash (sodium bicarbonate) instead of salt.

In recent years, salt-glazed ware has become very popular and is much used by leading potters. Unfortunately, it is a technique not available to those who use electric kilns – the salt would ruin the elements – and the lack of a flue for the fumes would make the process very dangerous.

Once firing

Glazes with familiar qualities on one clay may reveal different characteristics on another. The combination of a translucent amber earthenware glaze on a red clay makes a pleasing rich brown, and the effect of clay slips under glazes is mentioned in chapter 18. One glazing method which changes the qualities of the glaze considerably is raw glazing or once firing, where the glaze is put direct on to the dry green pot, and only once fired to the maturing temperature of the glaze. As might be expected, the glaze becomes closely combined with the body, and the surface is often less shiny than if the same glaze were used on a biscuit pot.

Lucie Rie and Hans Coper used the once-fired technique for all their work, and it is surprising that it is not more popular, particularly as it saves fuel. Economy of firing is counterbalanced by a high risk of failure, especially when the glaze is being applied, but once-fired ware has a unique unity and is worth trying if you have your own kiln. The person who packs a glost kiln for an evening class will not accept once-fired ware because of the danger of its shattering and thereby spoiling other students' work.

FAULTS AND REMEDIES

Unlike the medical student, who learns about the body before getting on to the general practice of curing maladies and weaknesses, most potters learn about their materials by trying to cure faults.

Crazing

The short unmusical ping of a glaze cracking on a pot fresh from the kiln is a maddening sound to the potter: it means that fine hairline cracks are appearing on a glaze, and will spread until the pot is covered with a network of lines which will catch the dirt and become ever more noticeable. Encouraged in some Eastern ceramics by rubbing oxide into the cracks and refiring, it is generally regarded as undesirable in tableware. A sudden change of temperature – like the shock of cold air to a pot taken too soon from the kiln – will encourage 'crazing', and it is this quick change of temperature which unhygienically disfigures serving dishes put into the oven to keep the meat warm.

The reason for this most common of problems is disharmony between the glaze and the body. Earthenware glazes are usually in a state of compression after firing, induced by the greater shrinkage of the body as it cools. If there is no compression, cracks will appear and spread.

To prevent crazing, some alteration must be made to the clay or the glaze. Oddly enough, the addition of silica in the form of flint or quartz will increase the amount of shrinkage in the body if added to the clay, and decrease the amount of glaze shrinkage if added to the glaze, effectively putting the glaze into the required state of compression in either case. For the amateur potter it is usually more practical to adapt the glaze to suit an existing clay. Unfortunately the addition of silica will change the glaze quality, so small measured quantities of silica should be added, starting with 1 per cent, and tested until the crazing fault has been cured.

In earthenware glazes, adding borax will correct a glaze with a tendency to craze, and (although itself a fluxing agent) borax can even be added to glazes in which lead is the principal flux. A really good safeguard against crazing on earthenware, however, is to make sure that the body is biscuit fired to over 1,100°C, as this causes the body to contract more at low temperatures, when the pot is subsequently glazed, giving the glaze a useful 'squeeze'.

At stoneware temperatures the relationship between glaze and body is a very close one, as both are vitrified, and the more alike they are chemically, the less likely is crazing. Sometimes a glaze will craze even when it is well matched to the body clay, if it has been applied to a pot unevenly or unreasonably thickly. If the door of a glaze kiln is opened too soon the shock of cold air strikes the glaze before it reaches the clay, and will cause crazing which could otherwise be avoided. Unfortunately the temptation to open the kiln while it is still warm is a very strong one, and hard to resist.

Glaze crazing is sometimes called 'crackle', especially by auctioneers and dealers, perhaps in the hope that it will sound more seductive, and less like a fault. Crazing or crackling is an essential feature of raku-ware, which is described in chapter 21.

'Shivering', 'shelling' or 'peeling' is a form of crazing in which the glaze, under excessive compression, is forced away from the body and chips off, especially on edges. This is a serious fault for commercial potters, as bits of glaze – or glass – coming off the pot can be mixed with food. Though it looks the same as crazing, shivering can usually be distinguished by feel: the network of lines is slightly raised to the touch, as small areas of glaze press hard against each other. Too much silica in the body or the glaze is the usual cause, and the best remedy is to scrap the glaze and prepare a new one containing less flint or quartz.

Crawling

This is a tiresome fault with a more disastrous effect on finished ware. It is the shrinking away of the glaze from certain areas of a pot, leaving a raw scar. There are two principal causes, both curable. The presence of grease

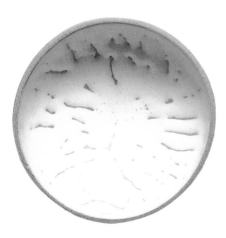

Crawling: it can be prevented.

or dust on the biscuit pot leads to crawling, and the normal greasiness of fingers is enough to cause crawling on a much-handled pot. A biscuit pot with less tactile appeal may lie around on a workshop shelf for a long time attracting dust, and this has exactly the same result. If the potter suspects that the unglazed ware is either greasy or dusty, it is worth biscuit firing the pot a second time, to cleanse the surface, even though it means waiting longer to see the pot finished.

Crawling is also caused if the glaze, when applied to the pot, dries out too rapidly and cracks on the surface like the mud in a dried-up puddle. Such cracking can be carefully smoothed over with the fingertips, effectively forcing powdered glaze into the fissures.

You should always inspect pots for surface cracks on the dried glaze before packing the kiln because if a newly glazed pot goes into the kiln with any kind of crack on the glaze surface, the surface tension of the melting glaze may cause it to curl back, especially if the glaze layer is thick, and the result is very ugly. Equally, if you put a newly glazed pot into the kiln before it is dry, then the surface cracking which leads to crawling may well happen as the pot is heated up and the moisture it contains evaporates as steam. The glazing of still-warm biscuit ware will often cause cracking of the glazed surface before firing, as will the application of a second coat of glaze.

Matt glazes are more likely to crawl than shiny ones, which are more runny, and in my experience glazes containing zinc or tin, or a combination of the two, often suffer from this malady, which can be cured by a progressive reduction in the proportion of these ingredients in successive batches of glaze. Finally, a glaze which is perfectly content to flow over a clay may well crawl back over a band of slip, especially if it is dark slip.

Blistering

An unattractive feature sometimes associated with the use of too much chromium in combination with other colouring oxides, blistering also occurs in earthenware glazes containing lead if the kiln atmosphere is oxygen-starved or 'reduced' (see chapter 20). Where the culprit is already in the glaze, the only cure is to start afresh with a new glaze, but sometimes blistering is the result of overfiring, in which case the cure is obvious.

Blistering also happens when two incompatible glazes overlap, and a small bubble of gas remains under the top glaze even when the pot is cool. It never makes a practical surface, but it is sometimes used to decorative effect on surfaces which are not to be used as tableware – by grinding all the bubbles away to create a lace-like pattern.

Pinholing

This fault is the result of volcanic activity during firing, either in the glaze mantle or in the body below. Small eruptions of gases from within the glaze leave ugly 'craters', and the cure is often to 'soak' the glaze for a few minutes, by maintaining a high kiln temperature with the glaze molten, so that an even layer of glaze will re-form over the scars. This is not a satisfactory solution, however, when the fault is in a matt glaze, as such a glaze is never very liquid on the surface of the pot.

When the eruptions come from the body they may make small pock marks on the surface, which can be quite attractive on stoneware of a certain rugged type. It is even encouraged by some potters, who introduce 1 per cent silicon carbide into the clay body.

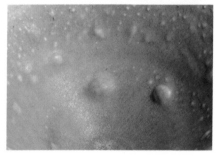

Top: Pinholing is a nuisance on tableware but can be attractive, as on this stoneware pot by Lucy Rie.

Above: Bloating – it is always ugly.

Bloating

The name given to big blisters made by gases still within the clay, 'bloating' is not strictly speaking a glaze fault, but it reveals itself in the glaze firing and can be caused by taking the temperature higher than that recommended for the clay or by working with clay which contains impurities or foreign bodies. A bloated pot cannot be corrected.

Dunting

If it happens in the glaze firing, then I suppose 'dunting' or breaking apart must be the ultimate glaze fault. One cause of dunting is over-rapid cooling, and another is the fact that pots without foot rings which stand on kiln shelves cool more quickly at the top than at the bottom.

A form of dunting which has caused me great pain and disappointment relates to porcelain. When the body is very thinly thrown, a glaze sometimes cools to a compression state which proves too much for the body, and instead of crazing simply breaks the pot up. There are two remedies: one is to make the glaze give less of a squeeze by adding flint, and the other is to maintain the kiln temperature at vitrification point by 'soaking' (see chapter 20) and then to cool it more slowly.

Underfiring and overfiring

Both are faults of kiln technique rather than of glazing. It is a sad waste of effort not to fire a carefully prepared glaze to its optimum temperature, and 10°C can make all the difference between a commonplace pot and a pot of distinction.

The characteristics of underfired ware are unmistakable: a dull dryness of surface reminiscent of an unripe pear. If it is not possible to vary the kiln temperature, for instance where the work of many students shares the same kiln, then a glaze which does not mature should be abandoned.

Overfired ware not only looks too runny and treacly, but the glaze will also probably have run into a pool inside the pot or run down the outside and stuck the pot to the kiln shelf. Gravity affects the quality of a glaze, and sometimes a glaze which holds together beautifully on a flat tile will run miserably thin if put on a pot with vertical sides. You should therefore always consider the shape of the pot when choosing the glaze.

Experimentation with glazes and bodies is an occupation for someone with a great deal of time to spare, but for the potter with limited time, who has laboured long over a single pot and then been disappointed by its glaze, there is a ray of hope: a second coating of glaze can be applied and the pot refired. The result of a combination of two different glazes fired at different times will look like neither, nor will it even resemble an intelligent guess at a mixture of the two. But it may be better than the original surface. To persuade the second glaze to stick to the pot, warm up the pot slightly and add a sticky substance of some kind to the glaze. Gum arabic or even sugar will help, and will not affect the glaze itself. Getting the new glaze to lie evenly over the glazed surface is not easy using the pouring method, and spraying the second coat on with an atomizer is strongly recommended.

Left: Blistering – one glaze overlies another. Ground away, the bubbles leave a pattern, as on this graceful porcelain bowl by Suzanne Bergne.

DECORATION BY DESIGN

*It's all been done before, of course, and so well done
for thousands of years that heart and hand sometimes falter at the
prospect of decorating a pot. Every culture I can recall has its
master decorators – think of the Minoan vases, Persian ware,
the Mimbres Indians of North America . . .
In pottery, form and decoration often merge, so that it is hard
to tell where the pot ends and the decoration begins. The handle or
spout of a functional pot may be part of a bold or intricate
concept. Or the decoration, if it is a painted design,
may be the reason for the pot.*

**Opposite: White slip and brown slip
applied in both conventional and
unconventional ways to a plate by
Katherine Pleydell Bouverie link the
heritage of East and West.
Diameter: 30.5cm (12in).**

17

MULTI-COLOURED CLAYS

'We', wrote Bernard Leach, 'have the whole world to draw upon for incentive beauty. It is difficult . . . to keep one's head in the maelstrom. . . .'

He goes on to relate how touchstones of beauty guided him, and how the two poles of English tradition and Japanese culture provided him with a lifetime's crusade as he sought ways to bring them together. No one has written more beautifully or with more passion about pots than Leach, but since he wrote, the bewildering variety of possibilities which confront the beginner has grown even greater, as the frontiers of pottery and its uses have extended and some techniques have become more accessible.

Those with a creative block, however caused, must remember that clay is *kind*, and is capable of almost anything. It can record, as a hand pressed into it will prove. It can faithfully reproduce, either identical casts from a mould or the print of a car tyre. It can make ceramic versions of interesting objects from lemons to lemonade cans; an art

teacher friend of mine once made a ceramic snake at least 3.6m (12ft) long, in reposeful coils, and with a convincing snakeskin glaze.

The inspiration should come before the pot. Always have in mind what you want to do, and plan any decoration when you plan the pot. The next two chapters are concerned with decorating a pot, as or after it is made, but this chapter describes decoration which is in the clay itself.

Colour and texture are the variables that clay has to offer. The danger of using clays which are too different is that they will crack apart when fired, because of their different rates of thermal expansion, but experiments show that strange bedfellows can marry well, and a single clay can be coloured with different oxides, grogged with fine or coarse grog, and even have materials such as cork added which will burn away in the kiln to leave pock marks, which can be decorative.

Ewen Henderson's technique of placing patches of flattened clay

together, sometimes as a sandwich, sometimes side by side in a variation on the traditional coiling technique, allows these contrasts to show. Structural striations using different clays are also at the heart of the integral decoration in Claudi Casanovas's ceramic sculpture, and although his work is massive in scale, the same technique can be used on a small scale by those who want to make interesting pots while learning the limits of the behaviour of clays.

Varying the colour

Mixing clays of different colours has a long tradition, the best known being the agate ware which dates from the seventeenth century in England. It uses the 'streaky bacon' effect of putting dark and light clays together, and deliberately keeping the colours apart by arresting the kneading process. Once the clay has been sliced up, it can be rolled into slabs for press- or hump-moulded dishes, and the surface scraped clean to bring out the distinct

NERIAGE

MILLEFIORI TECHNIQUES

A sandwich of dark and light clay, cut into strips and then into small blocks, can be rearranged to make patterned sheets of clay if carefully bonded.

Millefiori **is a glass maker's technique, but its pottery equivalent is centuries old. Here a dark body is rolled round a light core and chopped into units.**

One pattern is superimposed on another – a spiral of black and white streaky blocks will stand out against its paler neighbours when fired.

Left: A simple form – in this instance a hemispherical bowl by Jane Waller – is a sensible choice when a strong but random patterning is derived from the clay body itself. The technique is illustrated below. When pressed together, the coloured balls approximate to hexagons, and the pot's appeal depends on a harmonious relationship of colours once the pot has been fired. Diameter: 20.5cm (8in).

Opposite: A hand-formed plate by Ewen Henderson, made from large thin patches and sandwiches of oxide-stained clay, covered with a single glaze. Diameter: 25.5cm (10in).

COMBINING COLOURED CLAYS

1 Like items of confectionery, the piles of hand-rolled balls of clay stained with different oxides represent the first stage in a labour of love.

2 A plaster of Paris mould is lined with damp butter-muslin before the balls are placed side by side, chosen at random from the different colours.

3 To smooth the wall, a pestle presses the balls together. They will stick to it unless it is covered with butter muslin, dry or soaked in linseed oil.

colour boundaries that may have been blurred by the rolling pin.

An alternative name for pottery which is made from integrally patterned clay is 'scroddled ware', and in France *neriage* is the term used to describe the technique in which more controlled patterns can be created by laminating dark and light clays in a multi-decker sandwich, and slicing them vertically into strips of even width. If these are laid side by side, a wide slab of clay can be made, and a fine metal tool drawn across the clay will create a feathered pattern (as described on page 156 for slip). Again, once the slab is rolled out, it can be scraped to clean the pattern.

Varied rearrangements of such combinations of different-coloured clays are possible and can be an end in themselves, covered only with a clear glaze. However, junctions between dark and light can equally effectively be blurred deliberately with a sponge, or made to burn softly through an opaque glaze. A good example of the latter is seen in the famous spiral thrown ware of Lucie Rie. She simply threw with a lump of clay in which dark and light ingredients had been pressed together without kneading, so that an ever widening band of dark clay spiralled up the pot, and later burnt through the glaze. A good example of such a pot is shown on page 146.

Patterns of different-coloured clay can also be used in a more automatic form. The English potter Jane Waller has developed a technique of placing small balls of clay of equal size against each other in a press mould so that, when beaten firmly with a pestle, they take the form of hexagons, like the cells of a honeycomb. A fine layer of butter muslin lies between the mould surface and the clay to keep the fragile structure together while the pot dries, after which it can be peeled off.

Of course, the range of patterns which can be pressed against moulds is vast. Imagine, for instance, wrapping a coil of white clay in a thin blanket of dark clay, and slicing across the resulting tube to make a series of short sections like liquorice allsorts. Set on end, these can be rolled into sheets of

clay, to be cut into tiles or used in moulds. This process is extremely time-consuming, and depends on scrupulous cleanliness and tidiness, for only if the ingredients are kept distinct will the patterns be clear.

It is also disheartening if such patterns later crack apart in the kiln, and this can happen easily where there is no bonding between the surfaces of adjacent clays. The best way to avoid it is to make sure that the coloured clays have the same basic body: for instance, a special white proprietary clay known as T-material or a white stoneware can be prepared and cut into two lumps. One lump remains white while the other one is progressively coloured with oxides up to 7 per cent of its dry weight. Cobalt, iron, manganese or ochre can all be used separately, or mixed together. T-material already contains grains of molochite, but additional molochite or some other form of grog up to 10 per cent of the dry weight of the clay helps to keep the combined clays in one piece after firing.

THROWING MIXED CLAYS

When dark and light clay balls are pressed together without kneading a helical pattern emerges during throwing as clay particles spiral upwards.

GALLERY
MIXED-CLAY POTS

Above
ROBIN HOPPER
Modern agate ware. When dark and light clays are mixed, the clarity of the patterning is obscured by throwing or handling and can only be revealed if the surface is carefully scraped with a sharp knife or razor blade, and the result left unglazed. Height: 20 and 26cm (7¾ and 10¼in).

Right
LUCIE RIE
If dark and light clays are thrown from an unmixed ball on the wheel, a spiral design will rise up the pot. When the final form is assembled from two or three thrown pieces, as in this classic vase, much care must be taken to make a good marriage between the parts. Here manganese in the 'dark' clay burns softly through the thickly painted glaze. Height: 43cm (17in).

Below
EWEN HENDERSON
Right
CLAUDI CASANOVAS
Decoration is in the structure of the clay in these two pots. Regular stratification lines in Casanovas' twisted forms retain an inorganic and geological appearance. Henderson's more complex sculpture is made from porcelain and bone china clay, sandwiched with stoneware clay and loaded with oxides and glaze.

18

DECORATING THE RAW POT

The Greeks were great 'decorators' of pottery, in the sense that they used ceramics as a vehicle for a painted design. Their work was at once two-dimensional, because of the flat application of colour (though often figures were shown in perspective), and three-dimensional, in the way in which it filled or covered a curved surface. Sometimes the Attic pot was a masterpiece of decoration, but very often it was not, and these pots find more favour nowadays with social historians than with artists. Never did the red, black and white designs have a real unity with the materials of the pot, the fire-bound unity familiar in oriental and Persian ceramics. So superbly do their designs fill and complete the surface of their pots that they seem belittled by the very word 'decoration', which implies a treatment of a surface or an object subsequent to its making, rather than a part of the original concept. And there are West African vessels designed and decorated so harmoniously that you cannot say where one element ends and the other begins, and unglazed food vessels made by the Indians of the Brazilian Mato Grosso whose boldness of painted decoration hints at the irresistibility of a ceramic surface – a surface which cries out to the potter to be decorated, and decorated all over.

In the previous section I have discussed the clothing of a pot in glaze and I hope I have made it clear that a carefully balanced glaze alone is a fitting decoration for a finished pot. Many times have I watched a pupil, absolutely determined that his or her work was incomplete without a painted spray of flowers, resolutely spoil a competent pot by adding a stiff and unrelaxed piece of brushwork with no intrinsic merit and no relation to the form of the pot.

There can be no absolute rules for decoration, just as there is no longer any grammar of design. A rigid geometric pattern can succeed just as well as a free or organic ornament; a brutal or violent contortion of a pot can be as successful in its own terms as a delicately executed lacework in clay. In the following description of techniques there should be no conclusions drawn

as to one method's superiority over others. There is only one outstanding tenet which I would apply to the decoration of ceramics – that it should be *confidently done*, with assurance and no hesitation. The fiery atmosphere of the kiln has an unkind way of mocking tentative efforts and of making the muffed brushstroke look ridiculous, whereas it respects and underlines the emphatic mark, the clearly drawn line or the crisp-cut edge.

Impressed designs

Clay surfaces can be decorated by 'impressing' or stamping a design while the clay is plastic, or when it is leather hard. You could prepare a long list of household odds and ends which would serve this semi-automatic function, but it is important to avoid combining more than one or two impressions on a single pot. The simpler the design of the 'seal' the better, and of course effective seals can be specially made out of plaster of Paris or wood. Some natural forms make good seals, and the

Above: The designs impressed on to raw clay by Paul Soldner here are reminiscent of Egyptian bas-relief carving. They can be abstract or figurative and this example illustrates how well the decoration is married with the form – the two are quite inseparable.

Below: The tradition of making pots to suggest animal forms is both ancient and modern. By adding simple lugs and a head to a bowl, a bat pot was made by a Waura Indian from the Brazilian Mato Grosso in the 1960s.

'Elements of Chance'. Decoration is integral to the design process in this construction for wallhanging by Tom and Elaine Coleman. The low-fired units are glazed (or painted) in striking colours to emphasize the textures and contrasting character of the different parts.

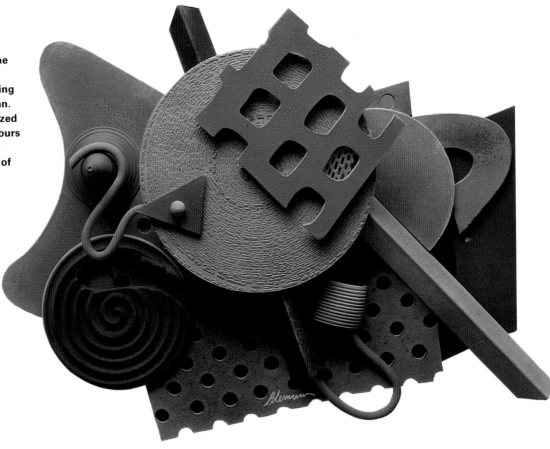

IMPRESSING

Experiment with everyday objects for impressing seals, or design your own by carving into small blocks of plaster of Paris or wood.

best one I have ever come across is the seed case of the eucalyptus tree, with a rigid star-shaped pattern on its end which is both geometric and lively. Within the pottery workshop, the beginner short of inspiration can use the ends of turning tools or Seger cones to gain practice in making repeating shapes.

A small seal like a button can look ridiculous in isolation on a pot, but used in a regular or linear way it can create a useful focus for the eye. A belt or band of impressions around a thrown cylinder, for example, can easily be made with an improvised roller, made out of wood, plaster or a cork, engraved with a design. However, when such devices are used to conceal inexpert throwing, they usually fail and simply make the pot look clumsier. Regular or random patterns can also be effective, if sensitively used, for the plane surfaces of slab pots. And impressed designs can be made on hand-made tiles at the leather-hard stage, although

pressure will distort their shape and the result is only effective when the tiles do not need to be precise in size or smooth in use.

Because clay is so good at taking up impressions, quite detailed designs, like cameos, can be accurately reproduced, and letter forms can be used both imaginatively and usefully. The wooden and metal letters which printers used in the days of letterpress have a new application as impressing tools in pottery, and can be bought in most antique markets, or sometimes from the printers themselves. They have the added advantage that they are cut 'backwards', or in mirror form, so that when pressed against clay they read correctly.

The use of complete slugs of type for identification purposes is familiar on old mineral-water and ginger-beer jars, and especially cider flagons, and some potters use a metal slug to advertise their names not only on the base of their pots but also on the sides. Many potters now sign their work, as a painter might, but an impressed mark or seal has a long tradition, and some beautifully elegant monograms have been created either by carving wood, or using plaster of Paris, or fired pottery. The most elegant designs I know were made by Hans Coper, who, like Bernard Leach, had different sizes to suit different sizes of pot.

An impressed design may often be enhanced by glazing. A light dusting of a colouring oxide will catch in the edges of the design and emphasize the pattern, whereas stoneware glazes, which usually break into a different colour on edges, will soften the contour of the impression without completely obliterating the design.

Embossed designs

These imply the addition of clay to the pot's surface, and if the pot is leather hard slip or water is required to act as a 'glue'. Small wads of clay impressed with seals, for example, can be added to finished pots as medallions, much like the glass labels added to the necks of old wine and port bottles.

The famous Wedgwood Jasper ware is the classic form of embossed design, in which delicately formed porcelain or white clay designs, cast from small plaster moulds, are added to a coloured pot as bas-relief – a decorative technique known as 'sprigging'. Sprigs, as in the case of Wedgwood, can be made in a different colour, but the same clay body should be used or adhesion may be poor.

Small modelled units added as handles or purely as decoration can be figurative – like the frog on a Bernard Leach lidded pot, or the fox heads on one of Ian Godfrey's hectic lidded vessels. But beginners who wish to emboss designs need not strive after natural forms, which are difficult to relate to the shape of the pot to which they are attached. Simple motifs, like strapwork whorls, are often the most striking, and it is important to consider the effect of any additions on the profile of the pot. The essence of this work is to keep the modelling crisp, to avoid over-larding the pot with stamps and to choose an appropriate glaze.

Carved and pierced designs

When carving into the surface of a pot, the state of the clay is all-important. If it is softer than leather hard, the pressure of the tool will affect the walls of the pot, and unless you *want* to make the pot wobbly, you must wait until it has stiffened up. A low-relief design can be made with metal sculptor's tools, modelling knives, sharpened wooden modelling tools or lino cutters, and designs can vary from the tightly controlled to the very flamboyant – the rim of a pot can, for example, be carved into a skyline shape, with an outline of a landscape and trees, but such pots are ornamental, not practical.

The leather-hard pot can also be decorated by 'piercing'. Cutting away parts of the wall is a delicate operation, and the pot must be tackled when dry enough to stand up to the cutting tool but not so dry that it will crack. Simple holes can be bored easily enough with a drill-bit held in the fingers, but other patterns have to be cut carefully with a sharp-pointed blade like a dissector's scalpel, and the more holes the weaker the structure. Very small holes will fill in with glaze when fired, a common oriental technique much borrowed by European potters. Designs where cut-away parts stay open are more effective.

Two wheel-thrown units form the starting point for this ornate carved and impressed container by Ian Godfrey.

Fluted and faceted designs

'Faceting' is a decorative technique which can alter the basic design of a pot. A simple thick-walled cylinder, for example, can be made into an interesting shape if the outside surface is cut into facets with a sharp knife when the clay is leather hard, or with a fine wire while the pot is still on the wheel. Mathematical figures and crystal structures are obvious sources of inspiration for potters who are primarily interested in the form of their pots, but these are most conveniently made out of slabs. Certainly there is less need to aim for symmetry with a faceted pot.

The most important advice for a beginner is to make sure that the cutting tool is used boldly and not hesitantly. Faceting is a good technique to practise before embarking on the more difficult technique of 'fluting', in which a series of shallow, rounded, concave grooves are cut into the outside surface of a thickly thrown pot.

Fluting is often spiral but can be effective when vertical. A cylindrical

FACETING

1 If facets are cut with a knife into the sides of a thrown form, the walls have to be thick – the fewer the facets the thicker the walls.

2 If neatness is your aim, then it is worth turning the base after faceting. The result will be an elegant scalloped profile.

FLUTING

Sometimes the leather-hard pot is turned first, then fluted, then damped down and the form squeezed, distorting the flutes.

form may be fluted from top to base, like a Doric column, using a loop-ended wire tool made from banding wire, which can be formed into the desired shape and will stay in shape when in use. If the fluting is only going to cover part of the pot, the termination of the flutes must be clearly defined by a shoulder or the sharply reduced diameter of the foot.

In oriental cultures, faceting is often done with a bamboo fluting tool while the pot is still on the wheel and the throwing continues afterwards (though from the inside of the pot only). In this way a pumpkin shape can be made from what was previously a squat cylinder, with the grooves broadening out at their centre. The use of a bamboo rib on the inside of a pot after throwing will also radically alter the plan of the pot, and can be decorative.

Chatter designs

Chatter decoration is achieved while the pot is still quite soft, by the use of a piece of springy metal, called a 'jumping iron' by Bernard Leach, which bounces against the pot as it turns slowly on the wheel. One revolution, and the pattern is made. The shape and size of the chatter depend on the profile of the end of the tool, and how hard the clay is in relation to the tapping of the tool. The distance between the marks depends on the speed at which the wheel is turning. The secret is in the springiness of the metal – the dead weight of a turning tool is *not* appropriate – and the best material is pallet banding-wire bent into an 'S' shape. It is not as easy as it sounds.

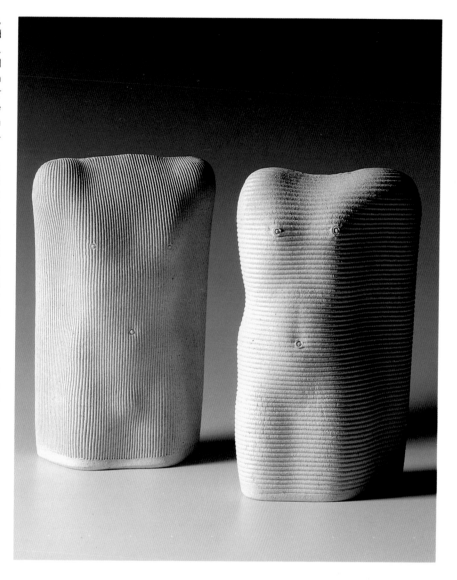

Above: 'Man and Woman'. A ceramic sculpture by Vladimir Tsivin. The contrast between the impressed details and the 'perfect' corrugated surface is essential – fingermarks would ruin it. Porcelain, with touches of glaze. Height: approximately 30.5cm (12in).

Opposite: A massive fluted stoneware vase with decorative lugs by Bernard Leach. Tenmoku glaze.

Left: A chatter design, emphasized by the later pooling of the glaze, inside a small bowl by Richard Batterham.

Inlaid designs

The decoration carried out on leather-hard or plastic pots is not restricted to changes in surface. Colour can be added at this stage, either by inlaying or in the form of slip (see below).

Lino-cutting tools or gouging knives can be used to cut a pattern in leather-hard clay much as a pattern is cut in lino, and a coloured body clay (or several different colours) can be impressed or 'inlaid' into the incised design, provided the coloured clay is soft enough to fill up the incised areas without distorting the edges. As it dries, the surface of the pot can be scraped down to reveal the inlay as a crisp design.

This technique is not confined to detailed and fine-line patterns, and when used boldly is a particularly powerful method of decoration, since it becomes part of the fabric of the pot under the glaze and not merely a superficial layer. It is appropriate to slab pots and moulded pottery as well as thrown ware. Incised patterns can also be filled with liquid slip and scraped down when dry – the technique used for floor tiles since medieval times.

Slip decoration

'Slipware' is, in its simplest form, pottery whose clay body has been overlaid with a thin layer of clay of a different colour. The decorative clay is poured in a very liquid form, like a glaze, over the soft leather-hard body, and the finished pot is coated with a transparent glaze. Most frequently, coloured slip decoration is used to cover the inside of bowls. It can be the starting point for a whole range of decorative techniques.

Decoration slip, as opposed to the casting slip described in chapter 13, is prepared by softening clay to a creamy consistency with water, and sieving through an 80- or 100-strand mesh lawn, together with colourants for a darker slip. A good black can be made with 15 per cent of iron oxide plus 3 per cent of cobalt or manganese, whereas 2 per cent each of copper and cobalt will make a strong peacock blue. If the body clay is red, a dense black slip can be made by adding 5 per cent cobalt oxide to the dry weight of the red clay.

INLAYING

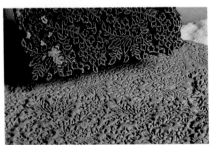

Above: A squared-off bottle by Tatsuzo Shimoaka, with a herring-bone design inlaid into its four faces before glazing and the overpainting of a calligraphic design in contrasting glazes. Height: 25.5cm (10in).

Below: A detail from a plate with an impressed design inlaid with copper, produced by the technique shown left.

1–2 Metal printing blocks can be used to impress plastic clay. The design is 'filled' with contrasting liquid slip, and then scraped down when dry.

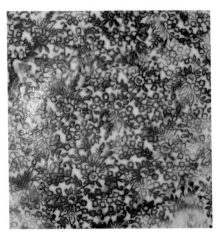

The clay for the slip should be the same as that of the body of the pot, though this is not possible when the pot is made of red clay and the slip is to be white. In this case a good white slip can be made out of china clay (3 parts), ball clay (1 part) and feldspar (1 part); or ball clay (4 parts) and china clay (1 part); or simply equal parts of china clay and ball clay.

A white slip, which as just explained differs from the coloured body on to which it will be poured, may not be a very good 'fit' and you may have to try several recipes before finding one which matches the expansion and contraction curve of your particular body clay. Cracks on the surface of the slip as it dries on to the pot are a warning sign, but the scaling off, like the shelling of a glaze, may not appear until the pot has been fired.

Like glazes and the casting slips mentioned in chapter 13, decorative slips must be kept smooth and even in texture, and the addition of bentonite as a suspender can help. Deflocculants

as used in casting slips are not necessary as the shrinkage of slip and body should be the same. The best method of keeping a slip in good condition, however, is to sieve it regularly – always before use – and to keep it in a bucket *with a lid*.

All shapes of pot can be 'slipped', in the same way as they can be glazed, by dipping and pouring, but a softish pot will readily disintegrate in the bucket if kept immersed for too long, and the slipping of a very thin shallow bowl is difficult, because the walls are always fragile until the pot has been fired. A favourite Japanese technique is to paint slip on to a vase on the wheel immediately after throwing, and to comb a design through the slip to the clay body as the pot slowly revolves. A beginner is advised to practise with a pot that has already been turned.

The most fruitful use of slip for the beginner is in combination with a press mould for here the walls of the pot are supported by the mould until the whole thing is dry. Two slips can be used in

quick succession, one all over the surface, the other over part of the surface only. When the mould is held at an angle and tilted to and fro, the slips will produce a marbled pattern.

A less random design is produced by running lines of contrasting slip into a slip layer or 'field' and drawing them into a delicate feathered pattern by running a fine point, the tip of a feather, or single bristle across the lines at right angles. A multi-toothed tool can also be used to 'comb' contrasting slips into striking patterns in the manner of marbled paper.

Sometimes these patterns are carried out on slabs of rolled-out clay before it is placed in or over a mould. Once the surface of the slip has gone dull – when the free moisture it contained has evaporated or sunk into the

Slip trailing with contrasting slip over a dark ground by Michael Cardew, whose stylized bird filling a shallow dish is reminiscent of Persian or Indian designs.

SLIPPING A PRESS-MOULD POT

A leather-hard cast in an octagonal press mould has liquid slip added and then poured out immediately, leaving a skin over the inside of the cast.

MARBLING WITH COLOURED SLIPS

1 By laying stripes of rather liquid slip on to a contrasting ground of slip while it is still wet you can direct the process of marbling.

2 Tip the pot on a board at an angle, and the slips begin to run. Hold the board steady at this angle until the effect is quite marked before turning.

3 Marbling is not as random as it seems. Like the streaks in real marble, the pattern comes from a combination of forces from different directions.

FEATHERING WITH SLIP

1 For hundreds of years, dishes have been decorated by feathering, and early examples are now much prized. Start by piping wet slip in parallel lines.

2–3 The lines can be dark on a light ground, or vice versa, but must be done while the base layer is still wet. Think of these lines as the warp of a textile.

Stroke the tip of a feather, or a natural bristle from a brush, across the slip at right angles and in both directions to make a feathery weft.

mother clay – the slab can be handled, though with great care. The feathered or combed side can be placed against the plaster mould, whether concave or convex, and the necessary finishing done on the reverse side, to avoid smudging the pattern.

Once immersed in the world of slip, the beginner can experiment with many techniques, more or less creative, which depend on the reluctance of two different-coloured liquids to lose their separate identity, like cream in black coffee. To say that there is a danger of slip decoration becoming automatic and lifeless is to invite the scorn and wrath of those who admire the famous slipware dishes of the seventeenth and eighteenth centuries, as well some of the best work of the Leach School.

By squeezing slip of the right consistency from a plastic or rubber bag through a fine nozzle, the inventive potter has at his or her command a means of drawing in liquid clay, and by using several colours yet another dimension can be given to the work. The only tool needed can be bought from any pottery supplier, or improvised, using a ballpoint pen with its refill removed, attached through a cork to a cycle inner tube.

Drawing with slip demands a strong colour contrast (white on black, brown on white) and a stiffer mix than for the feathered and combed techniques, with the lines standing out in relief even when dry and fired. If the slip surface or ground is inside a bowl, it should be allowed to dry to a non-tacky state before slip trailing is added.

A leading expert in slipware today is Mary Wondrausch, whose work shows the applications for commemorative ware. Though strongly associated with folk art, and with the potency of the political cartoon, these techniques of drawing and painting with a slip trailer need not be figurative. It is a most expressive medium. It can, and for many potters indeed has, become the obsession of a lifetime.

Top right: Confident patterns in slip on traditional ware by Mary Wondrausch.

DRAWING WITH SLIP

1–2 Bands of slip to contain the lettering are first applied with the wheel turning. The same slip trailer can be used for drawing the design in the centre.

3 One colour is used for the lettering and linear work. Contrasting coloured slips in more liquid form are applied to fill areas within the design.

A sharp point will scratch through slip to a contrasting clay beneath or into the body of an unfired pot leaving fine grooves. These can be inlaid with oxide or left as a textural pattern, as in this bowl by Lucie Rie.

Sgraffito and painting with slip

The decorative slip methods so far described, like glazing techniques, do not show the mark of a tool, but slip can be applied to a leather-hard pot like paint with a brush, or scratched away with a sharp tool, like scraper-board, to show the contrasting clay below in a technique called 'sgraffito'.

Painted slip, usually applied with a large mop-headed brush, will show marks of the paint brush when it has been fired, and these are often attractive if bold and big, and the reverse if they are small and repetitive. The Korean tradition of painting white slip with a rather stiff brush all over the surface of a freshly thrown pot made in dark clay is known as hakeme. The stiffness of the brush ensures that the coating is uneven and streaky, with the dark ground showing through, and no other decoration is needed, just a clear glaze. Because of its unevenness, painted slip is not suitable as a ground for feathering or trailing, and is best left alone or used in combination with sgraffito.

Any sharp tool, such as a penknife or turning tool, will scratch through the surface of a leather-hard slip, revealing the contrasting colour of the leather-hard clay below. This is a hard, non-fluid technique and attracts the inartistic. Lamentable examples of sgraffito work abound, with monochromatic heraldic shields, cartoons and mottoes leading the field. Drawing with a point is much less flexible than drawing with a pencil, but noble Roman or uncial lettering can be very impressive if incised through slip, especially if the potter tackles the fascinating typographical problem of letters in a roundel.

The technique of using a fine needle to scratch radiating lines or a cross-hatched reticular network into the clay body was perfected by Lucie Rie. In her case the coloured layer through which the lines were scratched was often not slip but painted oxide.

Combing through slip is another technique which involves revealing the clay body, and this is best done before the slip layer has dried out. The 'comb' can be cut from cardboard or soft plastic, and the width and spacing of the teeth control the coarseness of the design. Well suited to press-moulded dishes, the technique can also be used to decorate the sides of thrown vases before they are taken off the wheel.

Other methods of decorating with slip include stencils and paper resist, and the use of wax to make a negative design, and these techniques will be described in the next chapter, with majolica decoration.

Slipware is traditionally an earthenware form, finished with a glossy transparent glaze, which in the old days used to be made of galena, now banned for fear of poisoning. Through the glaze the slip, dull and matt when it is being applied, shows its true colours, often enhanced with richness and depth. Stoneware pots can also be decorated with slip, though the colours are less bright, and they are often left without a glaze, in which case the surface is called an 'engobe'. Such pots can have an interesting texture, but are not very practical if the surface is rough, as they attract dust and are very difficult to clean.

USING PAPER RESIST

1—2 Applying a pattern of thin damp paper to the leather-hard surface of a pot allows contrasting slip to be painted over the top. When the slip is dry, the paper 'resist' can be removed, leaving a sharp-edged design behind. This technique of paper resist is also used with glazed ware.

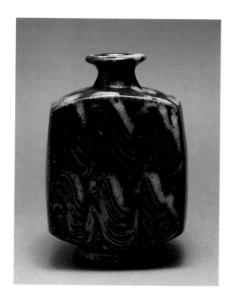

Above: Wave patterns combed into the sides of a flask by Bernard Leach.

Right: The hard bristles of the brush which applied the hakeme slip leave their mark on the background of this large vase by Shoji Hamada.

COMBING THROUGH SLIP

A flexible cardboard comb with coarse teeth is used to cut through dark slip to the light ground beneath.

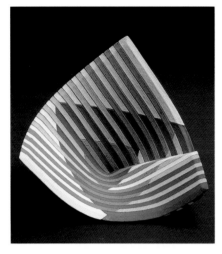

Above: Coloured slips are carefully painted between incised lines on this sculptural form by Rita Ternes. Unglazed, the slip fires dry.

Right: Oxide painted on to the clay gives a charred appearance to the cyclops face by Carmen Dionyse. Only the sparkling eye is glazed.

BANDING WITH OXIDE

Neat bands can easily be painted on to unfired pots slowing turning on an electric wheel, or a banding wheel, named after this function.

Painting with oxides

The same oxides that colour glazes can be painted on to a raw unfired pot with a brush, or sponged on to a hand-built pot which has a coarse surface texture. These powdered oxides, even if mixed with gum arabic or some other paste, are very susceptible to smudging until they have been fired, and when the pots come out of the kiln after the first firing the colour will be disappointingly muted and dry. It is only in or under a glaze that oxide colours shine out brightly, and most decoration with oxides takes place after the biscuit firing.

Burnishing

All the decorative techniques so far described are carried out before, but in anticipation of, glazing. Before facing the brilliant world of glaze decoration, we must consider two further forms of decoration which are an end in themselves, without glazing. One such method is saggar firing, which depends on carbonation in the kiln and is discussed in chapter 21. Another is burnishing, a technique increasingly popular with studio potters.

Burnishing is a labour of love. It is only appropriate for those with plenty of time, and is therefore never used in commercial potteries, even those operating on a small scale. It entails the polishing of the surface of the pot with a smooth tool – usually a hardwood modelling tool – until all the minute indentations in the clay surface are filled with fine grains of clay, and the pot shines with a special gleam half way between polished leather and metal. Some of the appeal of this very seductive surface derives from the fact that it is never totally even.

The sheen which comes from rubbing a firm leather-hard pot is sometimes lost in the firing, making the surface dull again. However, if the pot is coated first with very finely sieved slip mixed with an equally finely ground oxide, such as black iron oxide, the sheen is more likely to be retained, when fired to about 1,000°C. This temperature reflects firing conditions in Africa, where the technique has long been used on coiled pots. Thrown or moulded pottery can be burnished, though throwing lines are inimical, and thin rims difficult to burnish without breaking.

It is only reasonable to describe a burnished pot as 'graphite-like', if it ends up with the appearance of graphite. However, graphite added to the slip will produce a high sheen which burns away in the kiln. Iron oxide in the slip will produce a browner colour. The decorative qualities of a burnished surface are helped if it is fired in a kiln with a naked flame – using gas or oil – where the coloration will be more mottled. Incising fine designs through a burnished layer can be most effective if concentrated in small areas – in traditional African designs they are often in chequerboard fashion – so that the specially roughened texture contrasts with the surrounding sheen.

BURNISHING

1 Coloured slip assists the process of burnishing. When this coiled pot was dry, it was given an even painting with slip containing ochre.

2 The back of a bent spoon becomes an improvised tool. The aim is to move minute unfixed clay particles into crevices to give a polished surface.

3 Hand-made pots rarely have surfaces as even as cast or turned pottery. The finish comes from combining hand-building with patient burnishing.

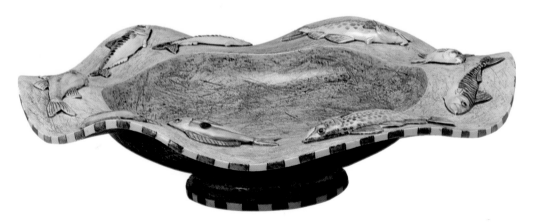

Above
JOHN GLICK
A huge plate is used as a vehicle for abstract decoration, employing a combination of techniques, including several slips, multiple glazing, wax resist and over-glaze trailing, as well as combing.

Left
ANNA LAMBERT
On this large coiled plate, realistically painted fish applied in relief lie stranded around the undulating rim.

Below
RUDY AUTIO
The painting of figures around pots has a tradition three thousand years old, and usually the figures have to accommodate themselves to thrown shapes. Here Rudy Autio characteristically creates a form which partially represents in three dimensions the figures which lie around it. It is a perfect example of the intertwining of design and form; neither the one nor the other would have much meaning in isolation.

Above
THOMAS HOADLEY
This decorated vase is made of coloured porcelain, with gold leaf on one side.

Below
ELISABETH VON KROGH
A symmetrical shape typical of modern studio slip casting, its multi-coloured painted decoration using underglaze pigments. Whichever way you look at it, it is a tiger.

19

DECORATING BISCUIT AND GLAZED POTS

In the minds of many beginners, decorating the biscuit pot conjures up images of a paint brush loaded with colourant poised shakily over an absorbent surface which will readily and permanently soak up any drops which accidentally fall. The decoration stage may mean a re-acquaintance with a small paint brush and a tussle with the formal elements of design, but painting is only one of many ways in which a biscuit-fired pot may be decorated, and some of the more automatic techniques should be learned first to gain greater confidence in the handling of ware at this stage.

Dipping

The glaze itself is the only decoration needed if the form of the pot is irregular or without convenient surfaces to contain a design. One glaze laid on top of another will create a contrast, especially if the glazes used are widely different. A popular way of avoiding the issue of creative design is to pour a

Picasso's genius shines forth in this inventive water jar which combines brush painting and sgraffito.

dark glaze over a part of a pot already glazed in a light colour, allowing the trickles to remain as they have run. The Christmas - pudding - and - white - sauce effect which results unfortunately has a very disruptive effect on the form and profile of the pot, and is only tolerable if the pot is a simple strong shape.

Controlled glazing is more satisfying. Imagine dipping one half of a plate vertically – to its widest point – in a bucket of glaze. When this is dry, the other half should be carefully dipped into a contrasting glaze so that the two lines of glaze just meet. When again dry, the plate could be dipped into a third glaze, this time held at a 90° angle to the previous dips. The result would be a 'quartered' design, and each of the four segments of the circle would be a different colour.

Even if the second glaze was used again for the third dip, there would still be four different surfaces, since one of them would be a double thickness. Variations on this technique can readily

CONTROLLED DIPPING

1 For quartering, take trouble to ensure that the pot is dipped exactly half way into the glaze, so the line is at the diameter.

2 The second dip coats the other half of the bowl in a different colour. Hold the already glazed half of the pot carefully; it must be dry.

3 Quartering a plate or bowl with different glazes is a simple exercise which neatly avoids the need to touch up the fingermarks.

be imagined, and they will be more dynamic if the resulting segments are unequal in size.

Contrasting glazes can be used alternately, with overlaps, to make stripes of different colour or texture on slab pots or thrown shapes, and advantage can be taken of the curved shape which results from a bowl or slab form being inserted into a bowl of glaze at an angle. This technique, known as 'window dipping', is often effective on simple shapes and the potter will soon learn that a glaze which is allowed to make its own 'edge' will often have a more natural appearance than a demarcation which is drawn or etched with a tool, though some potters use masking tape to gain a precise edge.

Wax resist

Glazes will adhere to biscuit ware and to one another, but they will shrink away from oily surfaces, and if wax or a similar substance is painted on to the biscuit pot, or between glaze coats, the next water-bound liquid which is poured on will shrink away from the waxed areas. When the wax, left bare, burns away in the kiln it leaves behind its own pattern. If this seems a long-winded technique for achieving a negative result, remember that painting with glaze is difficult, and the only way of getting a glaze to go around, say, an oak-leaf shape is to have something in the way, preventing the glaze sticking to the surface where the design is.

Scraping away the glaze to create a design is an alternative approach, like the sgraffito method with slip, but it is not satisfactory where large areas are concerned, and impossible where one glaze overlies another if both of them are in their unfired form. The strong designs on the much-prized bowls of Hans Coper were achieved by scraping away the dark glaze only *after* the first white glaze had been fired.

Wax-resist decoration is quick and 'forgiving', so it is popular with potters with a high level of production. The wax is prepared by putting a plain white candle broken up into short lengths into a small pan with turpentine or paraffin, and heating very gently until the wax is all melted. Fierce heating may cause

PAINTING WITH HOT WAX

1 Hot wax on the brush will dry as soon as it touches the pot, and therefore strokes must be firm and the design simple, like the stripes shown above.

2 When the pot is immersed in glaze, the attractive way in which the pattern reveals itself is seen. Waxed patterns before and after firing are shown at top.

the material to catch fire in the pan, so for safety the heating is best done in a double saucepan, or in a bowl in a saucepan of water: an evil-smelling smoke is a sign that the mixture has reached the correct runny consistency. Keep the mixture thin by making sure there is at least as much paraffin or turpentine in the mixture as there is wax. The wax 'freezes' as soon as it is painted on to the pot or glaze surface, and this restricts the type of design which can be successfully applied, but if the pot can be warmed, the working life of the wax will be a little longer.

Unfortunately, the hot wax has a disastrous effect on brushes, which can never be cleaned satisfactorily and quickly lose their hairs if left in the liquid for long. An improvised, very coarse 'brush' made from string can be used to make broad marks, thus cutting down the expense of lost brushes.

The wax-resist technique is very distinctive, as the glaze shrinks away from the grease in an attractive way, often leaving behind small globules of glaze which fire on to the pot as spots. It is also a practical method of keeping rims and feet clear when pouring glaze, and a wax-resist ring in the centre of a bowl will allow another pot with an unglazed foot ring to be stacked inside it in the glaze firing, a practical way of avoiding waste space and often successful aesthetically. When wax is painted straight on to the biscuit surface, rather than on top of a glaze, the resulting raw area will be porous if the pot is fired only to earthenware temperature, and vessels intended to hold liquids will be totally useless if they are decorated in this way on their inside surfaces.

Paper resist

Wax is not the only material which can come between glaze and ware. Cut-out paper patterns, cloth or scrim will have the same effect, and leaves with an interesting form (from the vine, for example) can be used direct. When such materials are used, however, they should be pulled off the pot before it is fired, as the glaze which sticks to them would make a mess either of the pot or of the kiln shelf.

All these 'resist' techniques are admirably suited to slip decoration on raw pots as well as on biscuit ware. The damp surface of the raw pot helps the adhesion of the paper pattern, while on biscuit pots it often has to be kept in place with some form of glue or paste, especially on vertical surfaces.

Paper patterns can come off when a pot is dipped in glaze and so spraying is a more appropriate glazing technique here. An atomizer (or even a toothbrush) can also be effectively used to spatter a second glaze or oxide round the edge of a paper pattern laid on top of a fired glaze. Or stencils can be used, and glaze spattered through them.

Latex glues like Copydex also repel glaze, and some potters use this evil-smelling stuff rather than wax.

Right: When two glazes are used, as on this plate designed by Janice Tchalenko, success depends on colour and on the tonal relationship between the two glazes as well as the pattern.

PATTERNING WITH SPONGES

1 A synthetic sponge (but not a natural one) can be carved with a knife or with scissors to give a raised pattern rather like that on a lino printing block.

2 A plate painted with a plain glaze is patterned with a contrasting glaze before firing, using the carved sponge. The result is shown at top.

Above: This mug from the Dartington Pottery shows the result of brush decoration and glaze trailing.

Below: A boldly decorated plate by Sandy Brown which shows the effect of soft-throwing lines as well as brush decoration and glaze trailing with oxides and bright under-glaze colours.

Glaze trailing

Most of the decoration which is applied to glazed ware is put on with paint brushes, but, before reaching for these, it is worth considering some of the techniques described under Slip decoration in the previous chapter.

Glaze can be used in a slip trailer on a glazed pot, not yet glost fired, or before the application of the glaze. It is an attractive technique which allows graphic skills to flower, and often the edge of the trailed line will have a special quality, as it merges with and affects the unfired glaze below. It can be the same glaze, with an added oxide or colour, or a totally different one, which will probably produce a contrast in texture as well as tone. The fineness of the line will depend on the consistency of the glaze in the trailer – it needs to be more solid than glaze used for pouring, and should not pool as it comes out of the nozzle. Sandy Brown has perfected the use of glaze trailing, but in combination with brush-painted decoration, described next.

Brush painting

Melting glaze has an effect on all linear and painted patterns, and 'under-glaze' and 'on-glaze' are terms which sometimes confuse the beginner. The distinctions are simple, though the results are wide ranging, and can occasionally confound the connoisseur. A transparent glaze applied over a design will blur it to some extent, depending on the stability of the materials used for the design. If an opaque glaze, white or coloured, is used over a design it will obscure it much more, even hiding it altogether if the glaze is a very dense one. A design applied on top of the glaze will not be blurred or obscured, but it may 'float' slightly at the edges as the glaze melts, and the quality of the painted surface may differ from the rest, since it lies on top of the glaze.

Potters' brushes are longer and more straggly than painters' brushes, and that first encounter with the 'feel' of painting on absorbent clay or glaze is a quite considerable shock to anyone already competent with a fine sable

GLAZE TRAILING

Trailed glaze merges more smoothly with the mother glaze than trailed slip, often with a slight but distinctive 'weeping', as shown at top left.

brush. The ware sucks the liquid out of the hairs, forcing you to develop a light touch, otherwise the brush will dry against the pot, leaving a mean and unattractive mark. It is like painting on dry blotting paper, or tissue, so practise a design by painting on these first.

The beginner will gain confidence with a brush by applying bands of colour to a cylinder, holding the brush steady against the pot and rotating the pot in the centre of a banding wheel or wheel-head. Similarly, circles can be painted inside bowls, but the beginner must beware of letting large drops of glaze fall into the bowl from a heavily loaded brush.

Ceramic suppliers are very ready to provide colouring stains for painting in a wide range of hues and tints, calling them 'under-glaze' or 'decoration' colours. Many studio potters prefer to make their own colours by using the metal oxides which are added to glazes, finely ground and mixed with water, or water and gum. Since these metal oxides are mostly leaden grey or black in colour, a sample pot or tile should be painted with a stripe of each oxide available in the workshop, carefully named, and ideally these should be tested both under and over each glaze which is used. Such a programme of testing would certainly occupy a once-a-week student's entire term, but there is no better way of getting to know the potential of colourants.

Most oxides burn through stoneware glazes at high temperatures, if they are applied before the glaze, but at earthenware temperatures they are more likely to be concealed or blurred. This is not necessarily a disadvantage, but it is important that a blurred result suits the style of the design. To avoid the smudging of an under-glaze design, some potters go to the length of firing decorated biscuit pots without glaze, and refiring a glaze coat later. This avoids the dragging of the design by the glaze on application, and it also prevents the adulteration of the glaze itself with colour from the design.

Painting with unfixed under-glaze colour or oxides on biscuit pots is slightly anti-social in communal potteries, where spots of colour pulled from the pattern by the glaze as it is being poured stay in the glaze bucket to alter the mix. On the other hand, under-glaze designs, as exemplified by the Water-weed Bowl on page 8, have a permanence which is unattainable by any other means.

Just how you use the brush, and what you paint, is personal, and no teacher can give firm rules because some student's pots will always confound the dogmatic. But here goes . . .

When planning any design, remember that many pots are circular in plan and have curved walls. Do not compose the design as you might compose a rectangular picture. Remember that a design on the side of a cylinder will disappear round the sides of the pot. It is best to choose a subject which is tall and thin, or to think of how ivy might grow on and around its surface. Forget about symmetry.

If the pot already has decoration or protruding features, such as handles or lugs, emphasize these in the design, rather than competing with them for

A human torso can be seen on this pot by Robin Welch when the drawings on the inside and outside coincide. Those who prefer to draw than to paint will want to try oxide-impregnated crayons (from ceramic suppliers) so the design remains strong after firing. Normally the drawing is done when the glaze has already been fired, and the pot is refired.

BRUSH PAINTING 1

Try experimenting with all kinds of brushes when applying glaze by this means – to see the different kinds of marks they leave on the pot.

BRUSH PAINTING 2

Brushes with long fine hairs called 'liners' are better than conventional water-colourists' brushes when painting bands or patterns in delicate strokes.

An inventive shape and fine calligraphy by Jean-Claude de Crousaz on a tile is enhanced by gold enamelling in an additional low-temperature firing.

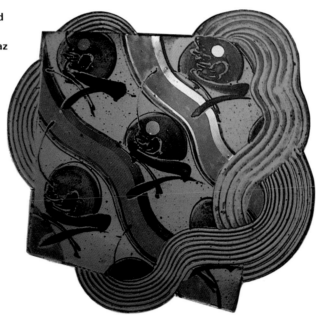

the eye's attention. Painters such as Picasso and Cocteau allowed the form of the pot to suggest themes for its decoration.

Repeating patterns and borders take a great deal of skill. They are likely to be more rhythmical if the potter stays still and the pot turns on a banding wheel.

Those without any drawing skills are best to think in terms of bands and blocks of colour. Designs should be bold – a few large bands will look better than a lot of small ones. Changes in shape, such as shoulders on a pot, should be emphasized by banding at or near to these changes, rather than somewhere else on the form.

If you have confidence in your drawing ability and want to paint something representational rather than make an abstract pattern, choose a simple, organic subject like an apple. Nothing in the present century has matched the painted decoration of Shoji Hamada, most of whose simple but vital designs were based on the image of a rice field after rain. If your passion is horses, or racing cars, you will need a fine illustrator's skill to express your obsession in pottery, though nothing is impossible: I can remember once seeing a wonderful open bowl, with a dashingly painted architectural design in green,

grey and red. It turned out to be based not on a fine historic building, but on the clubhouse of a golf course.

Calligraphic skills are useful to a pottery painter, and with the right brush, the thick and thin strokes of brush lettering can be the basis of handsome designs, as exemplified by the fine work of Caiger-Smith and de Crousaz.

Although the most convenient stage at which to apply painted decoration is after the pouring of the glaze, and before the firing, both glaze and pattern are very vulnerable to handling at this point. While application is not difficult, smudging or fingermarking of the design is all too easy, so the potter should handle the ware as little as possible.

On-glaze decoration

Painting on the glaze is the technique used in the famous majolica ware of Italy, where a design predominantly in blue is painted over a white tin glaze on an earthenware body. Though majolica reached its peak in the sixteenth century, freely painted designs of this type are still made in Mediterranean countries for domestic ware, such as plates and serving bowls. As far as I am concerned, such joyful but humble pottery makes northern European industrial attempts to bring liveliness to the

everyday dining table seem quite pathetic and graceless.

The later in the sequence of making a pot that a painted design is applied, the more superficial it appears, and some surfaces applied after the glaze firing eventually wear away with use. Two important decorative techniques which must be applied after the glaze firing are enamelling and lustre. Both are essentially low-fired techniques, the maturing temperature being lower than the temperature of the glaze. Enamels are fired to about 750°C, and similar temperatures are used for lustre ware.

Enamel colours, which are also available from ceramic suppliers, are mixed with turpentine or an oil mixture as a medium, and painting on pottery requires no special technique. Extremely fine and detailed designs can be painted on to glazed surfaces, and for some students painting ready-made ware is a satisfying long-term study.

Lustre is a form of decoration in which a film of metal is laid on top of the glaze. Most potters encounter lustre as a liquid preparation for on-glaze painting containing such metallic salts as copper sulphate, which, when burnished after firing, becomes a very convincing 'gold'. Lustre can also be mixed with low-temperature glazes to give an all-over metallic sheen as well as painted on to fired glazed ware, but it should not be mixed with other ware in the kiln. It is very sensitive to the atmosphere there, with the result that it can become unburnishable. Some lustre preparations require a reducing atmosphere, and this was certainly true of Persian and Moorish lustres of the early Middle Ages.

Silk-screen printing

The techniques of decoration so far described do not help the potter who wants to be able to repeat a design exactly on many pieces of ware. In industry, this is achieved with ceramic colourants, which are either 'transferred' to the ware on a thin transparent film which burns away in the kiln, or printed direct on to the pot through a silk screen.

Many studio potters borrow and combine these methods from industry, and, using a silk-screen printing press, print in one or more colours on to a film with a paper backing. The backing can be floated off in water, and the design fixed on to the glazed surface. Flat surfaces are best, of course, for keeping the design intact. Direct screen printing (that is, with the ware directly under the screen) must be done on a perfectly flat surface, and ready-made tiles have a rounded 'cushion' edge which will spoil the quality of a direct screen print which has to cover the whole surface.

Screen printing allows solid areas of flat colour with a very precise edge, and it is possible to reproduce photographs and detailed designs with great accuracy. When enamel colours are used in ceramic screen printing, they produce very bright results, and are most successfully printed on top of a white glazed surface for contrast. The technique is equally appropriate for small discrete patterns and large repeating or pictorial designs.

Designs on tiles

The decoration and design of tiles is a vast subject on its own, daunting to the amateur yet fascinating to many beginners. Tile making has been mentioned in chapter 11, and is both a lengthy and frustrating business when the potter lacks tile-making equipment. But thick stoneware and relief tiles can be successfully made, and it is worth remembering that they need not be square – only interlocking – to make an effective cladding. Hand-made tiles can have a textured surface or, like any other ceramics, can be impressed, incised or inlaid before they are dried and fired. If you want to create a practical flat surface such as the top of a coffee table, however, the surface must be smooth and the best way of decorating it is to use metal oxides or on-glaze enamels or lustres on plain white glazed tiles. It is difficult to find glazes to fit the body material of unglazed tiles without crazing and it is also difficult to find a manufacturer of tiles who will supply them unglazed.

Geometric and diaper patterns on tiles are often made by the assembly of four or more different units in such a way as to give a large-scale repeating pattern. Repetition, however, is not an essential part of tile design and decoration. The tile is a convenient manufacturing unit by which a painting the size of the entire west front of a cathedral can be made permanent. One of the most inspiring examples I know of the use of tiles for giant wall paintings is the Dominican Chapel at Vence, near Nice, designed and executed by Matisse in his old age. It is an object lesson in simplicity and in the adage 'Less means more.'

Bands, drops and spots of earthenware glaze can be arranged on glazed tile surfaces to great effect, creating a design which is complete in itself, as well as a strong single element for use in a decorative panel. But beginners should remember that a single well-decorated tile can look lost or downright ugly when combined with other tiles in a wall surface, and if the amateur has the perseverance to make a tile panel he or she must plan the total design in advance, and, if possible, fire all the units in the same kiln firing.

But now it is time to turn to the last stage in the pot's journey – the kiln.

Above: A linear design by Matisse in a single colour decorates white tiles on internal walls in the Dominican chapel in Vence, in the south of France.

Below: Modern tile design from Portugal shows how a large-scale pattern results from rearranging a single tile.

FIRE AND SPACE

The climax of the pottery experience is the kiln firing.
Some potters still use wood, so that flames lick around their
work, from ruby beginnings to the white heat of stoneware.
More will use gas or oil, each affecting the surface of pots in a
different way. A relationship is forged between kiln and potter,
like an old sailor with his sailing boat: every quirk, weakness
and strength is allowed for, used to advantage.
The moment of truth comes when the kiln is finally opened.
Lone professionals may have three months' work in a single kiln,
and the joy or disappointment is an experience unlike any other.
No wonder the Japanese make it a social occasion.

Opposite: Large coiled and burnished
pot, sawdust fired by Gabriele Koch.
Diameter: 56cm (22in).

20

KILNS AND KILN FIRING

The average pot has a double encounter with the kiln, once for biscuit and once for glaze firing, as explained in chapter I. However, many beginners do not encounter the kiln at all, because their pots are fired for them, and as they are not instructed in packing the techniques of kiln loading and operating remain a mystery.

All too often, inadequate small kilns or broken electric-kiln elements cause a bottleneck in the flow of work, and a pot, after waiting a fortnight or so to be biscuit fired, will wait again for a glaze kiln, and its vulnerable decorated surface may become damaged, chipped or fingermarked. Moments of delight, when a perfect finished pot appears from the kiln, occur to compensate for the disappointments of waiting and damage, but the beginner soon learns that a pot's path through the kiln may be far from swift and straightforward, and understanding the sequence of events can sometimes help to counteract impatience.

Kiln design

At one time kilns were all fuelled by solid materials – wood, charcoal, coal, coke – but now the majority are fired by electricity, both in industry and in art schools. Special glaze effects can be achieved at high temperatures using wood, oil or gas as a fuel, and kilns of this type are very popular with studio potters. By whatever means it is fired, a kiln includes a rigid chamber in which the pots are placed, and which must be able to stand high temperatures. Structural principles are important when the fabric has to cope with a temperature change of perhaps 1,300°C, and the chambers are normally made of refractory blocks with an arched or vaulted roof, ideally in the self-supporting form of a catenary curve.

An even distribution of heat in the chamber is desirable for larger pots and for consistent results, and this is achieved by the layout of elements (in an electric kiln) or by the routeing of draughts or fire pathways when combustible fuel is used. In the latter case, care is sometimes taken to prevent the pottery or ware coming into direct contact with the flame by stacking it inside

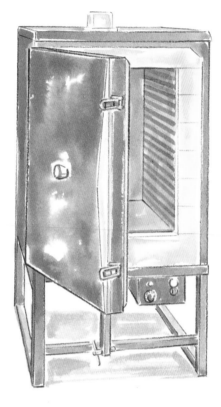

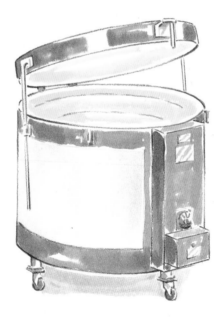

Electric kilns for studio pottery are of two main types: front and top openers. Both have spyholes in the sides and bungs on the top, which are left open during the early stages of firing to let water vapour escape.

protective refractory cylinders called 'saggars' or by packing the pots into a sealed area or 'muffle' in the chamber around which the flames play, but into which they cannot enter. The area immediately around fuel burners and elements is hotter than anywhere else, and it is not a good place to stand a pot. Even kilns without muffles have a so-called 'bag wall' where the flames are strongest, to protect the ware. This is not a supporting wall, which is just as well, since it is often distorted by the heat in time and needs replacing.

Heat rises, of course, and equally obviously a fire burns hotter when there is a good draught. Chimney design and design of the firemouth are just two aspects of the search for greater efficiency in the fascinating history of kiln design. The pattern of heat flow through the kiln influences the form of the outside, and the traditional bottle-ovens of the potteries in the English Midlands are a good example. These ovens, like factory chimneys, are usually demolished when they are no longer used and the few rare survivals of the industrial past are kept in musuems.

Any large-scale oven which has to be laboriously packed, heated and cooled cannot match for efficiency a tunnel kiln, in which the thermal conditions remain constant – hot in the middle and cool at both ends – and the pottery is drawn slowly through on refractory wagons, or a clamp kiln, lowered over ware which has been pre-stacked on a refractory base. These systems are justified where large and continuous production is required, but a studio potter or pottery class will be equipped with a chamber kiln, using energy only when it is needed. Recent developments have led to an increase in the use of kilns loaded from the top, sealed with a lid, though many kiln chambers are packed from the side and closed with a door or sealed with a temporary wall of firebricks.

The principles of packing are the same whatever type of kiln is used, and the beginner should take any opportunity to watch a kiln being packed for biscuit or glost firings, and of noticing the difference between them.

Packing for biscuit firing

It is wasteful to leave any empty space inside the kiln chamber, and so small pots are arranged in layers on stout but mobile shelves. These shelves, and the tubular props which support them, are called the 'kiln furniture' and they must be capable of withstanding high temperatures without changing shape. If the structural props and shelves collapse during a firing most of the ware is destroyed, especially in the case of glost firing, as pots will 'kiss' and be glued together by the glaze. The kiln shelves, made of sillimanite, are therefore strong and heavy, and the props interlock with one another for stability.

By means of the furniture a staging of pots can be built right up to the very top of the kiln. At the biscuit-firing stage pottery can be tightly packed, with pots touching, and small pots stacked inside large ones. Bowls are wasteful of space when packed side by side on a shelf, but they can be stacked rim to rim, a method which helps them to keep a level top. Strong pots can stand one on another but shallow or thin ware, such as wide flat dishes, should not have to bear weight,

especially on unsupported rims. It is tempting to fill the corners of a biscuit kiln by stacking plates on their edges, but unfortunately this can cause warping or cracking.

Unfired ware can be placed up against the sides of a muffle in a gas or oil kiln but should not be less than 1cm (⅜in) away from electric elements. If the elements are touched by the ware, they may burn out and melt, damaging the kiln wall at the same time. Not only the walls but the shelves themselves must be kept in good condition. Protection of shelves with batwash or 'placing powder' is described under Packing for glaze firings, but it is important even in biscuit firings to avoid using shelves which are spotted with glaze.

When biscuit fired, pots will shrink still more – there being a total shrinkage of up to 15 per cent from the wet plastic state, depending on the type of clay. Because of the variations in the amount of shrinkage it is quite possible for one pot to become trapped permanently inside another (which has shrunk more) during the firing, and such possibilities have to be considered when the kiln is packed.

Biscuit firing

The main cause of damage in the firing of green ware, however, is dampness. If any moisture remains in the clay it will turn into steam when the kiln temperature is raised above boiling point, and expand, cracking the pot apart. It is dampness in the centre of the thick walls of a heavy pot which causes explosions, not the thickness itself. Colour (light when dry) and feel (cool to the touch when still damp) are clues to the dryness of a pot, but even if all the ware packed into a biscuit kiln seems absolutely bone dry, it is still important to start the heating process very slowly and to leave open the bung and spyholes to let any steam escape. Most potters check to find out when a biscuit kiln has stopped 'steaming' by periodically holding a piece of glass over the bung or spyhole for a few seconds to see if there is any condensation.

As the temperature inside rises, the colour seen through the spyhole will change first to a dull red, then to cherry-red, to orange and on towards white. Colours are precise indicators of temperature, but unfortunately a potter's eyes are too used to adjusting to varying brightness to be able to relate colour and temperature by observation. He or she uses two principal aids. The 'pyrometer' is a gauge measuring temperature on a calibrated dial or a digital display by means of an electric current discharged between two metals, protected inside the kiln by an insulated sleeve. The advantage of a pyrometer is that the temperature can be read off from a distance, without looking inside the kiln, but it is notoriously inaccurate, and its margin of error – within about 30°C – is too big for the potter. It also indicates only the temperature, rather than the work done by the heat.

A burst of sustained heat achieves more work on a pot or a glaze than the mere temperature might suggest, and the device used to check the accuracy of the pyrometer is the 'Seger cone'. These cones are slender pyramids about 7cm (2¾in) long, made of ceramic mixtures designed to melt at certain precise temperatures. Shaped to stand at a slight angle to the vertical, Seger cones are often used in threes and placed in a specially shaped stand on a kiln shelf, close to the spyhole.

The cones should not be placed *too* close to the spyhole, and they are not always easy to position. A kiln with a hinged door will exclude all light when the door is closed, and when the kiln is being packed it is often useful to shut an electric torch inside to check that the cones are at the right level and visible through the spyhole. Positioning is important because cones are difficult to see at high temperatures when the light from inside the kiln is very bright, and staring too long through the spyhole, or too close, can become painful. Sun-glasses help, but plastic ones are inclined to melt in front of your eyes, which gives some idea of the heat coming out.

Biscuit firings for stoneware are usually taken to a temperature of 1,000°C, which provides a good porous surface for the application of the glaze. Industrial earthenware, however, which is often glazed to a temperature around 1,060°C, will always be biscuit fired to above 1,100°C, as a chemical change at this temperature causes a state of compression in the final glaze which makes the pots more hardwearing and more resistant to crazing (see chapter 16).

Pottery class work is usually biscuit fired all together, whether it is destined to be stoneware or earthenware, and the temperature of this first firing may vary between 960°C and 1,120°C. The correct sequence of firing the biscuit kiln is as follows. The kiln should be started on low for two or three hours, with the bung- and spy-holes open for any water vapour to escape. Then it should be stepped up to half power for two or three hours, during which time the escape of vapour will cease and the bungs can be closed. The final stage of the firing – perhaps another three hours or so, depending on the kiln capacity – can be completed under full power. Thus the temperature curve for biscuit is at first gentle, then steep. The curve for the second or glost firing is the opposite – steep at first, then slow as the temperature approaches the melting point of the glaze. Modern electric kilns can be programmed by a small computer built into the circuit to follow these heat curves, allowing modern potters to relax in a way which seems quite shocking to the traditionalist or to the potter with a wood-fired kiln, which needs stoking all through the day and night.

Packing for glaze firing

Both the packing and the precise temperature are much more crucial for the glaze firing than for the biscuit firing. Since glaze, at the peak of the firing, is a liquid, it can run down and even off a pot altogether. Certainly pots glazed on the base would glue themselves glassily to the kiln shelf if allowed to stand on it. Glazed pots will also stick to one another and the kiln packer must keep them apart, at least 5mm (¼in) for safety, and make sure that all glazed bases are lifted from the shelves on 'stilts' – the small refractory tripods with fine points which hold up the pot like fingertips. Stilts are not strong enough to withstand stoneware temperatures without buckling or causing the pot to buckle, and so stoneware pots stand directly on the shelf or on specially made rings of fired clay, but with no glaze on or near their feet. Porcelain pots actually change shape in the kiln, as the body of the pot becomes

Opposite: Kiln furniture and kiln shelves made of sillimanite. Tripod stilts are vital in earthenware glaze firings, but are useless when their points are blunted, and should not be re-used.

Left: A test ring withdrawn with metal tongs as a wood-fired kiln reaches temperature allows the potter to check if the glaze is mature. Seger cones (*below*) placed inside the kiln by a spyhole indicate temperature; the bend in H1 shows it has reached 1,100°C.

vitrified, and allowance has to be made for this in the kiln packing (lest pots should sag and touch) as well as in the making process.

A light sprinkling of the shelf with flint, molochite or a proprietary 'placing powder' will prevent any sticking, but care must be taken to avoid dusting this on to the pots already stacked on lower shelves. Old kiln shelves spotted with glaze can be painted over with a mixture of flint and water as a 'batwash' to serve the same purpose.

Variations in the behaviour of glaze in the kiln are dealt with in chapter 16 but it is worth mentioning here that no two kiln firings are alike, and any pots which are intended to match one another in colour, texture and feel should be put in the same firing, and preferably grouped in the same area of the kiln. This is particularly important in fuel-burning kilns, where the kiln 'atmosphere' can be varied by the operator. Many potters find that a glaze is improved by maintaining the maturing temperature for a period of 10 or 20 minutes rather than switching off the power or fuel as soon as temperature is reached. This process is called 'soaking the glaze'.

Reduced and oxidized firings

In earthenware, as in biscuit kilns, there is no decorative benefit to be gained by changing the kiln atmosphere, but a reducing, or oxygen-starved, atmosphere in a stoneware glaze kiln darkens the colour of the body clay, which in turn changes the colour of the glaze. It also has a dramatic effect on some of the metal oxides, drawing oxygen out of them to help in the combustion process. Thus copper is changed from green to coppery red, and iron from brown to green.

Reducing the supply of oxygen in the fuel burners of kilns without or with only partial muffles, or introducing through the spyhole of a muffle kiln something (like mothballs or firewood) which will combine with or absorb oxygen in burning is a simple way of getting a reduction. However, most home kiln-firers are uncertain how much wood they need, and at what temperature and for how long to sustain the reducing atmosphere. A steady supply

Flames show a reduction in progress, with the damper in to reduce draught.

of wood chips of the size used for fire-lighting should be fed into the kiln throughout the reducing period, so there must be plenty of wood handy. Half an hour is a minimum period and it is pointless to do it at all at temperatures below 1,000°C, but because it is sometimes difficult to get kiln temperature to increase much while the atmosphere inside the kiln is oxygen-starved, a short final burst of normal (or oxidizing) fire is needed afterwards to reach maturing temperature.

A precise technical description of reduced stoneware firings may seem unnecessarily specialized to the beginner, but it is important to know why similar glazes yield different qualities and something of the method which has produced the most harmonious and beautiful works of oriental art. Successful reductions are hard to achieve in electric kilns because there is no combustion or air current, and putting materials through the spyhole to burn has a harmful effect on electric elements, shortening their life, as well as damaging the ware inside the kiln.

Building a kiln

Though some potters are content to leave the entire firing cycle in the hands of an instructor or technician, to others the pyrotechnics of pottery making are its most fascinating part, and their enthusiasm is stirred rather than daunted by the prospect of building and

firing their own kiln. There is an undeniable sense of pioneering about the activity, though in reality you are only returning to a long-established tradition still practised in small potteries in many countries. Bernard Leach, in *A Potter's Book*, wrote:

'The firing is the climax of the potter's labour, and in a wood-fired kiln of any size it is a long and exhausting process. Weeks and months of hard work are at stake. Any one of a dozen things may go wrong. Wood may be damp, flues may get choked, bungs of saggars fall, shelves give way and alter the draughts, packing may have been too greedily close, or for sheer exhaustion one may have snatched an hour's sleep, handing over control to someone else and thereby altering the rhythm of the stoking. At white heat things begin to move, to warp and to bend, the roar of combustion takes on a deeper note – the heavy domes crack and tongues of white flame dart out here and there, the four-minute stokes fill the kiln shed with bursts of dense black smoke and fire. Even in the East, where hand work is usual and labour specialised, a big kiln firing has the aspect of a battlefield where men test themselves to the utmost against odds. This may sound like discouragement, but it is no more than the simple truth.'

The amateur potter need not build a large kiln like this, which is exhausting to fire, and most permanent home-built kilns are gas, electric or oil fired, unlike the wood-burning kiln described by Bernard Leach. There are, however, several kinds of solid-fuel-burning kilns which can easily be made, providing you have the outdoor space in which to site them. The first is simply a brazier – a metal canister or large tin punched with airholes all round and at all levels. Filled with fairly densely packed sawdust in which are buried the pottery forms like presents in a bran tub, such a 'kiln' will reach a temperature of 750°C by being lit from the top and allowed to burn slowly downwards. Dried peat instead of sawdust reaches about the same temperature.

A rather more complicated but temporary kiln can be made out of doors

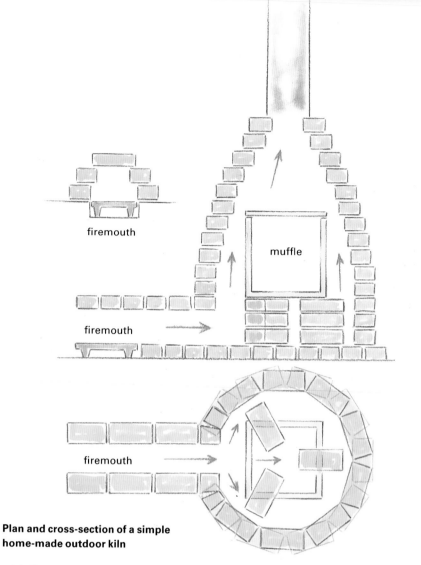

firemouth

muffle

firemouth

firemouth

Plan and cross-section of a simple home-made outdoor kiln

with firebricks and a muffle consisting of a single saggar or a cylinder with a base and a lid made from a 2.5cm (1in) thick slab of fireclay, shaped around a chimney pot or broad drainpipe. Naturally if no kiln is available in which to fire the muffle before its use in the temporary kiln, a ready-made saggar must be bought with the firebricks from a supplier. Alternatively, a box muffle can be built out of sillimanite shelves and fireclay cement assembled as shown in the diagram above.

A tunnel firemouth is made of firebricks, leading to a circular chamber of firebricks, in which the muffle is placed, raised on bricks upon a firebrick base above the level of the 'fireplace' in the tunnel. An even circulation of air around the muffle must be ensured, and the circular chamber should be reduced in diameter towards the top to increase the draught and the temperature, the walls being sealed with clay to prevent cold air being drawn in. This type of kiln is a miniature bottle-oven and fired with wood will reach an adequate temperature for low biscuit,

soft glaze or enamel. By smearing clay over the junctions of the bricks a better seal and updraught is achieved, and the higher the chimney, the greater the draught. The prospect of buying the right quantities of firebrick, tapered arch brick, insulating brick, common brick and heavy ironwork to hold the finished frame corseted together has deterred many of the potters fortunate enough to have space available from building their own kiln, but detailed plans are available in specialist books on kilns and kiln building.

If you are going to make salt-glazed pottery (see chapter 16), you will have to assign a special kiln to it outdoors because of the poisonous fumes given off by the salt. Sodium chloride in the kiln coats not only the pots but the kiln walls with the glaze, and this wall coating will become volatile again when the kiln is next fired, covering whatever is in the kiln so that it cannot be used thereafter for biscuit or conventional glaze. An outdoor kiln for salt glazing can be quite inexpensive to build, although it will only last a few years.

Lightweight kilns

The arrival of space-age ceramic fibre in the 1980s, and the equally revolutionary 'Sayvit' lightweight insulation bricks from the USA, have reduced the amount of insulation needed for a kiln to work properly. Because the weight and size of the structural elements have been reduced, the structure itself can be modified and simplified, just as a modern cathedral would no longer be designed with a stone vault. Lightweight bricks which take up heat, and ceramic fibres compressed into thin sheets like plasterboard, can form the fabric of a kiln with a chamber size of 0.14–0.16cu.m (5–6cu.ft) – a useful size for the studio potter – while weighing only about 100kg (220lb). A kiln like this can be fitted in an upstairs room, provided there is adequate ventilation and protection against fire. Such kilns come with safety-conscious instructions and recommendations for installation, including distances from walls.

Electric kilns with elements bedded in metal sleeves are now available, circular or octagonal in plan, ingeniously designed so that the chamber size can be increased or reduced by inserting or removing insulated rings, much as the volume inside a stack of rubber tyres can be changed by changing the number of tyres.

The flexibility which this gives is advantageous, and even more so is the energy economy. A lightweight kiln can reach a temperature of 1,300°C in only five hours, and while this is not appropriate for biscuit firing it saves much fuel for glost firings. Lightweight kilns are also inclined to cool very quickly, and traditionally this has been regarded as somewhat damaging to the glaze. It seems, however, that the mystique of slow cooling developed as much because the older generation of kilns *would* only cool slowly, as because slow cooling improved the pots. It is only at certain temperatures that rapid cooling induces crazing.

Although much of the mystique of the older types of kiln is swept away, a great deal of the uncertainty and labour has been banished too. The new fibre-lined kilns are an enormous boon, and best of all, they are cheap to buy.

21

RAKU AND SAGGAR FIRING

The potter making raku-ware has to be involved both with the firing process and the fire itself, and for the beginner it is a dramatic and compelling experience. Bernard Leach was a beginner when, in Japan, he first witnessed the firing of a raku kiln, and it was this that began his lifelong love of pottery making.

Raku means 'happiness through chance', and the process was first used in the sixteenth century in Japan. Modern techniques have now removed much of the chance, though results are still unpredictable and losses are high. It depends on the very rapid glost firing of biscuit pottery thickly glazed with low-temperature glazes and cooled very fast, often with the aid of cold water. This demands a sturdy clay that has low thermal expansion, and a glaze that most certainly will craze as it cools several hundred degrees in seconds. It is the nature of the glaze, which often has a high colour or lustre, that is much sought after by potters, and a quality best described as 'instant age'.

Some building methods are not well suited to the raku technique. Slip-cast or slab-built pots, for example, are likely to crack apart in a raku kiln. The techniques best suited to raku are coiling, pinching or thick throwing. Thrown pots, however, are made by stretching the clay, and have a structure less sturdy than well-formed coil pots, where the clay is compressed. Thin thrown pots will probably break, as will pots which are very asymmetrical or shallow. The 'safest' forms are bowls which are not too open and other forms without corners.

The clay needs to be open in texture, preferably with a high grog content. Now that raku has become fashionable and popular, pottery suppliers prepare a body specially for the technique, usually described as 'raku marl'. If you are making your own body, add about 10 per cent by weight of grog – coarse or fine – or silver sand to plastic clay.

Finished pots should be biscuit fired in the normal way to about 1,000°C and glazed with an earthenware glaze that melts at less than 1,000°C. The low temperature of the final firing and general reservations about toxicity should deter raku potters from using lead, even when in fritted form, and a low-temperature alkaline frit is the most commonly used for raku glaze, with an addition of 15 per cent ball clay, or ball clay and whiting. The typical crazing of alkaline glazes obviously presents no problem here since crazing is inevitable anyway with the rapid cooling, and desirable.

It is usual to paint the glaze thickly on to the pot with a mop-headed brush rather than to dip or spray it, and colourants such as copper, cobalt, manganese and tin can either be included in the glaze or painted on top of it in a water and paste mix (gum arabic helps adhesion). Detailed patterns should be avoided, since the way in which the fire works on the glaze is likely to obliterate painted designs. Hefty 'taches' of oxide or a second glaze made with the mop-headed brush, or with a slip trailer, can produce interesting results.

QUENCHING RAKU-WARE

1 Rakuists wear fire-resistant gloves when opening kilns at maturing temperature. David Roberts (*left*) raises a top-hat kiln, helped by counterweights.

2 Rakuist Ursula Rubens, wearing a heat-shield visor, takes a pot from a kiln with metal shovels. Because of fire risk, raku kilns are always outdoors.

3 The hot pot goes straight into a metal vessel containing sawdust (which quickly ignites) to achieve carbonation while the glaze is still 'open'.

Firing methods

The traditional method of raku firing involved a small improvised open-flame (wood or gas) kiln constructed outside using firebricks, with a chimney made from a stoneware drainpipe and old kiln shelves made of sillimanite which acted as doors, when supported. The process began with the pre-heating of the kiln with nothing in the muffle chamber, and the glazed pots heating up gently on the top to ensure complete dryness.

In order to get the pots into the muffle, long-handled tongs were used at a safe distance to open the side of the kiln and place the pots inside while the flames played around the chamber. The design also required a spyhole big enough to give the rakuist a clear view of the ware inside the muffle, so that

'Midsummer's Bay', a massive landscape pot by Wayne Higby, with the lustrous rich glaze coloration which comes from raku firing. Diameter: 47cm (18½in).

QUENCHING RAKU-WARE

4 More sawdust is poured over the pot, and the longer it stays covered in this smouldering material, the more thorough will be the reduction.

5 The pot, still hot, is put into a bucket of water which will 'freeze' or fix the sometimes iridescent colours of the reduction under the glaze.

6 Finally, the burnt sawdust debris is removed from the outside of the pot. The potter uses a scouring pad in water to reveal the bright colours beneath.

the pots could be removed – again with tongs – when the glaze was molten. Then came the most exciting bit of the raku experience: the removal of the red-hot pot from the kiln, its 'quenching' in a metal bin filled with leaves or sawdust which burnt smokily, and its subsequent, second quenching while still hot, but no longer red hot, in water. Cracking and splitting on removal from the kiln was commonplace.

Clearly electric kilns were unsuitable for such a procedure. All this has changed, however, with the simple concept of removing the kiln from the pot rather than the reverse, using the 'top-hat' kiln, devised by Paul Soldner, which makes practical the building of much larger pots.

Soldner is the king of raku in the West, and since the 1960s has been developing in America modern techniques of making raku-ware as large as any other kind of pottery, which accounts for the appearance of large and beautiful pots with rakued surfaces in studio potteries. The unpredictability of the result makes the technique of no interest to industry, and it is not easy to produce raku in pottery classes, although small traditional raku kilns can be set up for summer courses wherever there is open space and enthusiasm. The top-hat kiln tends to be used by individual studio potters who adapt their workshops for raku.

The light ceramic-fibre insulating chamber can be lowered by means of a pulley system on to a base on which the glazed ware stands. This allows the potter to heat up the chamber with oil or gas burners from below, and to cut off the heat just before raising the insulating chamber to reveal the red hot pot. It still has to be picked up with tongs at a safe distance and put into the sawdust-filled bin, because it is the sawdust, forced to smoulder by the heat of the pot, which seeks oxygen for combustion and so darkens the body of the clay under the glaze by reduction. The rapid crazing of the glaze allows carbon into the cracks and a pearly sheen usually appears on its surface as oxides such as tin are reduced by combustion to their metal bases. Thus copper is likely to blush pink, or turquoise. Moving the pot a second time with tongs into a water bath 'freezes' the glaze and sets up a secondary crazing, though not necessarily immediately, giving to the surface of the pot extra 'depth', and a mottled appearance. Ten minutes or so in the water bath is enough to finish the metamorphosis, and the pot can be scrubbed with a nailbrush to remove any loose dirt or scum.

Although the process sounds complicated, it demands only dexterity with the iron tongs, good organization and a safe outdoor location, as there is a lot of flame and steam about. The whole process takes just a few hours: David Roberts, a leading British rakuist, has a firing cycle of three hours from cold to 1,000°C to cold again. So there is an immediacy about the technique which attracts those who have not the patience to wait weeks to see a glazed pot emerge. With raku the chrysalis turns to a butterfly before your eyes.

Saggar-fired reduction

A more sombre but equally exciting surface is produced by firing pots in sawdust *inside* another ceramic form in a conventional open-flame kiln. This is not raku, nor is the end product sealed with glaze. The vessel traditionally used to contain pots fired in this way is called a saggar, as used for centuries in pottery making, but it can simply be a large expendable pot, and the technique has been developed with great aesthetic success by John Leach at Muchelney Pottery in Somerset. The biscuit-fired pot placed at an angle in a bed of sawdust inside the saggar burns black with reduction underneath the sawdust and is darkened into carbonation above it, while a pale ring encircles the pot, marking the place where flames burnt at the surface of the sawdust. Although the kiln is fired up to stoneware temperatures, smouldering sawdust inside the saggar lowers the temperature to around 1,150°C, so the pots are not fully vitrified, nor coated with glaze. They bear the marks of the fire, however, and delight those who see in the final stage of the ceramic process a touch of alchemy.

The hard-edged form of John Leach's bowl is reminiscent of African pottery. The smoky surface is the result of saggar firing: placing the pots up to their middles in sawdust in fireclay saggars imported from China (*above*) and then firing them in his wood-fired kiln.

22

THE HOME POTTER

Pottery can definitely *not* be made in the kitchen. An individual pot can, of course, especially if it is hand built, but once the simple creative act begins to turn into an absorbing spare-time activity, the stresses and strains of mixing clay with everyday household events becomes unbearable.

Pots in the making have big demands for space, and even for special atmospheric conditions, and most pottery processes have a constant demand for water. A bathroom, which provides this latter, can sometimes be persuaded to double as a photographic darkroom, but *not* as a pottery for there is rarely enough space to work, no facilities for electric tools and an uncharitable atmosphere which has something to do with the lack of comfort. If you don't believe me, try it and see.

Clay, though not an inherently dirty material, is persistent as dust, and leaves an opaque film when washed surfaces like table tops dry. It does not stain carpets or clothes, though a lot of the materials used with it, such as metal oxides, do and the potter who knows this needs a good deal of enthusiasm to overcome inhibitions about creating a mess, even if work is confined to making chessmen on a tray.

Siting the workshop

The ideal place for a pottery workshop is an outhouse – preferably a ground-floor room which has no other full-time function. Flat dwellers, and those whose homes yield no spare rooms, must forget about making pottery at home. Studio space is not difficult to rent, even in dense cities, but for the beginner the best bet is probably a pottery class workroom.

This book is no companion, however, if it cannot encourage those with the bare bones of a pottery workshop to use it effectively, and my own enthusiasm helped me in early days to make a pottery out of an old coal cellar, a room in a boot factory and a conservatory shared with a vine. None of these had any form of carpeting, and bare floors, which can be brushed out or scrubbed, are of the essence.

Funnily enough, pottery studios in new school and college buildings are often designed on the top floors, or in the basements, disadvantages which immediately become obvious when the heavy equipment and raw materials are moved in. School kilns rarely weigh less than 200kg (10cwt) and clay is usually ordered by the tonne. This, of course, need not worry the student overmuch, for the end products of his or her efforts are lighter and easier to move out, but it is worth bearing in mind when choosing a room for a private workshop. Ground-floor rooms are ideal and should have large wide doorways (vital for large kilns) and as much light as possible. All fuel-burning kilns need a flue, and normal chimney stacks are often unsuitable for such bursts of energy, so single-storey buildings are the most convenient, when chimneys have to be built. As running water is most important, a disused wash-house begins to emerge as an ideal starting point.

The trouble with such outbuildings is that they tend to be chilly places in winter, and although the kiln, when it is on, brings a great deal of comfort as a gratuitous spin-off, a regular form of heating and insulation against frost damage is most important. One-person studio potteries often produce batches of work, all at the same stage, and I remember seeing the sad results when one such potter's entire exhibition production was splintered by overnight frost while 'drying'. It is also hard to work well when hands or feet are cold in winter, and equally, in summer, when the kiln has to be fired and the ventilation is poor.

Choosing the equipment

The kiln is the most important piece of equipment. The home potter buying a new or second-hand kiln must take its measurements carefully, and make sure that he or she can get it into the workshop. All but the smallest electric kilns need an individual switch gear and special wiring from the mains supply. The capital cost of the kiln can be rather daunting, but either money or time must be spent in surmounting this initial hurdle and until this has been done there can be no pottery.

The kiln comes before the wheel, and immediately opens to the potter a vast range of possibilities. The home potter who is tempted to get a wheel first soon regrets it, and is faced with the prospect of taking green ware wrapped in cotton wool or newspaper, and often broken on the way, to be grudgingly fired at a school or at the local brickworks. It is a disenchanting experience, since the potter has no control over the firing, and if the firing is done by the brickworks or earthenware factory, it can be breathtakingly expensive too.

A sturdy work bench is the next requirement. A piece of smooth slate laid over it or marble from an old wash-stand, makes a good work surface for clay, better than wood, though both may be hard to come by nowadays, and Formica or a smooth kitchen worktop would replace them satisfactorily. Then, with a kiln installed, a work-bench, clay and running water, the potter has no obstacles and no excuse. Much more energy spent making the place right often pushes the end product farther into the future, and can even inhibit the potter. The tools for hand-made pottery are simple, and have already been described. Kitchen knives, wooden modelling tools, hacksaw blades and rolling pins can be easily acquired, as can sandpaper, cutting wire or nylon, and clay additives. Kiln furniture, if not supplied with the kiln, must be bought for it cannot easily be made.

Making and applying glazes requires slightly more sophisticated tools, principal among which is the phosphor-bronze lawn or sieve. A sieve, with a 100-strand mesh and 20.5–25.5cm (8–10in) diameter, is an essential, and it is useful to have a coarser and a finer one (80 and 120 mesh) as well. Those with time to go to country sales can still buy scales, buckets, pestles and mortars and enamel jugs and bowls quite cheaply, but the amateur potter with less spare time is well advised to buy new rigid polythene equivalents. He or she will do well, for rigid polythene is the potter's best friend in the workshop. It is easy to clean, and easy to see when it is not clean. Compare a bright orange-handled, nylon-bristled scrubbing brush with its wood and bristle forebear: aesthetics apart, plastics win every time. It is a matter of some shame for the potter that when it comes to pouring, the ceramic jug can never match for drip-free performance the moulded plastic jug, with its crisp lip and liquid-repellent surface. The wider top of this same jug is also vastly more convenient than its enamel equivalent, which is traditionally narrower at the neck than at the base. One jug, a scrubbing brush, two bowls and one bucket with a lid are the minimum requirements.

Balances and scales are very important to the potter, not only in measuring glaze ingredients but also in weighing clay. Spring balances are to be avoided; not only are they inaccurate, but often the pans are inconveniently small and they are much slower in use than beam balances, with weights on one side and a pan on the other. A good beam balance will be reassuringly accurate for very small quantities – down to 7g ($\frac{1}{4}$oz) – whereas a spring balance will never match it. Kitchen scales and kitchen rolling pins can be used as pottery equipment, but it is wise to get separate ones as some pottery materials are unhealthy, if not toxic.

A full list of all useful tools is tedious reading, and common sense will indicate the need and the solution in most cases. Storage jars made of glass, with well-fitting lids, as described in chapter 15, are helpful for glazes and dry materials that can absorb moisture (materials which absorb dampness from the atmosphere are not only no longer dry, they are also heavier, and therefore will give an inaccurate figure when weighed). Sponges, both synthetic and real, pins, corks and paint brushes are required and must be kept clean. It is equally important to have a regular place – such as a handy shelf over the wheel – to store the smaller tools like chamois-leather strips, as otherwise these can all too easily disappear into the clay waste and the slop bin.

Wheels

Points to look for in buying second-hand wheels are possible wear in the bearings within which the wheel-head revolves, and, in the case of powered wheels, the amount of resistance the power source can stand – that is, the amount of pressure on the wheel-head – before the driving mechanism slips. Test this by trying to stop the wheel-head when under full power by grasping its sides with both hands. If you can do it easily, then do not buy the wheel. This is a test which should also be applied to new wheels, for the power provided varies greatly. A problem for the buyer of a new wheel is that the product usually has to be bought from a catalogue, and the potter is committed to purchase, and to pay carriage, before it can be tested.

An electric wheel in a workshop will need a power point, but no special wiring. It should be located in a good light, preferably under a window. If there is drainage for the water tray under the wheel-head, it will probably consist of a short tube or pipe, poised ready to spew clay slip all over the floor. This should not be directed into a drain as the clay content will quickly cause a blockage, and ideally should go into a settling pan (like an old glazed sink) with an overflow leading to a drain. The settled clay can then be cleared out periodically and reused. If no drainage is available, aim the rubber pipe into as large a vessel as possible and try to remember to empty it before it overflows. Some wheels have a plastic water catching tray which can be emptied only by removing the wheel-head first, which can be hard work.

Storage space

Every pottery I have ever known has suffered from a lack of shelf space. Ware drying, awaiting glazing, finishing or firing, and completed work on display all need a place. Working surfaces must be kept clear, and batteries of adjustable shelves are most useful. The discovery that the only unfilled shelf is too low to accommodate a fresh-made pot always comes just as you are about to slide the pot on to it, and clearing suitable spaces before making a batch of pots repays the effort involved. Shelves consisting of loose planks of wood resting on dowels between uprights, like ladders, are easiest to adjust. Loose shelves can also be rested on angle brackets fixed to the wall.

A pottery studio at home may be in use every day, but even if it is not, a fairly frequent check on the state of freshly thrown pots can be made, and the need for a damp-atmosphere cupboard is less vital than at a weekly pottery class. The home potter can nevertheless be caught out when a batch of green ware dries overnight, especially if the kiln is in use, and a fairly airtight cupboard is a useful asset. If a so-called 'damp' cupboard is made of wood it will warp, and if it is metal it will certainly rust, so it is best to use something which is old and valueless. Polythene bags can be used to maintain a damp atmosphere around coil and slab pots in the making, but they cannot be used on wet thrown ware, which shows the mark of anything which touches it. The best way of preserving the dampness of a freshly thrown pot is to invert another pot or tin over it, and to seal the junction with the shelf by means of a ring of clay. Such extreme measures, however, are rarely necessary in a workshop when it is in regular use, and it is good for both pots and pottery room to keep projects alive and progressing.

Some work, like the drying of tiles, cannot be hurried and takes up space. So, of course, do glaze tests, glass jars, clay for reuse and kiln shelves and furniture. Successful pots soon disappear from the workshop but failures and near-failures linger. To have imperfect and stodgy work around has a very depressing effect, and the potter should make a determined effort, and throw it away.

Self help

I have an aunt who, with more affection than discrimination, has kept an embarrassing record of my early progress through the hazards of learning to be a potter. More depressing than a photograph album of one's childhood is to see arranged, but tactfully rarely in use, heavy tableware unsuitably glazed, experimental pottery, first attempts at wax resist and slip trailing, or composite structures so badly balanced

Ancient and modern peasant pots often put the work of studio potters to shame.

that a quick sudden breath should send them toppling but, alas, never has.

The sight of these all-too-permanent reminders of skills hard learned recalls the ultimate ignomiy of once, having decided to consign an ugly pot to oblivion, being quite unable to break it against the metal side of a dustbin because of the very thickness of its walls. Unlike the early mistakes of an architect, which loom large in the city to the general inconvenience of everyone, poor pottery, unless it gets into the hands of my aunt, has a short life. The heavy uncomfortable jug, the impractical and scratchy vase, the dull-ringing stoneware bowl, all these witnesses to bad design and execution undermine your pride in your work, and can be banished. Conversely, the senses collectively quicken to the beautiful pot. Dissatisfaction with the quality of your work is a route not to despair but to fulfilment, since a hand-made pot can always be better next time, and the amateur potter can devote time to making it so.

Results in pottery reflect people's moods, and it can sometimes seem as

if your work, especially on the wheel, is going to pieces rather than improving. Even expert throwers have 'off-days', when it is better not to work on the wheel but to choose another technique. There are so many styles and types of ceramics that you are never at a loss for something to do.

As a teacher, I am always delighted by the variety of intentions and abilities among people who are taking up pottery for the first time. My heart sinks a little, it is true, when someone makes it clear that the main objective is to provide Christmas presents for friends and relations (a nearly impossible task anyway if the course only begins in September), but beginners respond quickly to one technique or another, and variety of work and interests is good for morale. If the beginner wants to make tableware, decorated bowls, sculptural forms with no useful purpose, or painted tile panels, there is no obstacle.

Working with clay quickly makes people more responsive to pottery in general, more critical of manufactured ware and more interested in museum collections and contemporary galleries. A regular but short weekly lesson whets the appetite, and beginners in pottery can help themselves by seeking the stimulus of exhibitions, where other people's work and standards can revolutionize their whole approach to the subject. The expressive emotional use of clay in modern sculptural ceramics sometimes sends visitors reeling with shock from galleries, or simply angry because of the way in which ceramic artists are reacting against the traditions of the past. The imagination has always worked its way with clay, and five or six thousand years of experiment, tradition and reaction have brought no conclusion other than the inevitable continuity of the art form. The shaping of a small open bowl from clay is as basic now — and as full of potential — as it was in the time of Mycenae, Akhenaten or Atahualpa. The problem is that today's bowl is unlikely to be as good.

Suppliers of materials in several countries are listed on page 190. Many of these sources of equipment produce

catalogues which are well illustrated and extremely informative. Many excellent books are also available to help the potter, but outstanding is *A Potter's Book* by Bernard Leach, which conveys beautifully the excitement and satisfaction of pottery as a hobby or as a way of life.

National craft councils keep registers of crafts people of quality, some of whom welcome visits from pottery enthusiasts, while specialist magazines (see page 190) provide another method of keeping in touch with the latest developments, both technical and artistic.

There are hundreds of ceramics studios and cooperatives world-wide, and it is not too difficult to make contact with the potters who run them. It is not necessary, of course, to belong to an association or a group of any sort in order to progress in making pottery, though it does seem that a polarization of views is inevitable — the usual opposition of forces which produces good art. The emphasis is either on the functionalism and good design of a medium which started and continues to serve the table, or on the aesthetic and emotional potential of the medium, clay, as a means of communication. It is only this schism which is artificial. Good pots will continue to communicate their quality and beauty when the talking is over and done.

Four small tiles by Johannes Peters, decorated in relief and with white slip and then painted in cobalt oxide before adding a transparent glaze. Stoneware.

Definitions of most of the raw materials used in making clays and glazes are given in chapter 14, from pages 115 to 117. Italics indicate cross references to other glossary entries.

Banding wheel or 'whirler' A freely revolving metal *wheel-head* mounted on a pedestal base, the latter ranging from a few centimetres to a metre in height. There is no mechanical means of rotating the wheel-head; it is turned by hand and is used to help in the decoration of the pot (see page 125) or simply to turn the pot around.

Bat A flat portable working surface. Circular bats made from wood, metal, plastic, plaster or fired clay are useful surfaces on which to make or store pots. Kiln shelves are also sometimes called bats.

Batwash A mixture of flint and water, painted thinly on to kiln shelves which have become spotted with glaze droppings to prevent the sticking of ware.

Biscuit Pottery which has been fired to an insoluble but porous state, like a plant pot.

Bloat A blister caused by gas created and trapped inside the clay body during firing. Bloating is associated with high temperatures and the *glost* firing – if it occurred in the biscuit firing the ware would have been discarded.

Body The clay which forms the structure or fabric of a pot.

Carbonizing The permanent staining of clay by the introduction of carbon particles during exposure of the pottery to combustion. The dark lines in raku-ware are from carbon penetrating the glaze cracks when the pot is immersed in leaves or sawdust. Carbonizing of unglazed ware occurs at low temperatures in sawdust firings, giving more or less random patterning. See page 161.

Celadon *Stoneware* glazes containing iron which produce green, grey and grey-blue colours in *reduction* firing.

Chuck A hollow form, usually expendable and made of plastic clay, but sometimes permanent and made of plaster or metal, which will grip a pot on a *wheel-head* for stability during the turning process.

Combined techniques Applied to ware made by a variety of thrown and hand-made techniques. Thus a candelabrum may have a slab plinth, a coiled stem and thrown candle-holders.

Composite pots Ware which is usually the result of assembling separate thrown units.

Cottle The enclosing wall of clay or wood or linoleum built around a clay master to contain the plaster of Paris when a mould is filled.

Crazing The cracking of glaze on the surface of pottery caused by greater contraction in the glaze than in the body of the pot during the cooling stage. See chapter 14.

Crawling The shrinking back of glaze, often because of grease or dust on *biscuit*-fired ware, leaving scars which are invariably ugly. See chapter 14.

Deflocculant A substance which, acting chemically on *plastic* clay, gives it liquid characteristics with the addition of very little water. Sodium silicate and sodium carbonate work this magic.

Earthenware Glazed pottery fired to a temperature of 1,000–1,100°C and in which the body remains unvitrified.

Extruder or wad mill A device, usually wall-mounted, for producing from *plastic* clay under pressure even-section lengths of clay shaped according to interchangeable dies. See chapter 11.

Fettling Tidying up or trimming a pot in preparation for firing. The term is most commonly used in industry for the stage in which mould seams are shaved off *green* pots.

Flux A melting agent which causes silica to form glaze or glass.

Foot ring The circlet of clay at the base of certain thrown or hand-made pots which raises the form from the surface on which it stands. If it is part of a thrown pot, it is shaped and hollowed during the turning stage.

Frit A glaze material consisting of *flux* and silica which are melted together and reground to a fine powder.

Glost Glaze or glazed. Thus a glost firing is the firing of glazed ware.

Green Unfired pots are described as 'green' or 'green ware' when they are dry and awaiting their first firing.

Grog Ground-down fired pottery, varying in coarseness from the texture of granulated sugar to that of flour, added to *plastic* clay to quicken drying, add texture or decrease shrinkage.

Kidney A kidney-shaped tool made of flexible steel for finishing thrown pots, or made of stiff rubber for pressing and smoothing clay in a mould.

Lawn A sieve with fine mesh made from phosphor-bronze.

Leather hard or cheese hard An important stage in the progress of a pot from raw clay to finished ware. A leather-hard pot is dry enough not to stick to your fingers, but soft enough to allow some working of its shape without cracking or other damage.

Majolica or maiolica *Earthenware* glazed with opaque tin glaze and over-painted with oxides. Known in Italy as majolica (from Majorca), in France as *faience* (from Faenza), in England as Delft-ware (from Delft), its true origin is probably North African or Persian.

Maturing temperature The temperature at which a glaze exhibits its best qualities. A variation of 10°C on either side of the optimum or maturing temperature is enough to spoil the result.

Muffle The *refractory* chamber inside a fuel-burning kiln which contains the pottery and protects it from the flames.

Oxidized Fired with an adequate supply of oxygen, so that combustion is complete and oxides show bright colours.

Plastic When applied to clay, plastic means capable of being shaped and of retaining its shape.

Plunge pots Curious name for pots made by wrapping clay around a wooden dowel or former, and beating the walls into shape.

Porcelain White *stoneware*, usually translucent, made from clay prepared from feldspar, china clay, flint and whiting. Also known imprecisely as 'china'.

Press mould Strictly speaking , a press mould is a two-piece plaster mould which, when assembled, squeezes plastic clay like ham in a sandwich into a precise profile. It is more often used to describe a single mould into which *plastic* clay is pressed either by hand or with a tool.

Raw Raw clay is unfired clay and raw glazing is the technique of applying a glaze to an unfired pot, and heating both clay and glaze up together. The resulting ware is often described as once-fired ware.

Reduced or reduction Fired in an oxygen-starved atmosphere (either by restricting the inflow of air or introducing a substance which combines with oxygen in burning). Reduction firing is used in *stoneware* and the effect is to reduce the colour of metal oxides to the colour of the metals themselves. Thus green from copper becomes the orangey pink colour of the metal. Reduction is induced for a short period towards the end of the upward temperature curve.

Refractory Literally means resistant to heat. All clays are refractory in the sense that they do not burn, but the term refractory clay is applied to clay constituted especially for high firing temperatures. Glaze ingredients which raise the melting point are known as refractory ingredients.

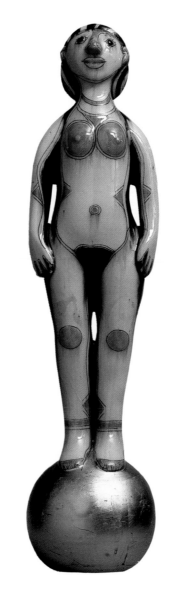

Figure by Jac Hansen

Saggar A protective fireclay box, usually round in section, for holding pottery in fuel-burning kilns without *muffles*.

Seger cone Named after their inventor and designed to indicate heat work by melting, Seger cones are not cones but small slender pyramids of fusible material like glaze which bend over as a precise temperature is reached.

Silk screening A common industrial decorative process, in which colourants in a liquid carrier medium are pressed through a very fine silk screen which has been partially obstructed with wax. The resulting design therefore appears where the colours have penetrated the unwaxed areas of the screen. Several screens can be used when making a multi-coloured design.

Slip Clay in a very liquid state, used in casting (see chapter 13) and in decoration (see chapter 18).

Slurry Thick slip.

Soaking This term is used to describe the maintenance of the vitrification temperature in the kiln by balancing the fuel intake. By 'soaking' a kiln for 10 minutes or so, instead of turning it off or damping down when the desired temperature is reached, the glaze can achieve a more mature appearance.

Spalling Splintering or chipping, especially of tiles, and associated with frost damage.

Sprigging A technique of applying relief designs to the surface of pots from moulds of plaster or wood. Examples are Wedgwood Jasper ware, where the design is in contrasting clay (white on blue or green, etc), and Lucie Rie's seal.

Stoneware Glazed pottery in which both body and glaze are fused together in a non-porous vitrified state, as a result of firing to temperatures above 1,200°C.

Surform tool A proprietary name for a self-sharpening planing device, much like a cheese-grater, sold either with two handles, for use with both hands, or with one handle, like a file.

Wad mill See Extruder.

Wedging The cutting and re-forming of lumps of *plastic* clay preparatory to kneading to ensure an even texture.

Wheel-head The flat disc attached to the revolving spindle of a potter's wheel, and on which the pot is formed.

SUPPLIERS

United Kingdom

Acme Maris Ltd (for clays and kiln furniture), Bournes Bank, Burslem, Stoke-on-Trent, Staffs ST6 3DW

Bath Potters' Supplies, 2 Dorset Close, Bath, Avon BA2 3RF

Blythe Colours Ltd, Cresswell, Stoke-on-Trent, Staffs ST11 9RD

Briar Wheels and Supplies Ltd, Whitsbury Road, Fordingbridge, Hants SP6 1NQ

Clayman (for general supplies), 251 Pagham Road, Nyetimber, Bognor Regis, West Sussex PO21 3QB

Cromartie Kilns, Park Hall Road, Longton, Stoke-on-Trent, Staffs ST3 5AY

Deancraft Fahey (for general supplies), 12 Spedding Road, Fenton Industrial Estate, Stoke-on-Trent, Staffs ST4 2ST

Dobles Fireclays, Newdowns Sand & Clay Pits, St Agnes, Cornwall TR5 0ST

Dragon Ceramex (for extruders), 5 Nomis Park, Congresbury, Avon BS19 5HB

ECC Ball Clays Ltd, 36 North Street, Wareham, Dorset BH2 4AW

ECC International Ltd (for clays), John Keay House, St Austell, Cornwall PL25 4DJ

Ferro (Great Britain) Ltd (for general supplies), Wombourne, Wolverhampton WV5 8DA

Fulham Pottery Ltd (for general supplies), 8–10 Ingate Place, London SW8 3NS

Kilns & Furnaces Ltd (for kilns), Keele Street, Turnstall, Stoke-on-Trent, Staffs ST6 5AS

Lotus Pottery (for wheels), Stoke Gabriel, Totnes, South Devon TQ9 6SL

Medcol (Cornwall) Ltd (for general supplies), Unit 17, Woods Browning Industrial Estate, Bodmin, Cornwall PL31 1DQ

Moira Pottery Co. Ltd (for clays), Rawton Road, Moira, Burton-on-Trent, Staffs DE12 6DF

Morganite Thermal Ceramics (for 'T' material clay), Liverpool Road, Neston, South Wirral, Cheshire L64 3RE

Pilling Pottery (for general supplies), School Lane, Pilling, nr Garstang, Lancs PR3 6HB

Potclays Ltd, Brickkiln Lane, Etruria, Stoke-on-Trent, Staffs ST4 7BP

Potterycrafts Ltd, Campbell Road, Stoke-on-Trent, Staffs ST4 4ET. In London: 2 Norbury Trading Estate, Craignish Avenue, Norbury, London SW16 4RW; 75 Silver Street, Edmonton, London N18 1RP

Ratcliffe & Sons (for wheels), Rope Street, Shelton New Road, Stoke-on-Trent, Staffs ST4 6DJ

Reward Clay Glaze Ltd (for high-firing colourants), Unit A, Brookhouse Industrial Estate, Cheadle, Stoke-on-Trent, Staffs ST10 1PW

Watts, Blake, Bearne & Co. PLC (for clays), Courtenay Park, Newton Abbot, Devon TQ12 4PS

Australia

Claycraft Supplies Pty Ltd, 29 O'Connell Terrace, Bowen Hills, Queensland 4006

Claymates Pottery Supplies, 120 Parker Street, Maroochydore, Queensland 4558

Houston Ceramic Supplies, 221 Macquarie Street, Hobart, Tasmania 7000

Jackson Ceramic Craft (for general supplies), 94 Jersey Street, Jolimont, Western Australia 6014

W. Mulder, Clayworks Aust. Pty Ltd, 6 Jonston Court, Dandenong, Victoria 3175

Mura Clay Gallery (for general supplies), 8 King Street, Newtown, New South Wales 2042

Newcastle Kiln & Element Service, 14 Hanbury Street, Mayfield, New South Wales 2304

Northcote Pottery (for general supplies), 85A Clyde Street, Thornbury, Victoria 3071

Potters' Equipment, 13/42 New Street, Ringwood, Victoria 3134

The Pottery Place (for general supplies), 44 McLeod Street, Cairns, Queensland 4870

Pug Mill (for general supplies), 17A Rose Street, Mile End, South Australia 5031

Quinja Potters' Supplies (for general supplies), 1–10 Ern Harley Drive, Burleigh Gardens, Queensland 4220

Sovereign Ceramics (for general supplies), 502 MacArthur Street, Ballarat, Victoria 3350

New Zealand

Arcadia Developments Ltd (for kilns, kiln elements and extruders), PO Box 87 088, Meadowbank, Auckland 1130

Bernies Clay Co. Ltd, Winchester-Hanging Rock Road, RD 2, Pleasant Point

CCG Industries (for general supplies), 33 Crowhurst Street, Newmarket, Auckland

Coastal Ceramics (for extruders and general supplies), 124 Rimu Road, Paraparaumu

Cobcraft Supplies (for general supplies), PO Box 32024, Christchurch

The Electric Furnace Co. Ltd, PO Box 76 162, Manukua City, Auckland

Furnace Engineering Co. Ltd, 6 Holmes Road, Manurewa, Manukua City, Auckland

Potters' Clay (Nelson) Ltd, PO Box 2096, Stoke, Nelson

Southern Clays Ltd, PO Box 6323, Dunedin

Waikato Ceramics (for general supplies), PO Box 12071, Hamilton

Wellington Potters' Supplies, 2 Cashmere Avenue, Khandallah, Wellington

South Africa

Gillian Bickell Potteries (for general supplies), 24 Staal Street, Kyasands Industrial, Randberg, Box 68624, Bryanston 2021, Transvaal

The Clay Pot (for general supplies), 3 Dunottar Street, Sydenham, Box 51151, Raedene 2124, Transvaal

Edgeware Ceramics (Pty) Ltd (for general supplies), 139 Old Main Road, Pinetown 3600, Natal

Ferro Industrial Products, Box 108, Brakpan 1540, Transvaal

Potter's Supplies and Mail Order (PSMO), 65 Meyerton Road, Daleside, Box 39, Henley-on-Klip 1962, Transvaal

Reinders Potter's Suppliers, Industria Avenue, Kraaifontein Industria, Box 194, Kraaifontein 7570, Western Cape

PUBLICATIONS

Pottery magazines have a special function in keeping potters, who are often based in remote rural areas, in touch with developments and exhibitions, and new work. The pioneer in this field in Britain was *Ceramic Review*, bimonthly, from 21 Carnaby Street, London W1V 1PH. It is a marvellous magazine, as is the highly recommended *Ceramics Monthly* in the United States, edited by William Hunt, from 1609 Northwest Boulevard, Columbus, Ohio 43212. *American Ceramics* is a quarterly published from 15 West 44th Street, New York, NY 10036. In Australia, *Ceramics: Art and Perception*, from 35 William Street, Paddington, NSW 2021, is a well-informed magazine produced to a very high standard, and *The New Zealand Potter* from New Zealand Publications Ltd, PO Box 881, Auckland, New Zealand, is a long established magazine which is well known beyond the shores of its native country.

Personally instrumental in making potters in France aware of what each other is doing, and in making outsiders more aware of French ceramics, is Sylvie Girard, editor of *Revue de la Céramique et du Verre*, 61 rue Marconi, F-62880 Vendin-le-Vieil. This magazine has a character all of its own, blending history and ethnology with the latest work of European potters. Articles are often in both English and French.

Keramik Magazin is published from Rudolf-Diesel-Strasse 10–12, Postfach 1820, 5020 Frechen 1, in Germany, and in Spain *Ceramica* is published from Apartado de Correso 7008, Pasoe Acacias 9, Madrid, and *Buleti Informatiu de Ceràmica*, quarterly, from Sant Honorat, 7, Barcelona 08002.

INDEX

Page numbers in *italic* refer to illustrations.

PICTURE CREDITS

The publisher thanks the following potters, photographers and organizations for their kind permission to reproduce the photographs in this book:

Endpapers Thomas Ward/Bonhams; 2–3 Robin Welch; 4 courtesy of Betty Woodman, Max Protetch Gallery, New York; 6 Cornelia Klein/Harald Mühlhausen; 8–9 photography by Michael Holford; 12 Rudolf Staffel – 'Light Gatherer', photograph by Eric Mitchel courtesy Helen Drutt Gallery, Philadelphia; 13 Catherine Vanier; 26 above Ursula Scheid; 27 right Herbert Wenzel, Germany; 32 above Thomas Ward/Bonhams; 34 above Edouard Chapallaz; 38 left Hein Severijns/Keramikmuseum Westerwald; 38 above right Robert Turner/Dorothy Weiss Gallery, San Francisco, California; 38 below right Janet Mansfield 'Flower Vase', woodfired in her anagama-style kiln at Gulgong, NSW, Australia, photograph by Roger Deckker; 39 above left Peter Voulkos, photograph by Joe Schopplein; 39 below left Michael Casson courtesy Ceramic Review; 39 right Thomas Ward/Bonhams; 43 above Jane Hamlyn courtesy Ceramic Review; 44 above photograph by Harry Foster/Canadian Museum of Civilization; 45 above Theresia Hebenstreit, Wiesbaden, Germany; 47 above Carol Roorbach; 49 right Stephen Brayne/Aberystwyth Art Centre; 52 above Peter Kinnear; 53 Thomas Ward/Bonhams; 54 above right Jane Hamlyn; 54 below left David Cripps; 55 above Los Angeles County Museum of Art, gift of Howard and Gwen Laurie Smits; 55 below right Michael Casson courtesy Ceramic Review; 59 above Duncan Ross; 61 Thomas Ward/Bonhams; 63 above Nicholas Homoky courtesy Ceramic Review; 64 left Thomas Ward/Bonhams; 64 above right Ruth Duckworth, Dorothy Weiss Gallery, San Francisco, California; 64 below right Thomas Naethe; 65 above Beatrice Wood/Garth Clark Gallery, photograph by John White, private collection; 65 below Paulien Ploeger, photograph by Erik Hesmerg; 66 David Cripps; 70 above David Roberts; 73 above Betty Blandino, photograph by G.O. Jones; 74 Galerie Besson/Alev Ebüzziya Siesbye, photograph by Michael Harvey; 75 Michael Holford; 76 above left Thomas Ward/Bonhams; 76 below left Thomas Ward/Bonhams; 76 right Martin Lewis, photograph by Bob Chegwidden; 77 Galerie Besson/Jennifer Lee; 79 above Thomas Ward/Bonhams; 83 Los Angeles County Museum of Art, promised gift of Howard and Gwen Laurie Smits; 84 below Cornelia Klein/Harald Mühlhausen; 85 above Philippe Lambercy; 85 below Evelyn Klam/Keramikmuseum Westerwald; 86 Carmen Dionyse, photograph by Bollaert; 87 above left Torbjørn Kvasbo; 87 above right Ard de Graaf; 87 below left David Cripps; 87 below right Paul Soldner courtesy of the Louis Newman Galleries, Beverley Hills; 90 left Richard De Vore; 93 above Mary White; 94 above left Elspeth Owen, photograph by Nicolette Hallett; 94 above right Mary White; 94 below Mary Rogers; 95 right Mary White; 95 below left Johann van Loon; 97 above Froyle Tiles; 99 above Emily Myers; 103 above Thomas Ward/Bonhams; 104 above Suzy Atkins, photograph by Soisson; 106 Sasha Wardell, photograph by Nicole Crestou; 107 above Jeroen Bechtold, photograph by René Geretzen; 108 above Dieter Balzar; 109 above Johann van Loon; 110 Janice Tchalenko; 113 Young Jae Lee; 114 Stephen Brayne/Ceramic Review; 115 Edouard Chapallaz; 116 Catherine Vanier; 117 Thomas Ward/Bonhams; 119 above David Leach courtesy Ceramic Review; 123 above Tove Anderberg, photograph by Tom Lauretsen; 124 above Stephen Brayne/Ceramic Review; 126 above Thomas Ward/Bonhams; 128 Vaughn Smith; 129 right Gilles Le Corre, photograph by Chris Honeywell; 129 above left Robin Welch; 129 below left Jac Hansen; 133 courtesy of Betty Woodman, Max Protetch Gallery, New York; 134 above left Stephen Brayne/Aberystwyth Art Centre; 137 Jane Hamlyn courtesy Ceramic Review; 139 above Thomas Ward/Bonhams; 139 below Peter Kinnear; 146 left photograph by Harry Foster/Canadian Museum of Civilization; 146 right Galerie Besson/Lucie Rie; 147 above Galerie Besson/Claudi Casanovas; 147 below Galerie Besson/Ewen Henderson; 149 above Paul Soldner courtesy Ceramic Review; 149 below Alphabet and Image; 150 above Tom and Elaine Coleman; 151 Thomas Ward/Bonhams; 153 above Galerie Besson/Vladimir Tsivin; 154 above Peter Kinnear; 155 right Thomas Ward/Bonhams; 158 above David Cripps; 159 right private collection, photograph by John Colls; 160 above right Rita Ternes; 160 above left Carmen Dionyse, photograph by Heyrman Graphics; 162 above John Glick; 162 below Anna Lambert, photograph by Jerry Hardman Jones; 163 left Rudy Autio; 163 above right Thomas Hoadley; 163 below right Elisabeth von Krogh; 165 above Thomas Ward/Bonhams, © Dacs 1994 (Pablo Picasso – 'Vase Itzteque aux Quatre Visages', 1968); 166 Sandy Brown; 170 Jean-Claude de Crousaz; 171 above Explorer/A. de Guise; 182 above Wayne Higby – 'Midsummer's Bay', courtesy of the Helen Drutt Gallery, Philadelphia; 187 below Johannes Peters; 189 Jac Hansen.

Every effort has been made to trace copyright holders and we apologize in advance for any unintentional omission and would be pleased to insert appropriate acknowledgment in any subsequent edition of this publication.

The following photographs were taken especially for Conran Octopus by Peter Kinnear:

8, 10, 11, 14, 15–17, 18, 19, 20–5, 26 below, 27 left, 28–9, 30, 32 below, 33, 34 below, 35–7, 40–2, 43 below, 44 below, 45 below, 46, 47 below, 48, 49 above left, 49 below left, 50–1, 52 below, 54 above left, 55, 56–8, 59 below, 60, 62, 63 below, 67, 68–9, 70 below, 71–2, 73 below, 78, 79 below, 80, 82, 84 above, 88–9, 90 right, 91–2, 93 below left, 95 above left, 96–8, 99 below, 100–102, 103 below, 104 below, 105, 107 below, 108 below, 109 below, 111–12, 118, 119 below, 120–2, 123 below, 124 below, 125, 126 below, 127, 130, 132, 134 top, 134 above right, 134 centre right, 134 centre left, 134 below right, 134 below left, 136, 138, 139 centre, 140, 142–6, 148, 150 below, 152, 153 below, 154 below, 155 left, 158 below, 159 above left, 159 below left, 160 below, 161, 164, 165 below, 166 above, 166 below right, 167, 168, 171 below, 172–4, 176–8, 180, 181, 182 below, 183, 184, 187 above.

ACKNOWLEDGMENTS

During the preparation of this new edition a great many busy professional potters and teachers have freely given their time to be photographed and to assist in sharpening the image and intent of the book. Picture research over five continents has meant the exclusion for space reasons of hundreds of marvellous pictures diligently provided by Abigail Ahern, Harald Mühlhausen and many others. The familiar faces of leading potters appear on the pages, as do their works, and they are too numerous to thank individually, but they know how much both photographer Peter Kinnear and I have appreciated their help. Our special thanks are due to Cyril Frankel, Anita Besson, Bonhams, Albert Clamp, John Leach, Bryan and Julia Newman, Betty Blandino, Gabriele Koch, David Cowley and the students of Goldsmith's College, London, Deirdre Bowles, Mary Wondrausch, Jane Waller, Jennifer Lee, Mike Levy, Ceramic Review, Sylvie Girard, Revue de la Céramique, John Ford, Alan Caiger-Smith, Claude Champy, Garth Clark, Gunnar Jakobsen, Thea Burger, Nicholas Homoky, David Roberts, Ursula Ströh-Rubens, Janet Mansfield, Stephen Course and Dartington Pottery, among a host of generous potters.